Maps and Compasses

2nd Edition

Stephen F. Bartold M.D.

Maps and Compasses

2nd Edition

Percy W. Blandford

TAB BOOKS
Blue Ridge Summit, PA

SECOND EDITION
FIRST PRINTING

Library of Congress Cataloging-in-Publication Data

Blandford, Percy W.
    Maps and compasses : a user's handbook / by Percy W. Blandford.—
2nd ed.
        p.   cm.
    Includes index.
    ISBN 0-8306-2141-5   ISBN 0-8306-2140-7
    1. Maps.   2. Compass.   I. Title.
GA151.B53   1991
912—dc20   91-12050
                                                                CIP

TAB Books offers software for sale. For information and a catalog, please contact
TAB Software Department, Blue Ridge Summit, PA 17294-0850.

Acquisitions Editor: Jeff Worsinger
Book Editor: Steve Moro
Production: Katherine G. Brown
Book Design: Jaclyn J. Boone
Cover Design and Illustration: Greg Schooley, Mars, PA   PFS

Contents

Introduction

THE SHORTEST DISTANCE BETWEEN TWO POINTS IS CLOSED FOR REPAIRS . . . so you need a map to find a suitable detour! And that's not the only occasion when you need a map. All of us who travel need maps, whether the place we want to find is in the same state or on the other side of the world. As travel becomes easier, the need for maps becomes greater. Even if you depend on someone else to transport you to your destination, your interest in traveling and arriving can be increased tremendously by using a map.

Maps and compasses go together. For many purposes it is possible to manage without a compass, but the ability to set a map with a compass helps you to get the map the same way as the country, even if you have doubts about where you are.

Most of us have used highway maps, but there is much more to mapping than that. Maps are available for other purposes besides getting from place to place by road.

In addition to travel maps, others can tell you about places you might never visit. If your interest is history, geology, population, or a host of other subjects, there are maps for you. If you want to make your own maps, that is possible without elaborate or expensive equipment. It is even possible to read maps competitively if you join in the sport of orienteering.

A map uses a sort of shorthand to tell us many things. Even a free state road map will yield information you did not realize was there, if you study all the explanatory notes.

The maps of wilder country, away from roads, might provide the most appeal. Your map and compass can take you into areas where you can explore in much the same way as our pioneer forefathers. There is a tremendous satisfaction in finding your way across such country on foot, by horseback, or in a canoe. By using your navigational skills with map and compass, you get where you intended without roads, signs, or other man-made aids.

Anyone who travels on the sea, whether he keeps in sight of land or crosses oceans, needs to use his map, even if he calls it a chart. With that and his instruments, he finds his way and depends on his navigational skills even more seriously than does the map user ashore. In a similar way, an airplane navigator is very dependent on his chart. From both of these important and essential mapping needs and skills have come developments of value to all who use maps.

For what they have to offer, maps and compasses are inexpensive. If you want to make map work more than just a minor sideline to other activities, you will find the essentials are few and the elements are easily mastered. Moreover, you will soon be engrossed in a hobby that has many practical advantages in other activities.

Learn to read all there is to be found on a map. Learn to use the map with a compass. Learn to make simple maps and plans. These are worthwhile accomplishments. They are what the book is all about.

Introduction
to Second Edition

CHANGES IN THE USES OF MAPS AND COMPASSES ARE NEITHER GREAT NOR rapid, but in the years since publication of the first edition of this book there have been advances that we should note. The first edition has proved a popular and most useful guide to those interested in the application of maps or charts and compasses in a great many ways. However, the time has come to revise, without altering the overall concept of the book—a concise and clear guide to anyone wishing to know how to make the fullest use of available maps and compasses.

Mapping has worldwide applications. Metrication is increasingly used, whether we like it or not, and necessary growing awareness has been noted by more use of metric measure in this edition. Although mapping technology does not change, and this edition is no bigger, several sections have been rewritten and illustrations redrawn to clarify points and allow for modern developments.

We hope that readers will find this revised book even more useful as a guide to the fascinating uses of maps of all types as well as compasses.

1

What Is a Map?

A MAP IS A REPRESENTATION, AT A REDUCED SIZE, OF PART OF THE surface of the earth. The amount by which it is reduced is its *scale*, meaning how much smaller the representation is than the actual area it pictures. All maps are necessarily smaller than what they represent, and this may be quoted as a fraction. If this is 1:1000, then a distance on the ground is 1000 times as far as it is drawn on the map. Another way of quoting the scale is to say that a distance on the map represents some other distance on the ground. It could be a scale of 1 inch on the map representing 1 mile on the ground. With the coming of metrication, which progresses in tens, the representative fraction is more easily converted to the second method of defining scale. You are then concerned with centimeters on the map representing kilometers on the ground.

Maps are usually drawn on paper. There are a great many different types of maps; much depends on what the map user wants emphasized. The map reader might want to know about the location of boundaries and the situation of cities. That is called a *political map*. Another reader might be more interested in the elevation of land, the courses of rivers or streams, and other details of the land. That is called a *physical map*. In some maps both features are combined, but that could produce a general map that has so many complexities that it is confusing.

Other sorts of maps show the densities of population, the distribution of wildlife, or just the meeting places of an organization. Maps for these purposes may start with one of the other maps as a base, but unwanted features are discarded and only things that are relevant to the particular purpose are retained and added to.

The term *map* does have other uses besides the representation of part of the earth's surface, but that is what is generally understood if the term is not qualified in any way. A representation of the sky, showing the positions of stars and other heavenly bodies is also called a map.

If the map is of a fairly small area and to a large scale, it is called a *plan*. This may be just the layout of a house and the surrounding yard and garden, plus the adjoining streets. It is not always easy to define the difference between what is a plan and what is a map. The large scale of a plan allows considerably more detail, including the actual sizes of things that could not be shown to scale size, if at all, on a map with much smaller scale. One guide is the way roads are shown. On a map, they have to be shown by parallel lines that are not to a scale width. On a plan the road width is drawn to scale and may vary as the actual road verge and boundary does.

If a map is primarily concerned with water, it is a *chart*. There might be a shore-line, but most of what is shown is concerned with depths of water and features on the sea or ocean. The chart is designed to suit the needs of those who navigate on water, and any land features shown are as they relate to anyone approaching from the sea. In general, a nautical chart is not much use to anyone concerned with matters ashore. Similarly, a land map might have an extensive coastline on it, but the details concerning the water are really given for the interest of a person ashore and would not be sufficient to provide navigational information for anyone approaching the coast from seaward.

PROJECTIONS

A problem with mapping—which might not be very obvious if the map is of a comparatively small area—is that the world is a sphere, but the map is flat. The difference between the curve of the surface of the earth and the flat piece of paper on which the map is drawn may be so slight as to be ignored if you are concerned with only 50 miles each way; but if you are thinking of 500 miles, something has to be done to allow for distortion.

The only accurate way of representing the shape of the whole earth or a major part is with a *globe*. A globe is really another form of map. Because of its shape and bulk, a globe is not a map to carry around. Even part of a globe would be an awkward package. A globe is an interesting and decorative thing to have in a home, school, library, or anywhere static, and it is useful for reference, particularly when you want to relate a flat map to the true shape and position of a country or other large part of the earth's surface.

There are many ways of *projecting* a map of the whole world, or a large part of it (as shown later), but all of these methods are attempts to portray what is really a sphere on a flat surface. This is impossible to do perfectly; all of these projections are compromises. This should be remembered when using world maps. Some distort shapes to get directions correct. Others aim to get shapes about right, but the relation between them is wrong—a straight line on the map would not follow the same course as a line between the same places on the surface of a globe. It is important to remember this when following air routes or other long distances on maps. Reference to a globe might be advisable.

Fortunately for most of us, we need maps of much smaller areas. When you are dealing with a local area, or even one the size of states, for all practical purposes the map is a true scale representation of that portion of the earth, and a scale measurement on the map can be safely interpreted as a particular distance on the ground.

We know that the earth rotates and the ends of the axis on which it turns are the North and South Poles. A compass points to a location quite close to the North Pole. Actually, the magnetic North Pole is on Bathurst Island, in the north of Canada, about 500 miles from the true North Pole. This information gives us map directions. Very early world navigators knew these things, even if they did not know the reasons behind them. They needed references on which to base their navigation and the maps they prepared as they explored.

The sun and the height to which it reached gave them one guide, and a line around the world where the sun rose highest became the equator. They drew a similar line passing through the poles. Quite early in the development of mathematics, a circle became divided into 360 degrees. It might have been some other figure, but that is the one accepted then and it is still the way angles are measured. Navigators projected angles from the center of the earth and drew circles where the angles broke the surface in both directions.

The circles around parallel with the equator are called *parallels of latitude*. The lines drawn around through the poles are called *meridians of longitude*. *Latitude* is measured north and south from the equator. *Longitude* is measured east and west from the meridian through Greenwich, England. Details are given in chapter 5, but here note that the lines are shown in the margins, if not across, most maps and they are the means of finding the exact part of the earth's surface that the particular map represents. The lines of latitude and longitude shown are not repeated anywhere else, so those given indicate that the area mapped is unique. There may be more maps of the area at many different scales, but the location indicated is of that place only.

MAP TYPES

There are a vast range of grades of maps, from the hastily scribbled sketch to show someone the way, to a work of great precision used in planning or laying out some vast project, but all of these have two things in common—if they are to be genuine maps. There must be a scale so that you have some idea of how big the real area is compared with what is drawn. This could be quite approximate, or it might have to be very exact. Then there must be an indication of direction; otherwise, the user does not know how the map lies in relation to the land it represents. Sometimes it might be sufficient to relate a major line on the map with what it represents on the ground, and which cannot be misunderstood. Usually, it is better to indicate north. The map can then be turned so the north direction on it agrees with a compass and it will then be set the same way as the land pictured on it.

Much more is said about scales in chapter 2, but the reader will hear about *large-*

scale maps and *small-scale maps* here and elsewhere. A small-scale map shows a very large part of the earth's surface on a piece of paper. A large-scale map shows a very much smaller part on the same size paper. The small-scale map gives an overall picture of a lot of land, but with not much detail. The large-scale map takes a very much smaller plot of land and describes it in much more detail. The small-scale map may have 1 inch representing 500 miles. The large-scale map may have 1 inch representing 2 miles. The terms are relative. There is no clear dividing line between large-scale and small-scale. They are more terms of comparison between maps.

A map cannot represent everything by a scale picture of it. Some early mapmakers tried to use illustrations, often with a side view of something that should have been viewed from above. Instead there are now symbols or conventional signs. These are a sort of pictorial shorthand. From the *legend*, which accompanies a map or is produced as a list that is standard for a whole range of maps, you can see what certain symbols mean and learn to identify them quickly. This makes for simplicity on a map. It reduces confusion where many things have to be shown close together.

INFORMATION

There is no universal standard for symbols and they may have to vary according to scale, but many are so well known that they are very nearly universal. For instance, almost all maps use blue for water and an upright cross representing a church. Fortunately, interpreting a map is largely common sense. Checking with a legend will show that there is more information available than is obvious at first glance. It is the use of symbols, as much as anything in mapmaking, that enables a small piece of paper to tell you so much about a piece of land.

Although symbols are typically used, with the coming of aerial photography we are accepting mosaics of photographs as maps. In such cases, actual views from above tell us what is there—with houses alongside roads and other features—all in plain view. Such photographs can be converted to the conventional map form and aerial photography becomes the modern way of correcting and checking maps.

Another section of information that many maps provide concerns *elevation*. A map that does not have any indication of heights could appear to be of a flat countryside when actually, there are mountains and valleys as well as plains. Some maps are drawn with shading to indicate hills, but this does not tell you their heights. A map could be made thickened and heavy so it has the hills and valleys built up to scale on it, but then it would cease to be something to carry around. *Relief maps* are made in that way, but they are used for display.

Instead, the flat map is marked with *contour lines* to indicate elevations. A contour line is drawn through all places that are the same height above sea level. Another contour line is drawn through more points higher and lower. These contour lines could be at 100-foot elevation intervals or any other spacing to suit the scale of the map and the type of country. Colors between contour lines may be used to emphasize their differences.

A figure set in the line indicates the height of that line. Reading contour lines can provide a considerable amount of information. If they are close, the land slopes more steeply than if they are far apart. More information on contours is given in chapter 4. Contour lines read in conjunction with other information can give a good idea of features of the land. You should be able to visualize what you will find when you get there.

In its most elementary form, mapping for many of us starts with a sketch on the back of an envelope to show someone the way they have to go. This might be just a freehand outline to represent roads, possibly with arrows to show the route and a few words, written or spoken, to show key points as landmarks or places to turn. You say or write that from here to there is 2 miles. You have then provided a scale. You might both know what road you are standing on and which way to go, so there is no need for a compass direction. That type of map is a rather crude large-scale one. If the directions you have to give extend to 30 miles, the map you sketch on the same envelope will be a small-scale one.

In those cases, both of you were clear about the direction of the map in relation to the ground, but on most maps there should be an indication of north. There is a convention that the top of a map is north. It nearly always is, but it is unwise to assume so. There should be an arrow in the margin of the map showing the northerly direction, and it is always wise to check that. Sometimes it is a very decorative arrow in the margin or on the body of the map. In some old maps, the cartographer seems to have spent more time on drawing the compass symbol than on drawing the map. On a nautical chart there are usually several north indications in different places, drawn with full circles of degree markings to help in plotting courses.

How are maps made? The sketch on an envelope came from our own observations. Many preliminary maps are made in that way, but for more precision the country is surveyed. Although the instruments used may be very advanced, the principle of most surveying is simple and based on the triangle. It cannot be pushed out of shape. If you establish a baseline and draw two more sides to the triangle at definite angles or lengths, that is it—there can only be that one size and shape of triangle.

Surveying consists of building triangles on triangles. This applies to horizontal and vertical measurements. From a first survey, a base map is prepared and all other maps are built on that, with the scales altered and more information added if required. This is done by the United States Geological Survey, as well as some other agencies and authorities.

SCALE PROPORTIONS

The first introduction to maps is usually a school *atlas* that shows the countries of the world and teaches us their shapes and relation to each other. We should be introduced to a globe as well as an atlas, or we may get wrong ideas about proportions. Many atlases do little more than show shapes of countries and their main towns on political maps, heights, waterways, and some general land features on physical maps. An atlas is a good introduction to mapping, but the scales are too small for you to be able to see local roads, small towns—and certainly not motels.

The next map to come your way is likely to be a state map (perhaps officially issued or provided by an oil company). Such a map is obviously directed to motorists who want to get from one place to another; therefore the main features are roads. What a motorist needs to know is there—road numbers, towns, and the distances between towns. If you want to know about rivers and streams, not many are there. If you want to know something about elevations, there might not be any contour lines. Because a modern car can climb just about any road, why bother with heights?

Quite a lot can be learned from state road maps. Study the information in the margin; it explains a lot you might not have realized was on the map. Get to know the symbols. A slight difference in a symbol could tell you more about the object than you expected. There is usually some way of indicating broad divisions of population.

Such a motoring map cannot give you much detail of towns on the main map, but there are usually inserted maps on a larger scale, showing streets in town and the routes through or around. Look at these *town plans* and note their large scales and the extra information that can be put in.

Such a road map is not much use to you if you want to walk, ride a horse, or paddle a canoe in wild, undeveloped country. The area that interests you could be just a blank space on a road map. There might be a considerable number of features in the area that interests you, but are of no concern to a motorist. This is where you need a *topographic survey map* of fairly large scale. Such a map gives plenty of contour lines as well as the situations of waterways down to the smallest, together with many natural features that form your landmarks.

With that sort of map and a compass, navigation becomes realistic. You are an explorer dependent on your skill to plan a route and find a destination without roads and signposts. An outcrop of rock or a stream becomes your landmark instead of some man-made object. It is this sort of map and compass work that many people find fascinating, and it is the basis for the sport of orienteering.

2

Symbols and Scales

BECAUSE ANY MAP IS SO MUCH SMALLER THAN THE AREA IT REPRESENTS, a scale has to be decided on and the layout arranged to suit this. Within the scale, the many things that are to be illustrated have to be represented. If the scale is very large, it may be possible to draw the actual shape as it would be seen from above, but in most cases the scale does not permit such things as buildings and roads to be drawn in correct proportions. If the scale is small, whole towns may be just dots. To indicate various things on a map, there have to be conventionally agreed-upon symbols, so that anyone accustomed to this form of representation will immediately understand what is meant and can read the map easily. In this way, a considerable amount of information can be packed into a comparatively small space.

There are no worldwide standards either of scales or symbols, but there are sufficient similarities. Anyone familiar with a map with conventional symbols and scales of one country should have little difficulty in interpreting a map drawn to the standards of another country. In America, the accepted standards are those of the United States Department of the Interior, Geological Survey, as found on the topographic maps they produce. Anyone familiar with these maps should have no difficulty in reading maps produced by commercial publishers, the British Ordnance Survey maps, or the majority of European and other foreign maps.

CONVENTIONAL SIGNS AND SYMBOLS

Mapmakers of a few centuries ago tended to use small pictorial representations that were sometimes grossly out of proportion and usually as viewed from the side, although the map itself was obviously drawn as a view from above. They also used their imagination and filled blank spaces with unlikely objects or such statements as "Here be dragons." With some old maps, it is difficult to decide what is the result of observation or survey and what is put in because the draftsman thought there ought to be something there. Many maps seem to have been regarded as art rather than science. Some of them may have been designed to impress the viewer rather than to be of much practical use.

A modern map should be a precision tool. Any part of it should be capable of interpretation, so the user can obtain information on the part of the earth's surface represented with a degree of accuracy dependent on the scale. He should not be confused by the mapmaker's desire to put in pretty pictures of features. (An exception may be where the map is intended to be decorative, such as a drawing of a state on a table mat, where places of interest are depicted to give an idea of situations without much accuracy.) Otherwise, a modern map will be found to use symbols to get a considerable amount of information in the minimum of space, so that the map is not cluttered with marks that obscure each other or make interpretation difficult.

LEGENDS

Many maps carry a legend giving details of symbols used and the way certain features are indicated, either in the margin or on a panel inset in the map. This often goes with a compass indication and the scale, possibly with details of how the map relates to adjoining maps and when parts were last revised.

Take note of the date of the last revision. Towns and natural features do not move, but a road made since the last revision may make a significant alteration to an area.

Symbols may be peculiar to the map, or they may follow the conventional practice of most maps. If it is a map intended for users with particular interests, there will almost certainly be some markings special to that map. For instance, a map of an area that goes over state borders may have special ways of showing state parks, national forests, wildlife refuges, and Indian reservations. The legend will tell you about that even if it is assumed you are familiar with the symbols common to many maps.

To a certain extent, symbols are common to maps of all scales, but there are practical limits. On a fairly large scale, a town may be drawn with an outline showing its approximate shape. But on a small scale it becomes a dot or a circle with a colored center. Individual buildings or features—such as schools, churches, and windmills—may be shown on maps down to certain scales, but as more of an area has to be included in a smaller space on the map it ceases to be possible to include them. Exceptions may be where the map area is otherwise blank and one of these is a prominent feature.

The reader of a map needs to relate his understanding of the use of symbols with the scale to which he is working. Fortunately, maps are usually fairly obvious and you can learn a lot after only a little experience. There is, however, always more information that is not immediately obvious, and which can be interpreted when you know what other conventional signs mean.

MAP COLORS

Colors will help to clarify details on any map. If a map is just in black on white, color is reduced to shading, stippling, or the use of printed words. Colors make some things immediately obvious. Blue is universally used for water, so the coast is there without any doubt. Without the color you might have difficulty in deciding if something drawn is an inlet or part of the solid ground. A map may have to be made without any colors; this applies particularly to a sketch map you make yourself. It is then very important to make sure that features that are obvious to you cannot be confused by a reader unfamiliar with the country.

In addition to blue for water in all its forms (sea, river, canal, lake, and marshes), red is the next most frequently used color. It is one of the easiest seen colors so it is used for emphasis. Roads may be drawn as parallel lines in black, but the most important ones are filled in red. Boundaries may be in various forms of red lines. Urban areas may be red dots or enclosed patterns of red tint or stippling (small dots). Red is usually the color of choice on special maps where something needs emphasis.

As might be expected, black is the main color for many drawn lines, but these tend to be man-made features, such as roads and buildings, railroads, and boundaries. Other colored areas may have their own darker shade. For example, the border of a blue lake will be darker blue.

Green is the color for woodland, either an allover shade or with patterns, if it is necessary to show such things as orchards and vineyards.

Brown is the usual color for contour lines, but the shade may appear almost red on some maps. Contour lines, however, are unlikely to be confused with other features, particularly in mountainous areas where they are drawn close together.

Purple tends to be associated with aircraft. Maps intended to be used in airplane navigation have some features emphasized with purple. Much mapmaking now makes use of aerial surveys. Where a revision is made from aerial photographs without field checks, purple is used on a map.

Those are all the colors normally used on topographic maps officially issued in the United States, but some other colors are used on commercially produced maps and foreign maps. A green that is darker than used for woodland may be used for some roads instead of red. A yellow or yellow-brown color may also be used to pick out particular roads. Sparing use of yellow can give prominence to state highway number symbols. Broad bands of any color may be used to draw attention to boundaries or other outlines drawn in black.

British and other European maps generally follow color patterns similar to American ones. Road quality may descend from red through brown to yellow and no color, but only hard-surfaced British roads are shown. Major motorways (equivalent of interstates) may be colored dark blue.

ROAD SYMBOLS

Roads are shown as parallel lines (FIG. 2-1A) with the more important roads usually filled in red. Some commercially produced maps use other colors to distinguish special roads from the primary highways in red. Examples are dark blue for free limited-access highways, green for toll limited-access highways, and yellow-brown for other four-lane divided highways in Rand McNally road maps. The choice of road representation depends on scale. On a smaller scale, a road may be just a red line, without the black parallel lines. The symbols for dual highways are only possible with larger scales.

If a highway is under construction, its outline is shown as broken lines when its alignment is known. This is the condition at the time of making the map or its revision. If you check with the date of the last revision, shown in the map border or with

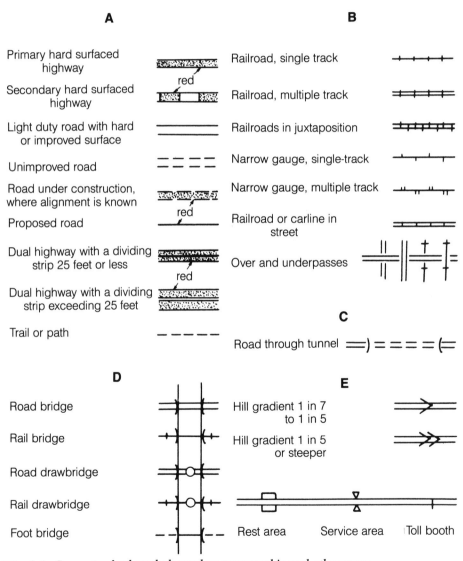

Fig. 2-1. *Some standard symbols used on topographic and other maps.*

the legend, you may assume that the road is now in use if the map is a few years old. A possible point of confusion comes with the use of broken lines for an unimproved road, but there the dashes are only about half the length of those indicating a road under construction. In any case, there is no color on an unimproved road. Therefore, color between broken lines must mean a road still being built.

On some foreign maps, broken lines mean that the road is unfenced. Any road shown with solid lines is fenced. If the line at one or both sides becomes broken, that part is without a fence. At the bottom of the series of road symbols is the path or trail, which is just a broken single line.

Railroads are always black. Even if you are not using a railroad, its presence is a useful navigational point, enabling you to set your map easier. As shown in FIG. 2-1B, the type of track can be discovered from the map, if it is of sufficient scale to allow the details. With small scales, all railroads are shown the same—with crossing lines over the one showing the route.

Highways and railroads may cross each other or water. On a small scale, they are drawn simply crossing. On a larger scale it is possible to discover which goes over and under. The one going under is broken. If a highway or railroad goes under for a greater distance than is necessary just to cross another, the tunnel is then drawn with a symbolic representation of the porticos and the buried part in broken lines (FIG. 2-1C).

Passage under a canal aqueduct would be shown in the same way, but if there is a bridge over a waterway, symbols show its type. The ends of the bridge are indicated (FIG. 2-1D). Roads or railroads are drawn straight across through these marks. If it is a drawbridge that swings or lifts, a circle in the middle indicates this. If it is a foot-bridge, the trail at each side is shown with broken lines, but the actual bridge is a solid line. On some foreign maps the portico signs are also used where road and railroads cross each other, looking like small representations of bridges.

A level crossing may be shown by the road and railroad symbols crossing each other. Level crossings are less common in some other countries and their presence may be shown by a small X over the crossing or by the road parallel lines being brought to a point at the railroad.

Some additional information found on some foreign and commercially produced maps include a circle on a railroad to indicate a station (red if available to passengers and open if not), with a red rectangle for a principal station on British maps. On some foreign maps a V on a road indicates a hill, with the V pointing downhill. Two Vs close together indicate an extra steep hill. The legend will show steepness, but typically a single V is a slope between 1-in-7 (14 percent) and 1-in-5 (20 percent), while double Vs mean it is steeper than that. Toll booths, rest and service areas, and wayside tables may be shown on road maps (FIG. 2-1E).

WATER

The blue color for water is treated in many ways to indicate its condition. If the map includes coast, but is intended only for users of the land, the sea may be just an overall blue. Some characteristics might be shown even if the map is not intended to be of serious use to navigators of boats. The coastline is usually shown as high water mark. If there is a flat foreshore of sand or shingle always exposed or uncovered at low water, it may be shown by dots (FIG. 2-2A). If there are rocks or coral reefs along the shore they may be shown diagrammatically (FIG. 2-2B). If soundings are shown, they will be like underwater contours in a darker blue with a figure alongside or enclosed indicating depth (FIG. 2-2C). Refer to the legend to discover what the figure represents. It could be in feet, fathoms (6 feet), or meters.

Features that may be hazardous to navigation, particularly if they are within view from the shore, may be shown. Pilings or a dolphin standing above the water is shown as a small circle. An exposed wreck is shown as a little black picture. A sunken wreck

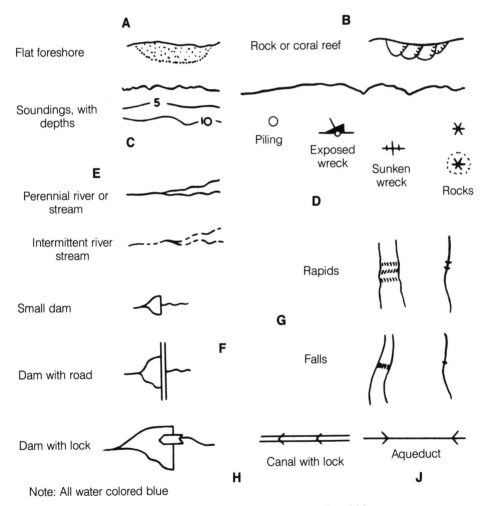

Fig. 2-2. *Symbols used in connection with water, usually colored blue.*

has its own black symbol. A rock awash is shown as a star, with dots around it if much is exposed at low water (FIG. 2-2D).

Where the scale width of a river or stream is enough to justify it, the outline may be drawn. Otherwise it is represented by a blue line following its course, but not indicating its width. If it is a stream that has only an intermittent flow, the solid outline or single line is broken with dots (FIG. 2-2E). If there is a small dam, that is shown as a black line across the resulting pond. A road may be drawn across the dam. If there is a lock in the dam, that is shown diagrammatically with gates pointing upstream (FIG. 2-2F).

Where there is a width of a river drawn, a rapid is shown as a series of small lines. If there is a fall, there is one set of lines. If the river is shown by a single line, two lines across mean a rapid and one line across marks a fall (FIG. 2-2G).

If the scale is large enough, a canal is shown with parallel dark blue lines with a lighter blue filling. A lock is then shown with a diagrammatic pair of gates (FIG. 2-2H). On a smaller scale the canal is a single blue line, usually without locks marked. If the canal goes through a tunnel, it is given broken lines and similar porticos to a road. If the canal is elevated over an aqueduct, it is drawn solid, but with the aqueduct ends indicated (FIG. 2-2J).

A water well is a small blue circle (FIG. 2-3A). If the well location is actually a spring and a stream flows from it, the circle has the stream joined to it. Similar circles are drawn in black to indicate other types of wells, but the type is always printed alongside, such as oil or gas.

A lake is an expanse of blue with a dark blue border. If the lake is an intermittent one, it has a broken border and diagonal dotted shading. If it is a dry lake bed, the blue broken outline contains a pattern of red dots (FIG. 2-3B).

A swamp has diagrammatic tufts with some light blue shading. If the marsh is submerged, there is an overall darker blue pattern. If it is a wooded marsh, it is drawn similarly, but the overall color is green (FIG. 2-3C).

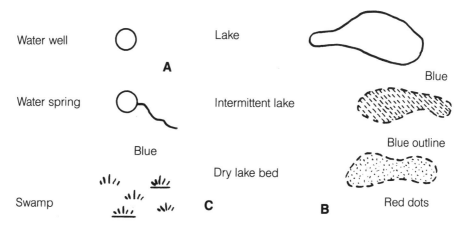

Fig. 2-3. *Symbols associated with inland water.*

STRUCTURES

How individual buildings and other erections are indicated depends on scale. If an exact location is to be marked on a small-scale map, it may be a dot at the actual position with a circle around and a name alongside, all in black. This may be a landmark visible from some distance. Tanks for oil, etc., are solid black circles. Water tanks are black circles with diagonal shading (FIG. 2-4A). A school is a small square with a flag above it. A church is a square with a cross above it and a windmill is pictured (FIG. 2-4B).

A power transmission line is a feature easily seen from a distance, and it is shown as a series of dashes between dots. If the scale is large enough to show metal towers, they are included as open squares in place of dots. Telephone and pipelines are a series of dashes labeled as to type (FIG. 2-4C).

Whether buildings are shown or not depends on the scale. If they are drawn to shape, small dwellings or places of employment may be solid black or filled with black cross hatching. Other buildings, such as barns and warehouses, may be open outlines or filled with diagonal hatching (FIG. 2-4D).

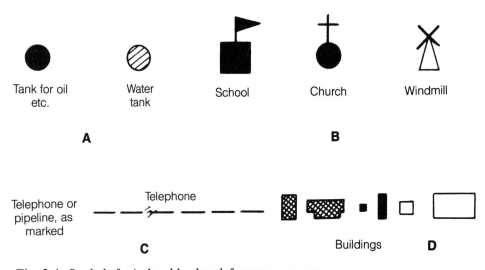

Fig. 2-4. *Symbols for isolated landmark features on a map.*

BOUNDARIES

Boundaries vary in prominence and intensity of line according to their importance. Black lines start with the heavily drawn national boundaries. There are similar, but lighter state boundaries and even lighter county or parish boundaries. Various lighter lines go down to the boundaries of such things as cemeteries and small parks (FIG. 2-5A). Further boundary lines are red (FIG. 2-5B), with some of lesser importance not very easily seen among other things on the map.

Brown contour lines are solid or dotted, but their significance and meaning are dealt with in more detail in chapter 4. A small triangle with a dot at its center indicates a control station or bench mark used in surveying maps. Such positions are usually high and command a good view all around. They are permanent features and may be marks on rocks or man-made erections that the map reader can locate on the terrain. The height above sea level is shown alongside the triangle. A small, green triangle may be used on some commercially produced maps to indicate a campground. A green tree alongside the triangle indicates a park with camping facilities. The tree alone means a park without camping. A small red triangle may be used for a youth hostel. An airport is usually shown with the outline of an airplane.

The foregoing symbols cover the majority likely to be found on maps, but there are others that may be only used at particular scales or on maps intended for particular purposes. Mapmaking is an ongoing science and new maps may be produced with revised symbols. Many have been found most suitable over the years and are regularly adopted, but some may be replaced as new series of maps are produced. If there are new or revised symbols, the legend will give details. That is why it is always wise to

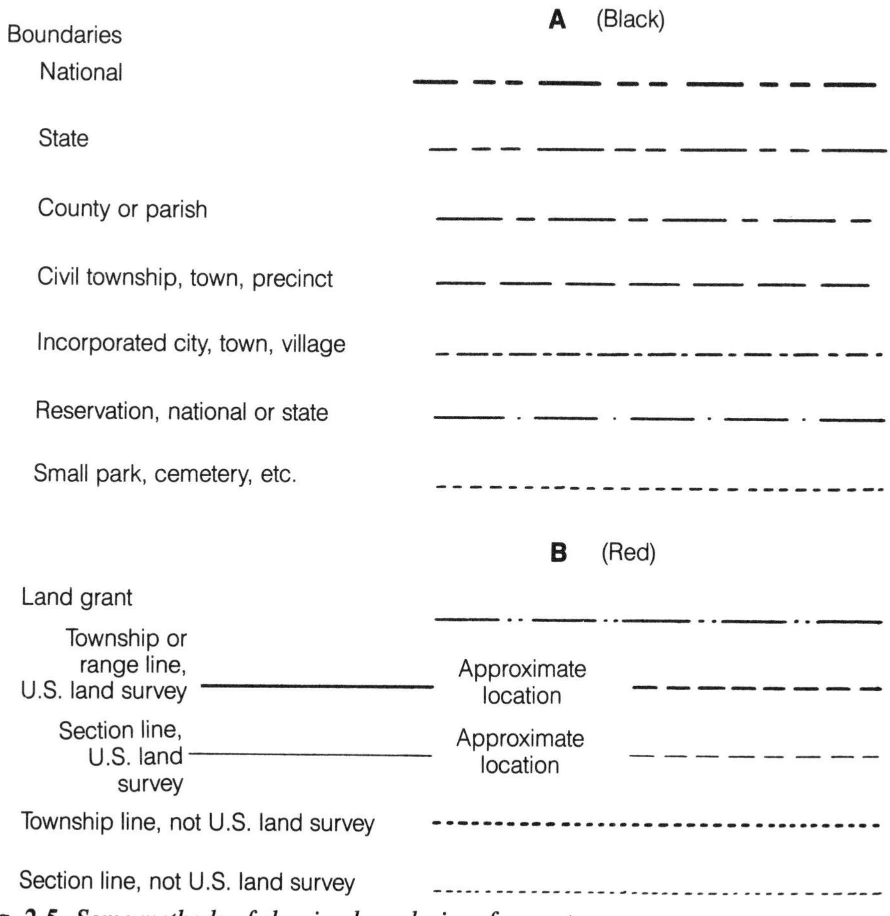

Fig. 2-5. *Some methods of showing boundaries of many types.*

consult it rather than assume that—because you expect, from past experience, something will be indicated by a certain symbol, that it will be so.

SYMBOLS ON OTHER MAPS

Besides officially produced topographic maps, commercially produced road maps, and the state maps mainly intended for motorists, there are others available that have symbols to suit their particular service offered.

The United States Department of Agriculture and Forest Service produces maps of the forests that range from small-scale maps covering large parts of the country and showing where the forests are to a map for each individual forest. From these individual forest maps are derived others to appeal to visitors. Forest visitor maps are the ones used by serious hikers and backpackers, but there are visitors' guides intended more for the casual visitor that indicate such things as points of main interest, car parks, information centers, and similar things, without including the more detailed information required by anyone going deeper into the forest.

A *forest visitors map* uses many symbols found on topographic maps, particularly where surrounding areas are shown. In the forest the user needs additional information. His landmarks are different from those in urban and developed areas. Consequently, primitive roads, caves, or quarries that would not be justified on a general map are important as key positions for locating where you are, possibly among an enormous number of lookalike trees.

Because the area is covered with trees, there is less need to use green everywhere. It may still be the predominant color, but other colors may be used for special areas. Roads within the forest are mainly of a much lower standard than outside, but they are indicated in a similar way (FIG. 2-6A). If restrictions are marked, the user should inquire at the local Forest Service station.

Railroads, transmission lines, and pipelines are the same symbols as elsewhere. Lookout stations are good landmarks, and they may be shown with hexagons (FIG. 2-6B). Buildings, including schoolhouses and churches, are shown the same as elsewhere, but many black symbols are used for places of navigational as well as other interest within the forest (FIG. 2-6C). Areas of special interest to visitors, particularly for their recreational activities, are shown in a red-brown color (FIG. 2-6D).

The National Parks Service uses the standard Geological Survey Maps, but they issue visitors maps that are more pictorial and diagrammatic for the use of tourists who only need to know the main features and the location of things of interest to them. Anyone exploring a national park more seriously will need other maps, but the visitors map shows height by two-color shading, with elevations marked at summits or overlooks. Water is blue; restricted boating areas are shown a darker shade. Roads and trails are drawn red over the basic shaded green of the map (FIG. 2-7A). Symbols are used for all the places of visitor interest, using a standard black base of a square with rounded corners (FIG. 2-7B). The symbols are rather large in relation to the map. If several have to be grouped at one point, they only give a general indication of place and are not the exact representation of position as found with symbols on a standard topographic map.

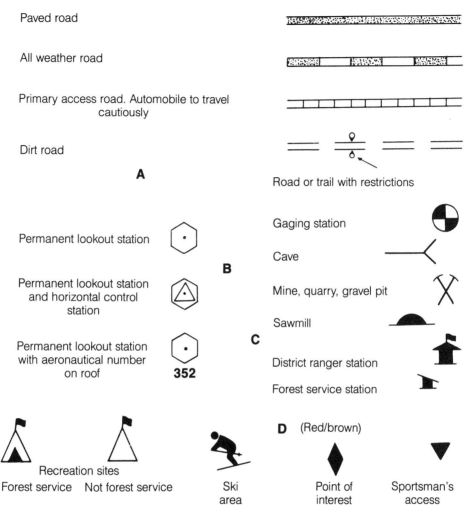

Fig. 2-6. *A selection of symbols used on forest and other maps of recreational interest.*

On the more precise topographic maps, a dot at the center of a symbol may be the mapped location of what it represents. The center of the base of the symbol is the location when it is blacked in or solidly colored.

SCALES

A map has to be drawn much smaller than the part of the earth's surface it is to represent. The relationship between what is drawn and the actual land and water it represents is the *scale*. There are many factors involved in the choice of scale. Convenience in handling the map is one: somewhere between 30 and 40 inches square is about the limit for a person to hold and use, and a map is usually better rather smaller than that. Folding allows parts of the map to be seen while the whole thing is kept compact, but

Paved road   One-way road   Gravel or dirt road   Trail

A

B

Information (Visitor center)

Gas

Picnic area

Amphitheater

Horse rental

Post office

Boat ramp

Interpretive trail

Ranger station

Campground

Lodging

Showers, laundry

Fire lookout

Marina

Store

Food

Medical service

Trailer sites

Parking

Fig. 2-7. *Symbols used on national parks maps.*

there will be occasions when the open map is needed. If the map is to be bound into a book, it has to be much smaller.

What goes on to that single piece of paper depends on requirements. If you want to show the whole country with state boundaries, you can get it on the sheet, but you cannot do much more than show capital cities in each state. Even then you will have difficulty in putting the name of the state and its capital in the outline of some smaller states. If you are only going to put one state on the piece of paper, quite a lot of detail will be possible, showing where places are in relation to each other, with the important roads and other features that are sufficiently big. From this map you can learn about the state in a general way, but you cannot find out about minor roads, footpaths, or the layout of towns.

At an even larger scale, the piece of paper of this size may represent only a mile or two each way, and then it can show such things as the actual outline of houses, fences, and even individual trees. A very large number of maps of this size would be needed to cover the same land area as a map of smaller scale. The scale of a map is determined by what information you want and convenience in handling. If you are travelling, a map of the scale that covers a day's journey is useful; this means that a motorist uses a map with a much smaller scale than a walker. If he used the walker's maps, he would be changing them at least every half-hour and the car would be packed with large-scale maps. If the walker used the motorist's map, he would only travel over part of it and would probably not find all the details he needed.

The possibility of greater detail, but smaller area, can be seen when maps are drawn to represent parts of another map (FIG. 2-8). In this example, each map is twice the scale of the previous one. Therefore, with the linear measurement halved, each map is one-fourth the size of the previous one.

This shows the need to compromise. You might want the advantage of greater detail on a map of large scale, but for the coverage of the next map you would need four maps and you would have to get 16 maps for the area of the next again.

A snag with using many maps for an area is the difficulty of visualizing through routes without spreading them all out on the floor. If they are bound as pages of an atlas, finding the best route across several sheets might be almost impossible. Small-scale maps of whole areas are needed for dealing with longer distances, but larger scales are what you must have if you want to know more about local parts.

METRICATION

In most countries of the world the unit of length is the meter (sometimes spelled metre). All other measurements based on it are in decimal steps: multiply or divide by ten. They have prefixes which indicate the proportion. The same system and prefixes are used for other measures, such as liquids or weights, but they do not concern map makers or users. The metric system was legalized for use in the United States by an Act of Congress in 1866.

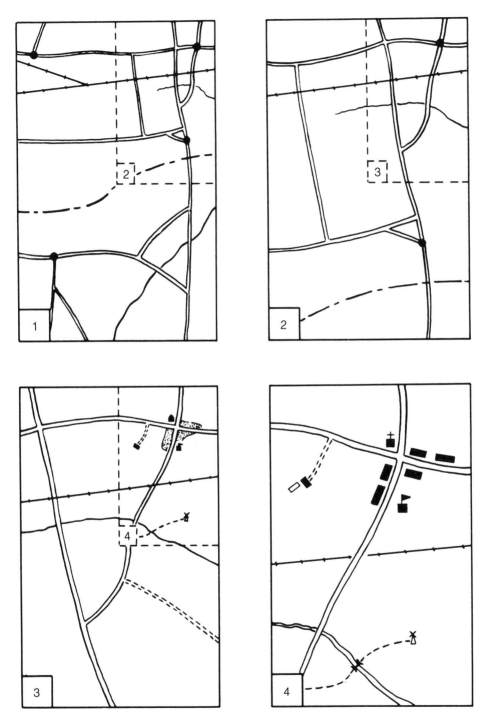

Fig. 2-8. *Map proportions at different scales. The dotted outlines on three maps show the area covered by the next map.*

The alternative to the mile in the metric system is the kilometer, which is one thousand meters. If you visit Europe or many other parts of the world and see a figure on a distance marker, it will be kilometers and not miles. There are some prefixes to indicate intermediate distances, but in general practice these are not used. You need to be aware of the centimeter, which is one-hundredth of a meter, and the millimeter, which is one-tenth of a centimeter. As with longer distances, there are some intermediate prefixes rarely used in practice. A metric rule, which will be marked in centimeters and millimeters, is useful for measuring scale distances on a map. With the decimal relationship between distances, conversion is easier than with inches and miles, because with most proportions you only have to move a decimal point.

If you will be using the metric system it is helpful to be able to think in it, but if you are used to inches and miles, you may first want to convert to the sizes you know. There are no exact equivalents, but it is helpful to know that $2^1/_2$ centimeters are about 1 inch, one meter is just over 39 inches and one kilometer is near $^5/_8$ mile. In practice you can assume that eight kilometers equal five miles. This is a sufficiently accurate conversion for most ordinary map reading. Differences only become apparent if you are dealing with hundreds of miles.

In the margins of many American and English maps you will find scales drawn (described in later sections) showing miles and kilometers, so you have a comparison and can convert easily. If you use a map intended for a country that only uses the metric system, do not expect to find a scale in miles. That is where it is better to think only metric and discard thoughts of miles.

It is usual when abbreviating metric measures to not use a period, so kilometer is shortened to km and not km., different from inch abbreviated to in., which most of us would write with the period. Tables showing metric distances and conversions are included in appendix B.

PROPORTIONS

There are two basic ways of indicating scale. You can say what distance on the map indicates a distance on the ground. It could be that 1 inch on the map indicates 1 mile on the ground. The scale is then described as "1 inch to 1 mile." It is better not to write "1 inch equals 1 mile." Obviously it does not—it represents it. The other way is to write the scale as a representative fraction, showing how much smaller the map is than the area of the earth's surface it represents. The proportion is shown with 1 as the numerator and the number of times the actual distance is bigger as the denominator, both in inches or similar measurement.

There are two lines of thought apparent in the choice of fractions. Until now, the English-speaking peoples have favored proportions of anything, not just maps, where we halve and halve again to whatever number of times gives us what we want: $^1/_2$, $^1/_4$, $^1/_8$, and so on. Countries where the metric system is used favor a decimal arrangement where proportions are in tenths, written as a common fraction or, more often, in decimal form: 1, 0.1, 0.01, 0.001, and so on.

The method we use tends to result in cumbersome representative fractions. The scale of 1 inch to 1 mile then becomes $^1/_{63,360}$ as there are 63,360 inches in a mile.

That is a rather unwieldly fraction that does not tell as much as quickly as the statement of what 1 inch represents. A representative fraction is clearer if its denominator is a round figure, as it may be when decimal measurements are involved. Measurements on the map may be in centimeters and those on the ground are in kilometers. One tenth of a centimeter is a millimeter. One hundred centimeters make a meter, and 1000 meters make a kilometer. As close approximations: 2.5 centimeters (25 millimeters) equal 1 inch, and a kilometer is $5/8$ of a mile (8 kilometers equals 5 miles).

With a scale of 1 centimeter to 1 kilometer, the representative fraction is $1/100,000$. With a scale of 2 centimeters to 1 kilometer, the fraction becomes $1/50,000$. This is fairly close to the scale of 1 inch to 1 mile and is nearer $1^1/4$ inches to 1 mile. Both scales are large enough to give sufficient detail for a walker and to put about 20 miles or more each way on a piece of paper that is convenient to handle.

It is possible to use any scale for a map, and it is sometimes necessary to have proportions that do not use standard measurements. For practical purposes, it is helpful to be able to use common measurements on the map. You can then put a rule between two points on the map and measure the distance in inches and fractions or in centimeters and millimeters and do a simple conversion to get the actual distance on the ground. Most of us are able to estimate distances in inches with reasonable accuracy, so we can look at a map of common scale and say what the distance is between points with all the accuracy we need for the moment. If it is a metric map and you think in inches, your estimate in inches must be multiplied by $2^1/2$ to get an estimate in centimeters.

Some scales used for American maps are tabulated in TABLE 2-1. As can be seen, some fractions are related to English measure and its traditional methods of halving, etc., but there is an increasing use of fractions with round figures as denominators, conforming closer to decimal division practiced in countries using metric measures.

Table 2-1. Representative Scales Used in American Maps.

Representative Fraction	1 Inch Represents	1 Centimeter Represents
$1/20,000$	about 1667 feet	200 meters
$1/24,000$	2000 feet	240 meters
$1/25,000$	about 2083 feet	250 meters
$1/62,500$	nearly 1 mile	625 meters
$1/63,360$	1 mile	nearly 634 meters
$1/100,000$	nearly 1.6 miles	1 kilometer
$1/250,000$	nearly 4 miles	2.5 kilometers
$1/500,000$	nearly 8 miles	5 kilometers
$1/1,000,000$	nearly 16 miles	10 kilometers

SCALE INDICATIONS

Among the information given in the margin of the map will be a scale. There may be the representative fraction and a statement of what 1 inch or 1 centimeter represents, particularly if this is not a round figure. But there will also be a scale drawn, and it is this that will probably be of most use to you when measuring distances on the map.

The scale may be in miles, kilometers, or a smaller unit—if it is a large-scale map. To avoid too much close detail, it is usual to put only whole units to the right of zero and fractions of the unit to the left (FIG. 2-9A). This means that you measure a distance by taking whole units to the right—until you cannot get another whole one—then take in parts of the unit to the left. If you start using the scale from its extreme left, as might have been expected, you will get a wrong distance.

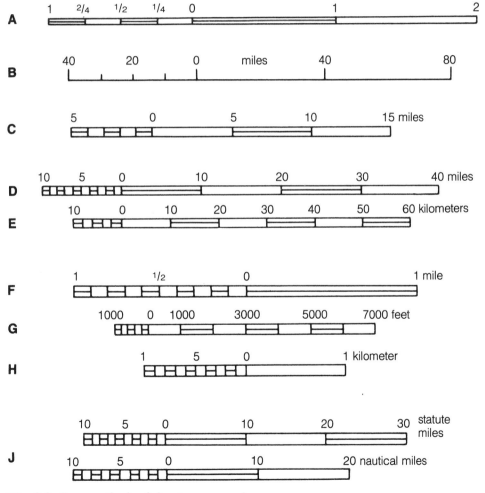

Fig. 2-9. *Some methods of showing map scales.*

The scale may be a single line with the divisions projecting from it (FIG. 2-9B) or, more often, parallel lines with the divisions between and alternate spaces shaded or marked with a line (FIG. 2-9C). What the divisions are depends on the scale of the map. For a scale of $^1/_{1,000,000}$ the main divisions may be at 10 mile intervals and the fractions to the left of zero are single miles (FIG. 2-9D). The same map may also carry a metric scale, which can conveniently be broken down to similar divisions: 10 kilometer divisions to the right and 2 kilometers to the left of zero (FIG. 2-9E).

If even more of the earth's surface has to go on a map, the scale divisions may be 25 miles or even more, and the fractions may have to be 5 miles or more. At a small scale, you cannot expect to do more than estimate individual miles. At the other extreme, a map of a comparatively small amount of land may have the fractional part broken down into eighths or tenths of a mile (FIG. 2-9F). There may be another scale alongside in feet, with the main divisions of 1000 feet and the fractional side divided into 200-foot spaces (FIG. 2-9G). There may also be a metric scale (FIG. 2-9H). As a help for comparison, the zero mark of nearby scales may be kept opposite each other, but that is not always done. Decimals may be used on metric scales. Be careful not to overlook the point, which may not be very obvious, particularly if there is no "0" in front of it.

A coastal map with a large expanse of sea on it may also have a scale in nautical miles. If a scale is marked *miles*, it can be assumed they are the normal land miles of 5280 feet. These are more correctly called *statute miles*, and they will be marked as such if there is also a scale in nautical miles on the map (FIG. 2-9J). A nautical mile is 6080 feet. This may be the only scale shown on a chart intended for navigation at sea.

MAP MEASURING

Where the scale to which a map is drawn can be related to a rule marked in inches or centimeters, the rule can then be used to measure on the map. A little mental arithmetic will give you the conversion to distances on the ground. There are scale rules available that are marked with commonly used scales. They will give direct readings without the risk of error that may come with conversion. An edge may be marked with two scales in opposite directions, usually one being twice the other. A flat rule marked on both sides and edges may then have eight scales. One with a triangular section can carry 12.

Anyone using maps of a particular scale frequently may find a scale rule worthwhile. For large-scale maps or plans, one is particularly useful if graduated in fine enough detail for measuring sizes of buildings, widths of roads, and such things as yard shapes and field sizes. However, most map users can manage without a scale rule when travelling on foot, by cycle, or by car.

A navigator at sea uses dividers for transferring distances from scale to chart or vice versa. They are useful for ordinary mapping, even if they are only school dividers or pencil compasses. You can set the divider points to the distance on the map and move the dividers to the scale to read the distance (FIG. 2-10A). Without dividers, you

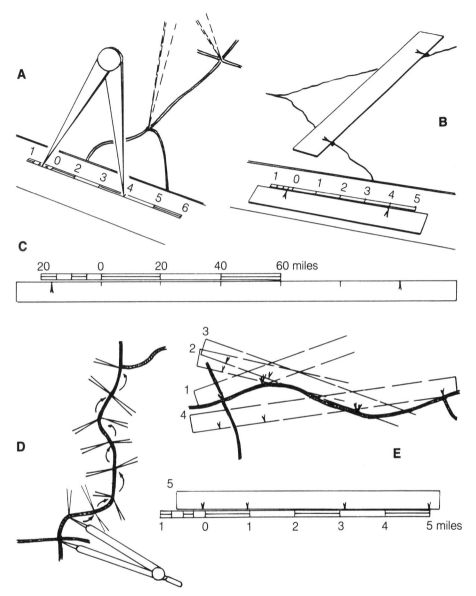

Fig. 2-10. *Transferring measurements on a map to and from the scale, using dividers or a strip of paper.*

can do this along the edge of a piece of paper using pencil marks in the relevant positions (FIG. 2-10B).

The scale drawn in the margin of the map is not usually very long in relation to possible distances you may want to transfer. For distances greater than its length, you can make marks on the edge of a strip of paper; then mark as much of the scale length as you can in steps along the edge and make up the difference against the scale (FIG. 2-10C). With dividers, you can step off whole divisions and make up the balance from the left-hand part of the scale.

Usually it is not distances in a straight line that are very important. You may have to follow a winding road. In wild country, you may have to go around a valley or avoid marshy ground. The distance may be considerably greater than a straight line.

You can set dividers to a short distance taken from the scale and step off along the route, counting the number of steps to get the total distance (FIG. 2-10D). You could put a starting mark on the edge of a piece of paper and move this around the route a little at a time (FIG. 2-10E) until you mark the final destination and can measure the length between the marks. It is possible to shape a piece of string or thread around the route, then straighten it, and measure between marks. But it is difficult in many cases to keep the string from slipping. With dividers or paper, you break the route into a series of short straight lines. There may be further shapings in those parts, so it is wise to add a little to the total distance you obtain.

There are several map measures obtainable that depend on running a wheel along the route being measured. A simple one has a wheel running like a nut on a screwed axle, which is mounted in a frame with a handle (FIG. 2-11). To use it, the wheel is screwed close to one side of its frame, and then run along the route so it unscrews away from the frame until it reaches the destination. Without allowing it to turn until put in position, it is reversed along the scale until it comes close to the frame again. The distance it travels straight along the scale should be the same distance it went along the route on the map.

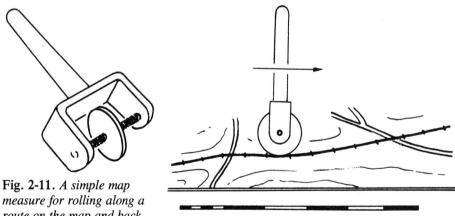

Fig. 2-11. *A simple map measure for rolling along a route on the map and back along the scale.*

A variation on this has the wheel on a plain axle, but connected by gears to a dial. The dial may be marked with a hand passing over one or more scales so distances on maps drawn to those scales may be read direct after running the wheel along the route (FIG. 2-12). For other scales, the hand may be set at zero on the dial; then the wheel runs along the route and reversed along the scale until the hand returns to zero to obtain the distances. That sort of map measure may have a lens on the handle and a compass on the reverse of the dial, with the whole thing light and compact enough to be carried in your pocket. The rather basic compass usually included should be regarded as a reserve. You should have a better one for normal use, particularly if you are undertaking wilderness travel.

The world is spherical. A map is flat. Most maps we use refer to such a small area of the earth's surface that the difference between distances represented on the flat paper and the curved earth surface they represent is so slight as to be ignored. There is a problem of scale when the flat map represents a considerable area of the earth. In an extreme case, this can be seen with a map of the whole world. A globe is the truest representation of the earth. If a flat map of the whole world is compared with it, places far from the equator will be seen to be drawn much bigger than they are more correctly represented on a globe. More information on this problem is covered in chapter 5. There are many schemes of projection that attempt to make an allowance for this difference, but no flat map can be truly representative of a global surface, and scales have to vary between different parts of the map. A map of the whole United

Fig. 2-12. *A map measure with a wheel to run along the route on the map, and a dial showing the scale distance traveled. A lense at the other end of the handle is useful for seeing map details.*

States is big enough to be affected. Although allowances are made in projecting the map, distances scaled should be regarded as very close approximations rather than precise measurements.

The inability of a flat map to deal with long distances is seen in diagrams of intercontinental flights or long sea voyages. The shortest distance between points on a globe is a curved line on a flat map or chart. The distance along this apparently curved path is actually shorter than along what appears to be a straight line, when drawn on the flat map.

3

Directions

MOST OF THE TIME MAN HAS BEEN ON THE EARTH, THE MAJORITY OF people have assumed it to be flat. With their limited local movements, their knowledge of the earth certainly indicated that all around them was basically flat. Some early scholars may have had ideas about the world being spherical, but they were in a minority. Even up to about 500 years ago, most people thought the world was flat. When Columbus, Cabot, and other great explorers sailed west from Europe, many people, including some on board their ships, expected them to fall off the edge of the flat earth. It was not until Cook and other explorers continued to sail west, and eventually arrived home in a circumnavigation, that the round shape of the earth became an accepted fact. (There is, however, still a Flat Earth Society.)

If you can identify the place where you are standing as a spot on a map, you know where you are on the map. That does not allow you to discover directions on the ground from the map. You can turn the map in any direction, but you cannot tell which way you are facing. If there is some landmark visible from where you are standing that is also marked on the map, you can turn the map so an imaginary line between where you are and what you see on the map is parallel with your sight line on the ground. The map has then been set in relation to the ground and other places on it will be in their correct relative positions on ground.

That is a common way of relating a map to part of the earth's surface that it represents. Some other way of identifying directions is preferable, for use in any circumstances, such as when you are using a map at home to plan a journey elsewhere.

Compass directions are the answer. We all know that a compass points north, so if north is indicated on a map we can relate actual directions with those drawn.

The Chinese are credited with discovering that a free-swinging magnet will settle on a north-south line. They used naturally magnetic iron ore called *lodestone*, and floated it in a little boat in a bowl of water, to function as the first primitive compass. Modern magnetic compasses use the same principle, even if their sophisticated make-up gives them the appearance of greater complication. There are compasses that do not depend on magnets that can be used in ships and on aircraft, but these are large, fixed, and are unsuitable where portability is important—as it is for most map users.

Even flat-earth believers appreciated the value of a compass, although they may not have understood exactly where it was pointing. North was a direction, but what was attracting the compass that way was a mystery. Man had not yet been very far into the polar regions either way.

With the realization of the shape of the earth and the knowledge that it turned on an axis through the North and South Poles, the poles became fixed points that could be used for navigation. Man had found his way using natural landmarks and by observing the sun and stars, but these were not as definite as the use of North and South Poles. Globes were made as the obvious alternative to flat maps to give a truer representation of the earth's surface. The science of navigation that we know today was founded.

It is still necessary to use flat maps as representations of parts of the earth's surface, even for long-distance flights, because parts of a globe of sufficient size would obviously be impractical as a portable piece of navigational equipment. Flat maps, however, are projected in such a way that allowance is made for the curvature of the surface they represent, and this can be seen by lines on them, which are described later. The area covered by most of the maps we use might be regarded as flat without noticeable errors, but anyone using a map of a large area for a long-distance journey needs to allow for the way the spherical shape has been opened to flat—a straight line around the globe is a curved line on the map.

SIMPLE COMPASSES

It is possible to improvise a compass to see how the early users discovered its properties. Iron and steel can be magnetized. No other metal can. If a steel needle is stroked one way with an existing magnet, it will acquire some of its magnetism. There are ways of magnetizing using a coil of wire with a current through it, but getting the magnetism from an existing magnet is simpler. Cut a disc from a bottle cork or make a small light wooden boat and put the needle on it in a bowl of water (FIG. 3-1A). It should swing to settle at a north-south direction as it finishes gyrating.

Another way of supporting the needle is to attach a long hair to its point of balance with a small piece of clay (FIG. 3-1B). If you hold the other end of the hair and let the needle hang, it will eventually come to rest on a north-south line. This is more portable than a floating needle and might be used—at least experimentally—for finding your way.

The simplest compass that may be bought has a needle supported with a bearing

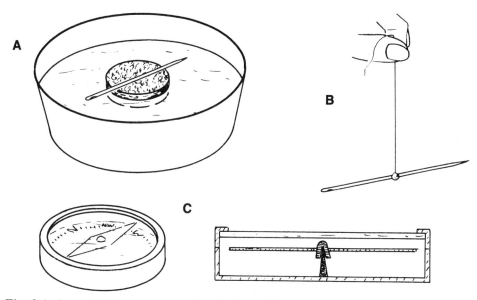

Fig. 3-1. *Improvised compasses and a simple needle compass.*

on a pointed pivot on which it is free to rotate. This is in a circular case with glass or plastic cover, close enough to prevent the needle bearing from lifting off its pivot (FIG. 3-1C). One end of the needle might be colored to indicate north, or it could be pointed or otherwise shaped so that there is no doubt about the way it is pointing. Otherwise, you could read it in the opposite direction.

A snag with such a compass is that you have to wait for the needle to swing from side to side and settle eventually on the true bearing. In many compasses this tendency to swing is dampened by sealing the case so the needle moves in alcohol or other liquid. The effect of this is to bring the needle to its final true position after only slight swinging.

Even the most basic and small compass has its uses—many wartime bailed-out airmen found their way out of enemy territory with a tiny compass concealed in a tunic button. There are compasses to wear like a finger ring. Some very good compasses are on wrist straps, but most compasses used by walkers, cyclists and canoeists are made to carry in a pocket or hang by a cord around the neck. Waterproof versions are available for divers. Compasses for the navigation of aircraft and ships are more complicated and intended to be fixed down.

COMPASS DIRECTIONS

Besides north, the basic directions are east, south and west at 90° intervals taken clockwise (FIG. 3-2A). These are the universally accepted cardinal points. Intermediately there are points at 45° indicated by putting together the cardinal points each side of them, with N or S first (FIG. 3-2B). Less commonly used are the intermediate points indicated by putting together the points each side of them, with the single letter first

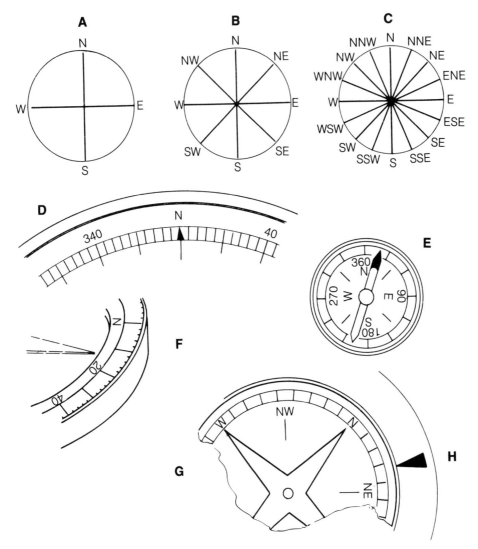

Fig. 3-2. *Examples of compass points and degree markings.*

(FIG. 3-2C). The old-time seaman, who regularly used these terms, tended to leave out the "th" and speak of "nor-norwest" instead of "north-northwest," and "east-sou-east" and "sou-sou-east" where appropriate. Besides those 16 points, the seaman had a total of 64 points.

If you have difficulty in remembering the directions east and west, imagine facing the sun (south). East has an initial before west. Left has its initial letter before right. The early initials go together (L and E) and so do the later ones (R and W). The 64 divisions were suitable for reading on a tossing ship, but they were not very scientific. It is better to use degrees (such as are used for dividing a circle).

On most compasses, reading in degrees is done clockwise starting and finishing at north (FIG. 3-2D). In practice, single-degree markings are too fine and it is more common to mark at 2-degree intervals. A modern compass user tends to name the eight main lettered markings, but use degrees for other directions when laying a course. It is worthwhile knowing what is meant by the 16 lettered directions, but degrees are the usual terminology. The whole circular pattern, no matter how it is marked, is called a *rose*. The circle on which it is drawn may be called a *card*.

With degree markings, north is 0° or 360°, east is 90°, south is 180°, and west is 270°. Intermediate angles that may be lettered, such as NW at 45°, are easily defined. But except for the four cardinal points, it is usual to define directions in degrees. Thus, you speak of a bearing of 225° rather than southwest. For most bearings, the nearest you are usually able to judge an angle is at 2° intervals, which will be marked around the rim, base, or card of the compass.

Degree markings are in general use throughout most of the world. It is unlikely that you will need to know any other markings, but there are two that may be met. For use with the metric system, there are *grads*. In a complete circle there are 400 grads. This means that a right angle of 90° is the same as 100 grads, so south is a bearing of 200 grads instead of 180°. In the metric system, the grad is further divided into *centigrads*, which are one hundredth of a grad, or *centisimal minutes*. That can be further divided by 100 into *milligrads*, but these smaller angular measures are much finer than any map user need bother about—any more than the smaller division of degrees into 60 minutes and then into 60 seconds.

Another system divides the complete circle into 6400 *mils*, so 90° becomes 1600 mils. This is less frequently used and has military applications for gunnery.

There are three ways of arranging the compass card. The markings may be on the bottom of the case, so the needle swings over them (FIG. 3-2E), or on the bezel or rim of the case, so the needle points at them (FIG. 3-2F). In both cases, the whole or part of the instrument has to be turned around to bring the north marking opposite the end of the needle before a reading can be taken. In another case, the card is a disc attached to the needle so that it turns with it (FIG. 3-2G). With this type, the markings are always in the correct relation to the needle and the extra action is avoided.

Having a floating card rotating with the needle is simpler, and particularly suitable where the compass is mounted in a car or ship. Afloat, the compass is in *gimbals* so it remains level, whatever the motion of the ship. The case containing the compass and gimbals is called a *binnacle*. The card rotates with the needle, and a point that coincides with the fore-and-aft direction of the ship, is called a *lubber line* and is marked on the forward edge of the compass case (FIG. 3-2H). The reading of the calibration opposite this is the compass heading of the ship. A car compass may have a domed card and a reading showing at the side of its case, but its action is the same as the flat card of the mariner's compass.

Floating cards are found in other compasses, but the type mostly used for general map reading and navigation on land has the calibrations on the rim and a needle alone inside (FIG. 3-3). To obtain a bearing with this type, where the complete compass part can be turned in the rectangular base, the case is turned until the north marking comes

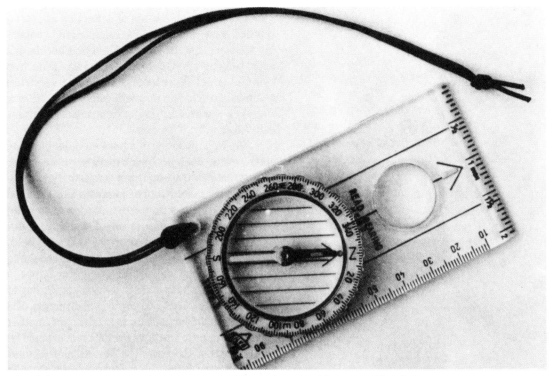

Fig. 3-3. *A Silva compass has a rotating calibrated rim and lines to aid sighting.*

opposite the north end of the needle. The direction is sighted across the markings on the base, and the bearing is read at the mark serving as a lubber line visible through or near the rim. With this and any other hand-held compass, it is important that the instrument is held level. The needle will function at a slight tilt, but at too much angle it will become lodged and cease to move.

This type of compass is popular for general use with a map. The base of the compass and the rectangular piece on which it rotates are transparent. There is at least one lengthwise line on the base for setting. Edges are calibrated, and there may be a built-in magnifier. Vital parts may be luminous for use at night.

COMPASS READING

It is important to avoid *errors of parallax*, caused by looking at a compass at an angle. You may think the needle is pointing at the letter N, when it is actually a little way out. If you look directly down on to the compass, that can be avoided. There are, however, occasions when you want to look across the compass. A help then is a series of lines across the base of the compass parallel with north direction, as can be seen in FIG. 3-3.

This problem is accentuated in the cockpit of an airplane where practical considerations make it necessary to mount a compass where it has to be viewed at an angle.

One type of airplane compass has two parallel lines indicating north and south on a cover glass inside a calibrated rim. The compass below has a line and arrow indicating north and a mark showing the fore-and-aft direction of the airplane (FIG. 3-4). If the calibrated rim is turned to get the desired heading opposite the mark and locked there, the pilot turns his plane until the north-south line of the compass can be seen to be parallel with the lines on the cover, and he knows he is going the correct way.

Fig. 3-4. *An airplane compass with a rotating rim and grid to set to the required direction.*

Looking across a compass may give sufficient accuracy for many purposes, but for greater precision there are compasses with sighting arrangements, usually a pair of sights (comparable to rifle sights) and a prism that allows you to read the bearing on a rotating card without moving your eye. One type, favored at sea, has a vertical handle containing a battery and flashlight that can be used to illuminate the markings at night (FIGS. 3-5 and 6).

Such a compass would be too bulky for normal use by a walker or other person travelling light, but there are other sighting compasses, which allow you take more accurate bearings than merely looking across a simpler compass. One type used by military personnel, and which may be available from surplus sources is little bigger than a pocket watch; it opens to allow sights and a prism to be used in a similar, but more compact, way to the nautical compass shown in FIG. 3-5. Another popular type is made like the simple Silva compass, but a mirror with a sighting line is swung up. You look across and can read the bearing reflected in the mirror.

Fig. 3-5. *This hand-held bearing compass has a handle and a prism below the sight, so the liquid-damped card can be read through it as the object is sighted.*

Fig. 3-6. *A sight is taken across the bearing compass and the prism adjusted with the side knobs to show the reading on the card.*

ERRORS AND DEVIATION

Any compass can be deflected by iron or steel nearby. Make sure that when you use a compass it is as far as possible from these metals. Electrical gear can also affect it. Any compass in a car can only be an approximate instrument. If you need to navigate a car with accuracy, you should stop and take a hand-held compass some way from the car to read it.

Other possible causes of deflection are steel-rimmed glasses, a mountaineering helmet containing steel or, at waist level, a steel belt buckle or a knife hanging on your belt. Keep away from iron tanks or steel fence posts. Operating electrical equipment can have a magnetic effect for some way and even a wire carrying current near a compass may affect it.

We talk about a compass needle pointing north, but it does not point exactly to the North Pole. What is attracting it is a magnetic field some way from the pole. From most points in the United States the compass needle will be found to point west of *true north*. This is called *magnetic north*. There is a slight movement in the magnetic field. For general mapping purposes this is not enough to matter. What the angular difference is between magnetic north and true north will vary according to where you are. This is shown in the margin of a map, with an arrow pointing true north and another pointing magnetic north, as the difference would be at the center of the map. The deviation or *declination* on a map of part of the eastern states is about 7° (FIG. 3-7A).

It is usual for a map to be laid out so true north is at the top, but it would be unwise to always assume this and the compass arrow in the margin should be checked. A simple arrow is usual, but there are variations (FIG. 3-7B), particularly on maps intended to be decorative as well as useful. On a nautical chart there are several complete compass roses drawn. This is because a navigator needs to read off courses on the chart by lightly penciling them and taking parallel rules or other devices across the chart to repeat the course through a compass rose and to read the actual bearing from it. At one time, a complete compass rose might have been found on a land map, but that would be unusual now.

If a map is drawn showing the route of a road or other feature elongated, it may be more convenient to have north other than at the top to bring the map vertical or horizontal to suit the paper (FIG. 3-7C). If it is a road or river that changes directions, it can be broken into separate sections with the north direction different on each section for a neat layout on a page (FIG. 3-7D). That does not matter, and each piece of the map can be set with a compass, but it emphasizes that it is unwise to assume that north is always at the top.

DIRECTIONS FROM THE SUN

There are ways of finding compass directions without a compass, particularly by using the sun and stars. Observations of nature may give you a guide, but not great accuracy.

The sun rises in the east and goes through an arc southwards to set in the west. The sun is highest and nearest south at noon: that means *local noon*, which is not necessarily noon on your watch. In the summer, noon in states that have daylight saving

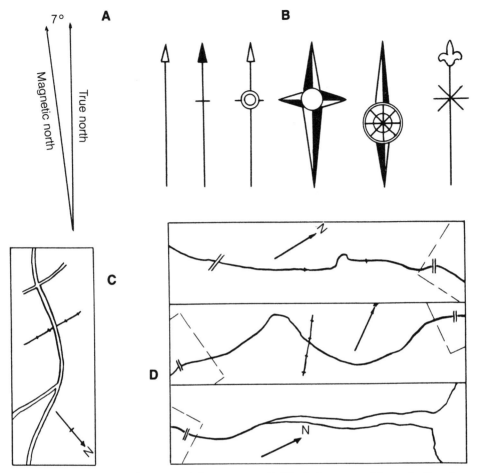

Fig. 3-7. *Methods of indicating north on a map (A,B). Strip maps with north directions arranged to bring the maps within the borders (C,D).*

time will be at 1 P.M. on your watch. For accuracy, you need to know where the time in your zone is set. Supposing you are about 100 miles west of that, local noon will be nearly 10 minutes later. For most purposes, that may not matter. For practical purposes, the sun is east at about 6 A.M. and west at 6 P.M. Add an hour if your watch is set 1 hour fast.

If you have a watch that you know to be reasonably accurate or, better still, a radio set on which you can get a time signal at noon, you can determine a north-south line by putting a stick vertically in flat ground so the sun casts a shadow of it. At noon, put a small stick or pebble at the end of the shadow. A line through the stick and the pebble will run north and south, with the pebble at the north end (FIG. 3-8A).

If you cannot check the time, it is possible to use a similar method. When you judge the sun is approaching its highest point, set up the vertical stick and mark the end of a shadow. Wait and do this again and continue placing pebbles. You will find

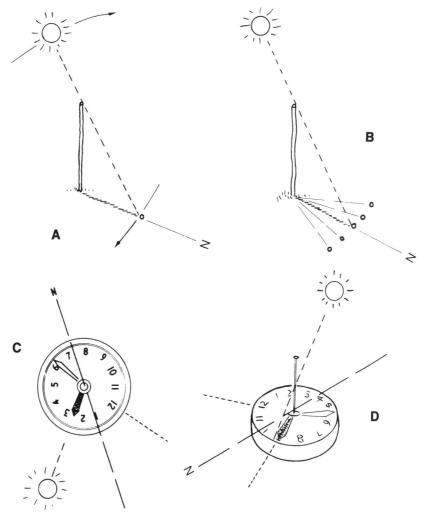

Fig. 3-8. *The shadow cast by the sun can be used to find north, either on the ground or with a watch.*

that the shadows will get shorter and then start to lengthen again (FIG. 3-8B), due to the sun working up to its zenith and then passing it. A line through the base of the stick and the pebble marking the shortest shadow will be approximately north and south.

That method applies to any part of the world; the sun's apparent movement is the same anywhere. Accuracy is easier the further you get from the equator as the shadows are then longer and differences are easier to see. Nearer the equator, the shadows are shorter, and at the equator the sun is overhead at noon.

You can use a watch that has hands, and is known to be correct, to get a close approximation of north. This is effective in the north temperate zone, but is less accurate if the arc of the sun goes very high or very low. You can get good results in most of the United States.

For the basic method in North America, hold the watch level and point the hour hand at the sun, and then bisect the angle between the hand and noon (1 P.M. for day-light-savings time). That line through the center of the watch runs north and south (FIG. 3-8C), with north on the side of the watch away from the sun.

A problem with that method is being certain that the hour hand is pointing exactly at the sun. A more accurate way uses a knife blade edgewise to the sun or a pin or other thin object held vertically over the center of the watch, so that it casts a shadow along the hour hand (FIG. 3-8D). That puts the arrangement the other way around by turning the watch through 180° (so that north is the other direction in relation to the watch face).

USING STARS

At night, if the stars are visible, you can make use of the North Star, which is over the North Pole. All other stars appear to move around it. It can be seen from anywhere in North America. The North Star is not one of the most prominent, but there is a con-stellation that is a good guide to it. This has many names, including *Great Bear*, *Plow*, and *Big Dipper*. The last two give a clue to its shape. There are seven stars, and the two at the end are on a line that can be extended to reach the North Star (FIG. 3-9A) at a distance equal to six to seven times the distance between these pointers. A help to con-firm your findings is the M or W formation that keeps the same relationship to the Big Dipper. Remember that the formations are moving around the North Star. What you are looking for might be upside down or in some other posture, depending on the time of night you make your observations.

Viewers in the Southern Hemisphere are not as well provided for. There is no star over the South Pole to use as a guide. Instead, there is a constellation called the *South-ern Cross*, with two stars that point to a position over the South Pole (FIG. 3-9B). You have to estimate the distance, which is $4^1/2$ times the distance between these two stars to the point above the pole. Two other stars, called *Pointers*, help in getting the esti-mated location. A line square to a line between them should cross the other projected line at the position above the South Pole.

USING NATURE

Natural signs that are helpful in finding directions cannot always be relied on as indi-vidual indications. There are always exceptions. Anyone with a little skill in wood-craft will observe several things and average his findings, therefore allowing for signs that do not conform to the rule.

On an exposed tree, moss may be more plentiful on the north side of the trunk, due to being away from the drying influence of the sun. Trees tend to bend and develop away from a prevailing wind. Some plants always point in the same direction. Even some types of ant hills will have a north-south axis. For natural signs in your vicinity it is advisable to consult a local woodsman.

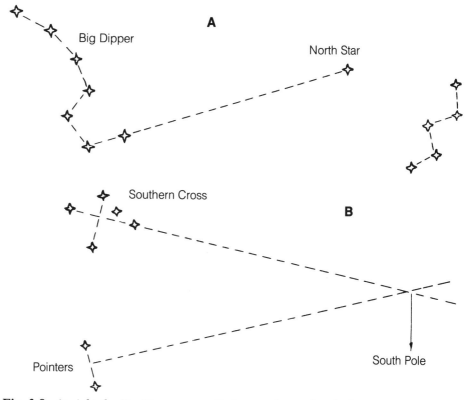

Fig. 3-9. *At night the Big Dipper constellation can be used to find north in the northern hemisphere, or the Southern Cross can be used in the southern hemisphere.*

With observations of natural things, one example may give you a clue. However, you need another example to confirm it, or you might have to average results. Another example may confirm your findings, but if you find the trees are contradictory, you cannot trust any and might have to look for other signs that may prove one or more of the earlier signs are correct. That is woodcraft and it is outside the scope of this book. The modern explorer in wilderness country is unlikely to be without a compass and map. Natural things are interesting and can be checked when found. If an emergency arises, you should know how to make use of what nature has to tell you.

COMPASS ADJUSTING

If a compass in good condition is used sufficiently remote from the influence of iron and steel or electric current, it should give you accurate readings on any bearing. If it is affected by nearby interference, this will vary according to direction—so much so that the error could be enough in some directions to be as much as 90°. Obviously, the compass is then useless. When you are using a hand-held compass, you must make certain it is away from interference when you read it. If the compass is mounted permanently somewhere, it may have to be corrected to allow for nearby interference.

This applies especially to compasses in use afloat in anything from a tiny yacht to the largest liner. In ocean travel, there are none of the landmarks that we can use ashore to check direction, and an error of only a few degrees could be serious on a long voyage. Compass adjusting is a skilled occupation. The ship's compass is corrected with additional small magnets to get the minimum errors on all headings. Even with electrical gear and iron parts kept away from the immediate area of the compass, there will be errors to correct. When the best adjustments have been made there will still be slight errors. A list of these at various headings will be kept on a card near the compass. The deviation card may be a list of bearings at, perhaps, 20° intervals, or it may be a diagram of a compass rose with another circle similarly marked a little way outside it, with lines from one to the other according to errors. If a particular course is to be steered, it can be noted on one calibration and a line followed to the other calibration to discover how the ship has to be headed in relation to the compass to be on that course.

Fortunately, it is uncommon for such adjusting to be needed ashore, but it does arise with a compass in a car as well as on boats used on inland waters—even in a canoe—if it is mounted and there may be iron or electrical gear on board.

The position of mounting a car compass depends on a compromise between putting it where it can be seen and keeping it away from interference. In the first locating of the compass, it is advisable to compare it with another compass held some way away from the car—with and without the engine running and with the car pointing in several directions. There will be errors, but try to find the position where they are least and then mount the compass there.

A car compass may have a view through a window in the side, or there may be a transparent dome with the card visible through it. In any case, the card will be in a fluid to dampen its swinging and there will be a lubber line marked where you are to read the direction. The mountains should have an adjustment so you can get this lubber line and the center of the compass on a line parallel with the fore-and-aft line of the car. Set this correctly and tighten the screws or other attachment to lock it.

On the compass should be two or more adjusting screws (FIG. 3-10). These screws control magnets that you can adjust to reduce deviations in various directions. Before putting the compass in the car, and while keeping it away from iron or electrical interference, "zero it in" by adjusting the screws. It is largely a matter of trial and error; average out the faults until you have them as small as you can get them. A compass in a car is in a bad location anyway. You will not achieve perfection. In many cars it will be far from true in some directions. If you know this, and can allow for it, the car compass will serve as a general guide. When you need to use a bearing with some precision, you will have to stop the car and get away from it to use a hand-held compass.

Use a compass away from the car as a guide to setting the car so it is facing north (FIG. 3-11A). If the compass in the car is also showing north, you are lucky. If it does not, turn the adjusting screws until the car compass reads correctly. Because a steel screwdriver would affect the compass while you are turning the screws, file a screwdriver end on a piece of brass rod or taper the end of a piece of wood. The screws should turn easily.

Fig. 3-10. *This car compass has a liquid-damped card and screws below for adjusting to reduce errors due to surrounding steel or electrical interference.*

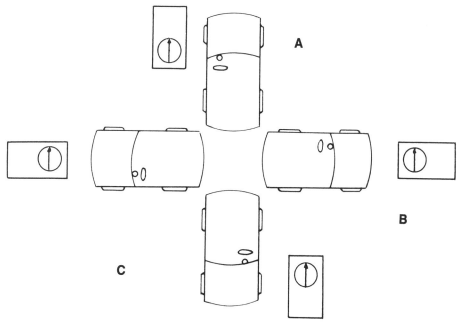

Fig. 3-11. *Car and separate compass positioned for setting the car compass.*

With the guidance of the outside compass, turn the car to face east (FIG. 3-11B). Check the car compass again. There will have to be some adjusting, but keep this to a minimum. Repeat with the car facing south and west (FIG. 3-11C). Each adjustment will affect previous ones. From the first circuit you will have to estimate what settings will give you the closest approximations in all directions; then go back to each heading again and try averaging the adjustments until the arrangement is as close as you can get it.

Ideally, you get a result that is not very far out in any direction. In some cars, it is possible to get quite close results in three directions, but the adjustments to get that put the other direction a long way out. You may have to decide that the compass can be trusted in all directions except, for instance, easterly, when it will have to be ignored.

Ship compass adjustment allows for a great many headings, but with a car compass, which is only an approximate guide in any case, it should be sufficient to adjust on the four cardinal points only. When you have your compass adjusted as close as you can, make a note of the errors on a card or label kept close to the compass. You will then know that, if you want to head the car north, you have to follow the compass slightly west of north (or whatever the error is). For intermediate headings between the four noted errors, you have to judge what allowance to make.

There may be a difference between when the car engine is running and stopped. It is better to do the adjusting while the engine is running because that is the condition when you are likely to use the compass. If the engine and car are stopped, you can get out and use another compass away from the vehicle interference.

Try windshield wipers. They are plated steel and could cause the compass to move with them and give a different reading, from when they are not working. You can probably locate the compass far enough away from the wiper motor so that it does not affect it. Screws in automobiles are normally steel. If there are any in the vicinity of the compass, you might replace them with brass screws before adjusting the compass.

When using a map while travelling in a car, it is always best to orient by using landmarks. That is the normal way; in any case, you usually know what road you are on. The compass can be useful if you are doubtful, and come to a junction without knowing if you should turn right or left. Even with its errors, it should tell you that much. If you are using an off-road vehicle to go across unmarked country, it may be wiser to decide on a course with a hand-held compass away from the car. Then note the car compass reading, and keep to that even if it differs from the other compass. At intervals, check and correct your course—if necessary.

PROTRACTORS

You can use a compass to find a bearing on a map by putting the compass over the map and turning the map until the map's magnetic north and the compass's calibrated north coincide. Put the center of the compass over the point you want to take the bearing from; a straight line through the compass center and the place for which you want the bearing will pass over the marks around the compass dial or card. You can then read the bearing.

That method is satisfactory, except for several possible difficulties. If the compass has a transparent base, it can be located fairly accurately. If it has an opaque base you have to estimate the position. There is a way out of that difficulty; the compass does not have to be placed directly over the spot from which you want the bearing. Pencil a line between the sighting place and the one being sighted. Put the compass anywhere over the line, and turn map and compass until they both point north (FIG. 3-12A). See that the compass is central on the line. Even if you cannot see through it, it can be brought to the exact position by getting it located so opposite bearings agree. The bearing at one side should be 180° more or less than the other. This is called a *reciprocal bearing*. If the bearing one way is 30° the other should be 210°. If one bearing is 157° the bearing the other way is 337° (FIG. 3-12B). Manipulate the compass over the line until opposite bearings match. Then the one in the direction you want is the correct bearing.

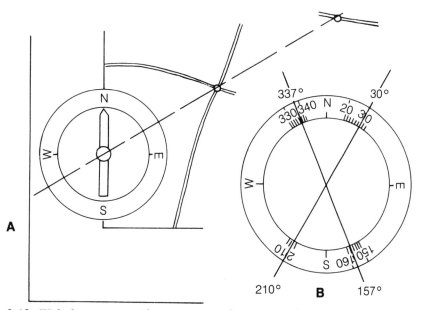

Fig. 3-12. *With the map set with a compass, a bearing can be read across the compass.*

This may be satisfactory as a guide to a route you are travelling at the time, but suppose you have a map spread out on the table at home and are planning a future trip. It would be a nuisance if you had to turn the map upside down and continue reading it that way for the sake of orienting it to suit the compass. If it is a compass where the needle swings over a marked base or rim, and not one where the card turns with the needle, you could turn the markings to match north on the map and ignore the needle. You are then using the compass for something different than what it is intended; there is a better instrument available.

The instrument is a *protractor*, which is a device with a baseline having a center marked on it, then a rim marked in degrees from that center. Some protractors are made of wood or other opaque material, but for mapping a transparent, plastic is more useful, so you can see map details through it. A protractor may be round or semicircular (FIG. 3-13), but many other shapes are possible. If a protractor is made rectangular, it gives you straight edges for drawing lines and one or more edges for scale markings, where they do not conflict with degrees. Angles are the same whether they have their degree markings on curved or straight edges (FIG. 3-14A).

Another advantage of a rectangular transparent protractor is that there can be one or more cutouts for such things as measuring proportions in a grid square (FIG. 3-14B). It is also possible to have scales drawn away from an edge (FIG. 3-14C), because you can see through when you apply them. There have been protractors obtainable with a considerable amount of information on them, but it is important to remember the prime purpose of a protractor; avoid complications that might make it difficult to read degrees.

Accuracy is easier to obtain with a large protractor—the further the markings are from the center, the less risk there is of an extended line through a bearing being inaccurate. A very large protractor may be cumbersome, however, and a diameter no more than 6 inches is a reasonable choice of size.

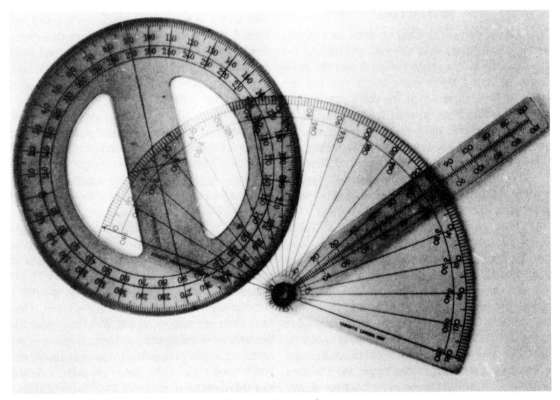

Fig. 3-13. *Two transparent protractors for measuring angles on maps.*

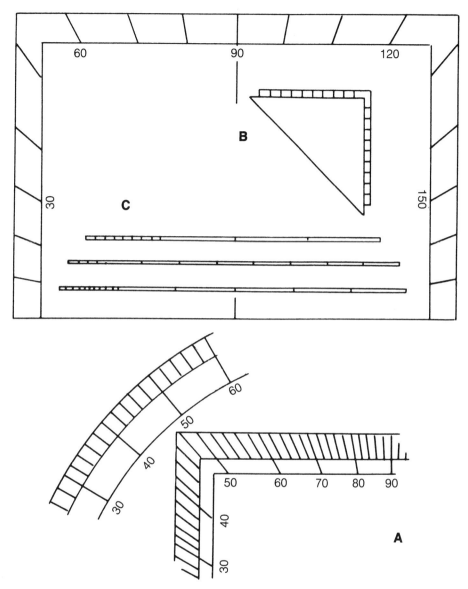

Fig. 3-14. *Protractor degree calibrations may be on straight, or curved edges and other information may be provided in the body of the instrument.*

To find a compass bearing on a map (called an *azimuth*), pencil a line through the points concerned and draw another line north and south across it (FIG. 3-15A). If the edge of the map is north and south, you can use that instead, if you extend the bearing line to it (FIG. 3-15B).

Put the center mark of the protractor over the crossing and the 0°/180° line through that on the north-south line so that you can read the bearing on the rim (FIG. 3-15C). The

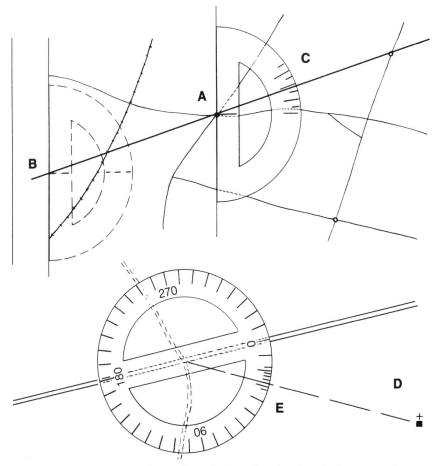

Fig. 3-15. *A protractor may be used to obtain a bearing in relation to north on a map (A,B,C), or it can be related to a road or other feature (D,E).*

baseline on a semicircular protractor might be the actual edge or a line drawn parallel to it on a transparent instrument. Be careful to get this positioned correctly.

Many protractors are designed for drafting and other purposes besides mapping, and are marked in degrees both ways. Use only the clockwise markings for compass directions. Some protractors are marked in 90° segments for other purposes. A degree is the same whatever the numbering, but examine a strange protractor and be prepared to adapt the readings on some.

A protractor can be used to find the angle between two directions when neither is north and south. Suppose you want to find the angle of a church in relation to a road from which it is visible at a certain point. Draw a line through the point on the road and the church (FIG. 3-15D). If you place the protractor over the crossing, with the zero line along the road, you can read off the angle of view of the church in relation to the road view point (FIG. 3-15E).

PELORUS

There is a further aid to measuring angles on a map, or in relation to landmarks on the ground. This is really a protractor on a compass base, marked in degrees, but without a magnetic needle. One type looks like a compass from which the needle has been removed. A protractor may have an arm arranged to turn on its center (FIG. 3-13). The transparent arm has a line marked along its center. Therefore, you can turn it to the direction you want to read and can see through the arm where the line crosses the calibrations on the rim (FIG. 3-16A). There could be a scale marked along the arm, which gives you a long reach over a penciled line or may be long enough to reach the destination point without a drawn line. Putting an arm on a protractor makes it a *pelorus* (the name comes from the reputed name of Hannibal's pilot). The arm is a refinement that helps when measuring angles, either in relation to north or the direction of a road or other route.

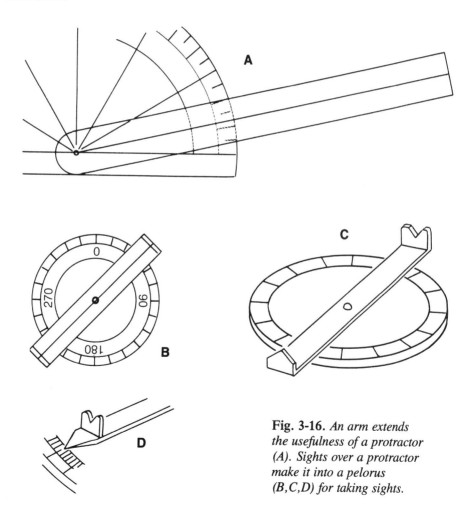

Fig. 3-16. *An arm extends the usefulness of a protractor (A). Sights over a protractor make it into a pelorus (B,C,D) for taking sights.*

Another pelorus has the circular compasslike base markings, but over them turns an arm with sights (FIG. 3-16B). For precise measurement of angles in surveying or for other exact purposes, the sights may be telescopic and capable of adjusting to minutes and seconds between degree marks. For general use in mapping, a much simpler pair of sights like those on a rifle will serve (FIG. 3-16C). If the degree calibrations come outside the length of the arm, it may be pointed to give the angle sighted (FIG. 3-16D).

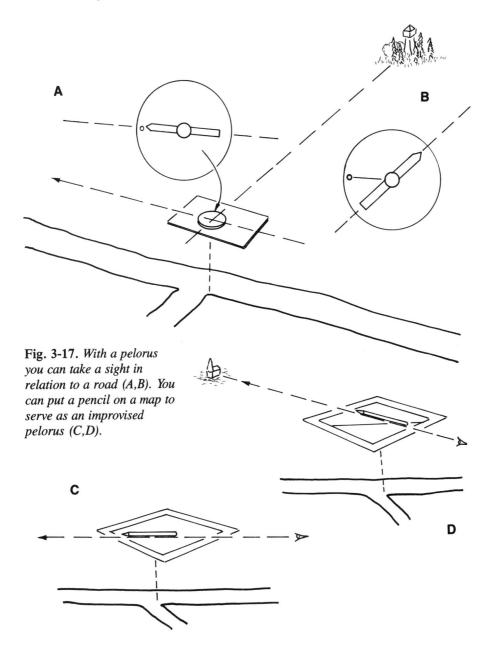

Fig. 3-17. *With a pelorus you can take a sight in relation to a road (A,B). You can put a pencil on a map to serve as an improvised pelorus (C,D).*

If the arm is longer, it can be transparent with a line over the calibrations, or it can be cut away to allow viewing through.

Such a pelorus can be put on a map and used as described, but it is also intended for use in the field where it is particularly useful for getting a bearing of a point in relation to a route. Suppose you are standing on a straight road at a crossing that you can identify on a map. It helps to support the map on a flat and level surface. It may be a board, the top of fence, or the roof of a car. You do not have to worry about the possible deflection that steel nearby would cause to a compass in the same location.

First have the pelorus arm pointing through 0°. Turn the whole instrument, so you can sight along the road (FIG. 3-17A). Without moving the base, turn the arm until you can sight the landmark that interests you and read its relative bearing (FIG. 3-17B). That is the angle between road and the direction of the object. There may be several similar landmarks in the same general direction; you want to identify one of them. If you return to the map and use the pelorus or a protractor, you can draw a line at the angle you have found. It should pass through the symbol of the landmark.

A cruder way of improvising a pelorus, that might still be sufficiently accurate for your purpose, is to use a pencil for sighting. Have the map on a level surface. Put the pencil along the road on the map and sight along it; sight it the same way as the road on the ground (FIG. 3-17C). Do not move the map, but turn the pencil with one side through the point representing where you are standing until you can sight the landmark (FIG. 3-17D). Draw along its side. That might give you all the information you need (by locating the landmark with its symbol on the map). If you need to know the angle, it can be measured with a protractor or the calibrations of a compass.

4

Heights

A MAP IS A FLAT TWO-DIMENSIONAL THING. THE SURFACE OF THE EARTH it represents may be flat and horizontal, but is more likely to be undulating, even to the extent of differing in level by many thousands of feet in the area represented by the map. There is no way that a map can be shaped to reproduce scale heights, except by being made into a three-dimensional model. Such models are sometimes made for display, but they are necessarily bulky and heavy and would not be suitable for carrying with you as you explore the area represented. A model may be put in a visitors' center, or similar place, and it then gives a good idea of the terrain to be visited. Once away from this three-dimensional model, the map user has to depend on his flat and folded sheet of paper.

Without any indication of changes in heights of the land represented, the reader of a map may assume that the shortest route between two points is a straight line on the map (FIG. 4-1A), when there is actually a mountain or hill in between (FIG. 4-1B). It might be an impassable ravine instead of rising land. In either case, the shortest practical, and maybe only, route has to follow a curve to miss the obstacle (FIG. 4-1C). We need a map that shows us variations in the heights of land.

This is best done by *contour lines*. A contour line is drawn on a map to represent an imaginary line on the ground through points that are all at the same elevation. Contour lines are drawn to indicate different heights. The interval between them varies according to the scale of the map, the type of surface represented, and many other considerations. The height interval should be indicated in the legend or the margin of the map. If the land represented does not vary much in height, contour lines at fairly

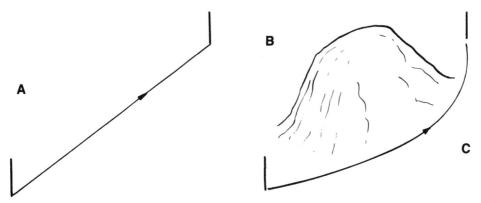

Fig. 4-1. *The straight line route between two points (A) may be impeded by high ground (B) and a way around might have to be used.*

close height intervals will be needed if they are to be of much use. In mountainous areas, such close vertical intervals would result in lines being so tightly packed as to be confusing; then, a wider interval has to be used.

The application of contours can be illustrated by using a built-up wood block. Imagine many pieces of wood temporarily joined together, and then turned in a lathe to make a cone (FIG. 4-2A). If the pieces are separated, each will show a different size circular shape to the next (FIG. 4-2B). If the shapes are drawn in the correct relation to each other, you get a plan or map of the cone with its shape at different levels (FIG. 4-2C).

Suppose the cone is turned with a concave profile (FIG. 4-2D). The shapes at the different levels will still be round. Although they will not be spaced at even intervals on the flat plan, they will be further apart at the lower levels than at the top (FIG. 4-2E). Suppose the cone is turned so the profile is convex (FIG. 4-2F). The resulting circles on the flat plan will be closer on the outside than they are toward the center (FIG. 4-2G). Knowing this, you can interpret a plan to tell if the cone it represents has a steady slope from its base to its apex, or if the slope of the side is concave or convex. With a little experience, you could decide if these slopes were more at the bottom, top, or regular all the way. The same reasoning can be used to visualize the forms that hills and valleys take from reading their contour lines on a map.

CONTOUR HEIGHTS

Contour lines usually represent heights above sea level. With tidal movements, the actual level of the sea varies. With a tidal range of a few feet, the difference does not matter to most users of maps. We usually need to know differences in height from where we are at the moment, and therefore other heights have to be related to that. Only if we were standing on the shore would sea level datum have much meaning to us. The sea level used as a datum for geodetic survey is a mean level that has been agreed upon. It would be unsatisfactory to take local tide ranges into account because they vary from the world record 88 feet in the Bay of Fundy to only a few feet in the Gulf of Mexico and many other places.

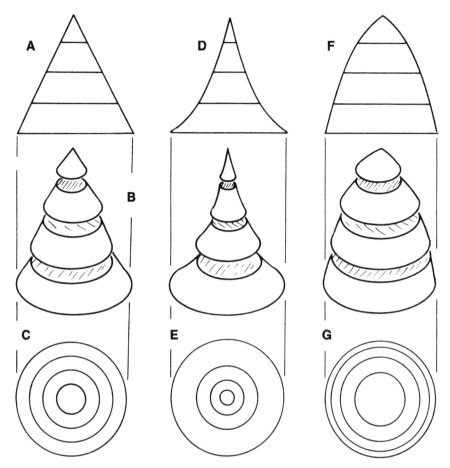

Fig. 4-2. *Layered conic shapes show by their sections how contours can be interpreted to show the types of slope.*

Contour lines on most maps are usually solid brown. The color does not conflict with lines drawn for other features and is distinctive. It may require careful investigation to find them on maps where other features are closely packed. It is in more open country with many hills and valleys that contour lines are more obvious and valuable. At intervals, usually of four or five lines, depending on the basic height gap between lines, a contour line is drawn wider and has a figure indicating the elevation set into the line or alongside it to serve as an *index contour* (FIG. 4-3A). To discover if the terrain slopes up or down, a check from one index figure to the next will tell you.

Sometimes there is a hollow, possibly among otherwise rising contours, with insufficient depth to warrant more contour lines within it. In that case, the closed contour line around the hollow has *hatches* (*hatching*) inside it. These are small ticks at right angles to the line pointing into the hollow (FIG. 4-3B).

If the contour line is approximate, it is drawn broken (FIG. 4-3C). A problem comes when contour lines may be fairly widely spaced, indicating a moderate slope, but at one

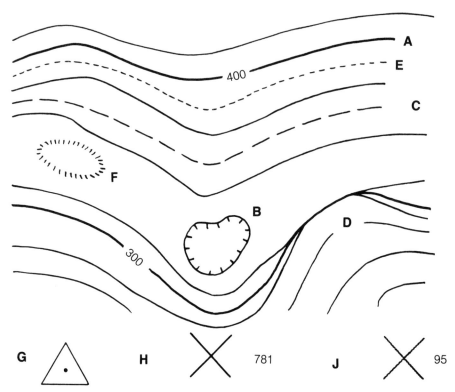

Fig. 4-3. *As contour lines pass through points having the same elevation they can be used to show different slopes. Intermediate lines give greater emphasis. Spot heights are shown by triangles or crosses.*

point the drop becomes sheer over a cliff or other nearly vertical edge. The contour lines then have to run together and these are known as *carrying contours* (FIG. 4-3D). On maps of fairly flat areas, the standard contours may be very wide apart on the map. If intermediate elevations are also shown, they are supplementary lines made up of dots or dashes much shorter than those used for approximate contours (FIG. 4-3E).

There is an increasing use of meters as the unit of measuring height, even if miles and feet are used for horizontal distances. What the elevation difference or contour interval is on a particular map will be detailed in the legend, probably adjacent to the scale. For instance, a map to a scale of 1:24,000 (about 2¹/₂ inches to 1 mile) may have contour intervals of 20 feet. One at 1:250,000 (about 4 miles to 1 inch) may have contour intervals of 60 meters, with supplementary intervals of 30 meters in some parts. One at a scale of 1:50,000 (about 1¹/₄ inches to 1 mile) with contour intervals of 20 feet may show a very complex arrangement of contour lines in a country of mixed hilly terrain. To anyone able to interpret the meaning of contour lines, a very detailed picture of the formation of the land will be given.

If contour intervals have to be converted from feet to meters or meters to feet, a single meter is about 3¹/₄ feet, 20 feet is just over 6 meters, 25 meters is about 81 feet, and 60 meters is about 195 feet. For a quick round figure conversion remember that 4 meters are about 13 feet.

Contour lines pass through points all at the same height. What they cannot show are minor differences in the terrain. If the contour interval is 30 meters, that is a difference equal to more than four times the height of a two-story house. Between the points on the ground at these levels, there can be quite large spurs, crags, and undulations, all less than 30 meters above the lower contour, but not shown on the map. If an individual difference between marked contour lines goes more than 30 meters above or below the levels of those lines, it should be shown by small enclosing contour lines.

If an individual rise between main contour lines is fairly large—and therefore quite prominent—and a feature to be noted by the user of a map, it may be indicated by hatches (short lines radiating from the feature). An example is a mine dump (FIG. 4-3F). What the prominence is will be labeled. There could be an excavation, due to quarrying or other activity. In that case, the hatches point inwards from an outline (FIG. 4-3B).

When the ground is surveyed for the preparation of maps, certain spots are located with extreme accuracy, so that they can be used for the further location of other points. Those used for horizontal control are marked on the map by a small triangle with a dot at its center (FIG. 4-3G). Bench mark vertical control stations or *elevation points* are marked on the map with a cross and figure beside it indicating the elevation (FIG. 4-3H). If you find one on the ground, it is a metal tablet from which surveys are made.

Of lesser importance, but of equal use to the reader of a map, are *spot elevations*. The bench mark crosses are black, but the spot elevation marks are brown (FIG. 4-3J), also with the elevation figure alongside. All of these marks are more accurate than the contour lines. For most map users, the contour lines degree of accuracy is far greater than they will require. If you can locate a marked cross position, you know the elevation quoted is exactly what it says.

If you need to work to a height that comes between marked contour lines, you will have to assume a regular slope and estimate height. Be prepared to find that the actual position on the ground is rather different, due to undulations. Your estimate will probably be as near as you require. If you need to have an intermediate contour for a particular project, you may lightly pencil in one midway between printed contour lines; remember that it is an approximation.

INTERPRETING CONTOURS

From the example of the wooden cones, we learn that contour lines can show the type of slope. Contour lines at fairly regular intervals indicate a slope that is uniform. If they are far apart in the direction that interests you, it is a gentle slope (FIG. 4-4A). If they are closer, the slope is still uniform, but steeper (FIG. 4-4B). If it is a hill where the line we propose to take shows higher lines closer than the lower lines, it is steeper toward the top (FIG. 4-4C).

If the lines are closer toward the lower level, the hill is flatter at the top and gets

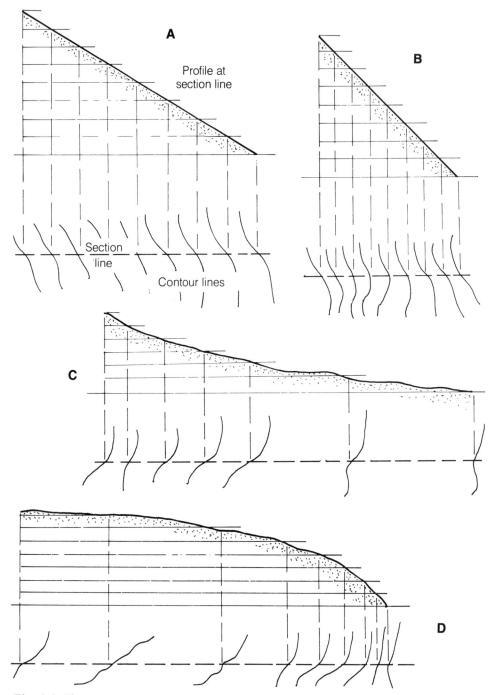

Fig. 4-4. *These sections show how the spacing of contour lines can indicate relative steepness (A,B) and if the slope is hollow or rounded (C,D).*

steeper toward its base (FIG. 4-4D). The curve across the contour lines is convex; the other is concave and the first slopes near a straight line. If you are walking, you may find it easier to mount a hill at a nearly regular slope. Choose a route from the contour lines away from where they show what could be an impossibly steep part on a straight path. If your map shows a trail, you can be certain that those who have gone before you have found the best way, even if from the map you think there are other ways across the contours.

If a hill or mountain goes to a peak, the contour lines will enclose it. Elsewhere they may appear to wander across the map as they follow points all at the same level. If the land rises to a single high point, the closed contour lines show you that it is an isolated rise. If you are finding your way in wilderness country, such a hill may be a good landmark. This would be particularly true if you interpret its shape from the contour lines. A fairly regular spacing without any obvious accentuation toward the top means a smoothly rounded hill (FIG. 4-5A). If the highest contour encloses a fairly large area, the top of the hill is flat or nearly so, because there is not enough rise to go another contour interval.

If the contour lines tend to get closer toward the top of the hill, it is more pointed (FIG. 4-5B). If the highest contour encloses a fairly small area, the top may not be a point, but the general form of the apex will look pointed from a distance.

If it is a hill or mountain of some importance, either in its own right or just as a landmark, the actual apex (FIG. 4-5C) may be marked with a dot and a figure beside it, indicating its elevation.

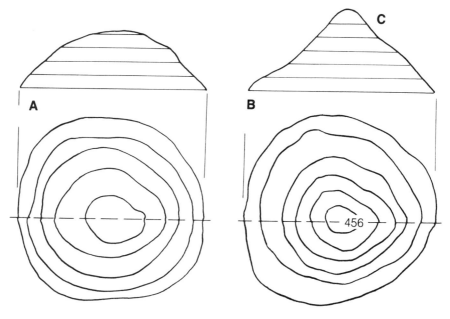

Fig. 4-5. *Sections across contour lines show the form of hills.*

CONTOURS AFFECTED BY WATER

Because water will always try to flow to a lower level, streams and rivers have plowed out grooves to form hollows in the ground. These may be anything from slight indentations to broad valleys. The presence of a natural waterway of any size will affect the lay of the land, and because of that the contour lines on a map. Even quite a small stream will have worn away the ground, so contour lines curve upstream. The breadth of this deflection will tell you what sort of hollow to expect to find in the ground. If the lines come together with quite narrow and nearly pointed V shapes (FIG. 4-6A), the stream has worn out a narrow fissure. If the Vs are short, the groove is not very deep.

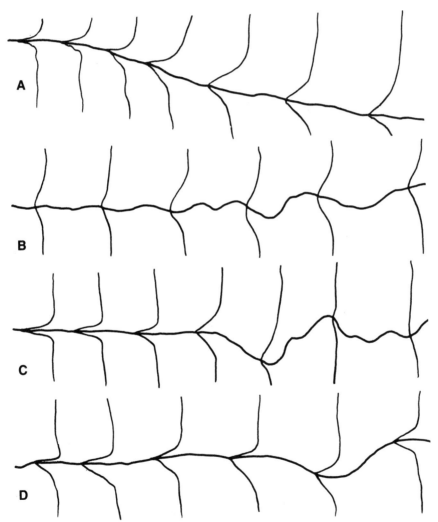

Fig. 4-6. *Where a stream cuts across contour lines, its effect on the lines can be interpreted to indicate if it has worn a deep or shallow hollow, and if one side is higher and harder than the other.*

If the deflection goes some way upstream at one or more contour lines, there could be quite a deep, but not very wide chasm at that point.

If the deflection of the contour lines shows fairly broad curves, the stream valley is very broad. The stream has probably worn away earth and soft rock over a broad channel at some time, although its normal flow is much narrower. A slight deflection in the contour lines means the stream is not set in very deeply (FIG. 4-6B). The greater the deflection, the more the stream has worn away a fairly broad hollow.

Of course, a stream does not necessarily flow over rock of uniform hardness or softness. This means that a part might be deeply grooved and another part might be in a broad and shallow hollow (FIG. 4-6C). From this you may decide it could be possible to wade across the stream where it is indicated as broad, or you may be able to jump over it where it should be narrower at a deeply grooved point. A stream might skirt hard rock on one side that has not worn away very much. The other side of softer material might have worn away considerably during flood conditions. Such a place would be shown by a contour line coming up close on the hard rock side, but the lines spreading out on the other side (FIG. 4-6D). When you get there, you will probably find a nearly vertical cliff at one side and gently sloping land on the other side. The stream usually sheers away from the high side. That is likely to be an outside curve against which the water flows quite fast. There could be rapids—and that is something of importance to canoeists.

The amount of fall of a stream will be indicated by the spacing of the contour lines it crosses. If they are wide apart, it will be quite slow and probably meandering in its course, as it originally sought out the easiest path to lower levels. With closer contour lines crossing the stream, it is indicated as flowing more steeply and therefore faster. Its course will depend on how it has been able to wear away its bed, but it is usually much less of a wanderer than the stream flowing over flatter country.

All of these stream features are found in larger natural waterways. A river may have used its much greater volume of water over thousands of years to wear away much more soil and rock, so it now flows in a broad valley with contour lines mostly confined to the higher land at each side and only contour lines crossing the river occasionally (FIG. 4-7A). Exceptions are mountain rivers that fall steeply and have usually worn out quite deep and narrow beds (FIG. 4-7B). In their lower levels they usually empty into broader valleys, with progressively slower flows, and therefore more widely spaced contour lines.

HEIGHT LANDMARKS

Apart from giving you details of rises and falls of the land you intend to travel over, the contour lines can provide guides to directions. If you check elevations on your map, you will know where the highest points are, and you should be able to see them on a clear day if they are within a reasonable distance. The map will also show you the elevations of other places between you and the highest points. All this comes from contour lines and helps you orient the map.

In addition to individual heights, the contour lines can tell you how a distance

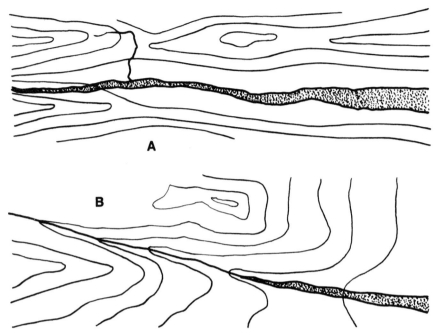

Fig. 4-7. *A river may have worn away the land, and contour lines will show if the valley formed is a deep gorge or a broad plain.*

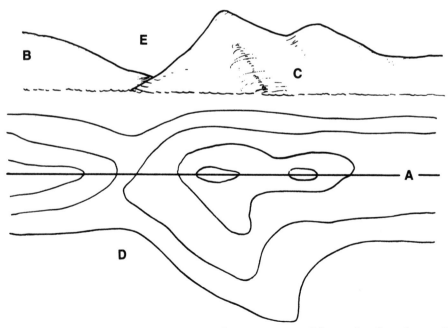

Fig. 4-8. *From a section across contour lines, it is possible to visualize the profile expected to be seen.*

range of high ground should appear. There will be lines showing how it goes up and down. You are first concerned with what happens along a line square to your line of view (FIG. 4-8A). It may help to lightly pencil a line through what appear to be the highest points on your skyline on the map. From this, you can sketch or visualize what the appearance should be and identify the hills or other features (FIG. 4-8B).

There may be other features that you can identify from the contour lines. If there is a pronounced projection of contour lines toward you from one point, you should be able to see the spur (FIG. 4-8C). If the contour lines around two adjoining high parts do not meet, but curve back around their own areas, the space between must be a valley (FIG. 4-8D). It could be the gap you have to aim for to get to the other sides of the hills (FIG. 4-8E); use your compass to get a bearing on the pass.

If the contour lines run together on the map (FIG. 4-9A), it should be fairly easy to identify the cliff or escarpment that they indicate (FIG. 4-9B). Anything of that sort gives you a positive position to work on in your navigation.

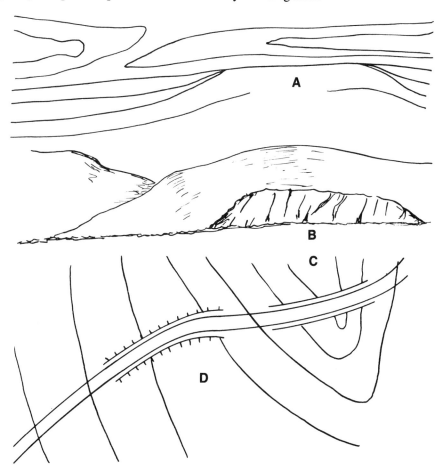

Fig. 4-9. *Contour lines running together (A) indicate a cliff (B). A roadway cut through contour lines (C), or have to be raised above them (D).*

If a road or railroad or other man-made feature has to be taken across the land-scape, there may be considerable work done to keep it reasonably level. When the Romans invaded much of Europe, their surveying and engineering made their roads as straight as possible, going up and down hills in their path so as to get the shortest distance between points. Presumably, the legions could be expected to take the hills in their stride. Their locations can still be seen and some modern European roads follow at least part of the Roman routes. Where there would be unnecessarily steep parts, newer routes take the easier slopes around obstructions.

A modern road, which is level or only has moderate slopes, might cut across contour lines. A cut through a hill may have nearly vertical sides and the road there is drawn with other parallel lines (FIG. 4-9C). Where there has to be fill to make up the road level, there are similar parallel lines on the map, but with hatches outward to indicate the slopes away from the road (FIG. 4-9D). Of course, there may still be some contour lines drawn across the road where it is on the elevation.

WATER CONTOURS

Where a valley has been flooded due to a dam being built, and the resulting large expanse of water goes over many levels that have been previously indicated by contour lines, these contour lines are still drawn on a map as submerged contour lines. There will be an indication of the elevation of the normal water level and the spillway elevation for times of low water level. From this information, the depths at various places can be deduced. This type of information is of value to boatmen who want to anchor, as well as to those with more technical needs.

Besides underwater contours (which are in the same brown color as those on land, but over the blue indications of water), there may be *depth curves*. These are dark blue and indicate depth measured from the normal water surface level. If there is an old river channel passing through the reservoir or man-made lake, depth curves may be there. Underwater contours appear on the surrounding, more recently flooded parts.

Around the coast, depths from the normal surface level are shown on many maps. Much depends on the design and purpose of the map. Where it is assumed that the user is concerned only with dry land use, the sea may be merely an expanse of blue. Where depths are shown, they are drawn similar to contour lines, but are dark blue. The depth they represent is a figure alongside a line. Usually, each line has a figure—not every four or five as on land contours.

The information on tidal water is not there for the use of extensive navigation by craft able to travel far at sea. Their navigators should use special nautical charts that contain more information and that are regularly corrected. Features at sea, and such things as navigation lights and buoys, will change more often than comparable features for land travelers; the seagoing navigator needs to be aware of them.

PROFILES

It is sometimes worthwhile to draw a vertical section of a route to be followed to get a better idea of its rising and failing. In the days when the bicycle was very popular and before the coming of automobiles, there were route books published that contained maps. The books also had sections or profiles of popular routes. Cyclists knew in advance which hills were steeper than others, and where they could look forward to a long freewheel downhill or where they would have to dismount and push uphill.

Most of us do not have that need, but a profile is a good way of familiarizing yourself with ups and downs of your journey. A drawn section gives you a good idea of how much you will ascend and descend between your start and your destination.

In its simplest form, the profile can give you a clue to steepness between the crossings of contour lines. The slope you will arrive at will assume a straight line from one contour to the other. It may fluctuate and be far from even, but you will get an average result. You will have risen a certain amount in a certain distance, even if not smoothly.

Note the contour intervals between the lines you are using. Measure the distance between them in the direction you want (FIG. 4-10A). You do not have to work square to the contour lines (unless that is the way you will go). The more acutely you cross the lines, the longer is the distance between them and the more moderate the slope. Suppose the contour interval is 60 meters and the distance you are using is 450 meters. You then have the lengths of two sides of a right-angled triangle (FIG. 4-10B) indicating the slope between the two marked elevations.

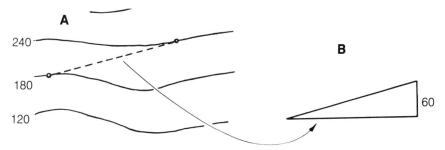

Fig. 4-10. *A section scaled across contour lines can be used to show the angle of slope.*

SLOPE INDICATIONS

There are three ways of indicating the amount of slope. You can speak of a rise of slope in a certain distance; you can give the slope as a percentage; or you can use degrees to horizontal.

In this case, there is a rise of 60 in 450. To bring this to terms of a ratio, divide 450 by 60, which is 7.5. The rise may be described as 1 in 7.5 or 1 in $7^1/_2$. Some slopes may give a denominator taken to several decimal places; they should then be brought to the nearest simple fraction.

If the slope is to be described as a percentage, the vertical distance is divided by the horizontal distance and multiplied by 100. In the example, 60 divided by 450 and multiplied by 100 gives a slope of $13^1/_3$ percent; the fraction would be ignored.

Slopes in degrees are not so satisfactory for the more moderate angles. They are quite small and it is necessary to go to several decimal places to show differences. For the angles of slopes suitable for vehicles, degrees are best avoided; although, they would be better for the steeper slopes that interest climbers. The angle can be found by trigonometry, but for practical purposes it is simpler to use a protractor on a scale profile.

If the slopes you are measuring are to be used for vehicles, 1-in-4 (25 percent) is getting near the practical limit and 1-in-2½ (40 percent) is as steep as most vehicles could go. At that angle, a walker almost finds himself scrambling—using his hands as well as his feet.

LONGER PROFILES

For a profile over a distance, showing the ups and downs of a projected route across many contour lines, a section drawn with the same vertical scales as the horizontal one may prove too flat to give much indication of differences. If what you plan to draw is very hilly, with considerable differences in elevation, such an arrangement may be satisfactory. Otherwise, it will be clearer if you increase the vertical scale so heights and angles are exaggerated.

In the simplest form, draw a line on the map marking the direction of the section you want (FIG. 4-11A). Use a piece of plain paper with a straight edge longer than the line you have drawn. Find the elevation of the highest and lowest contour line that your drawn line crosses. Draw lines on your paper parallel with the straight edge, enough

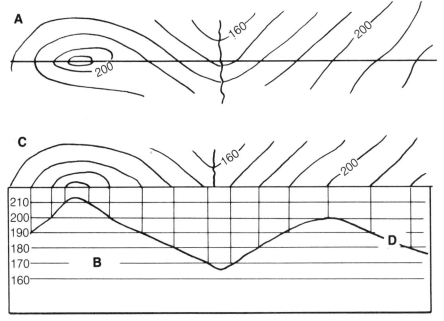

Fig. 4-11. *A strip of paper marked with elevation lines can be marked to form a profile of the land its edge crosses.*

to go one contour higher and one contour lower than the limits on the map. The scale you use for spacing the lines depends on the amount of exaggeration you want to provide. This could be twice the horizontal scale (FIG. 4-11B). Write the elevation figure at the end of each line.

Put the edge of the paper on the drawn line on the map, and project squarely everywhere that a contour line crosses it. Mark where the projection lines cross the appropriate elevation line (FIG. 4-11C). Join these points to obtain the profile (FIG. 4-11D). Because scale vertical heights are twice what they are in fact—in relation to horizontal distances—remember that the slopes of your profile are twice as steep as they are on the ground. How you draw the profile line depends on the land. If a stream is crossing the line, a hollow there will usually be V-shaped, but otherwise hills and valleys are rounded. You have to do some estimating of shapes as you draw through the known points on the curve. Although the example is a straight line, you can draw a profile of a meandering route in the same way.

OTHER HEIGHT INDICATIONS

On many maps contour lines are shown, but they tend to be obscured as background to many other features, such as roads, rivers and towns. In wilderness country there are fewer of these other features; the user may be much more concerned with slopes and heights. Special maps may be colored in layers between the contour lines. There is no standard range of colors, but a chart in the map margin will show those used. Colored layering makes visualizing the form the land takes much easier.

Another method of drawing attention to slopes is by *shaded relief*; this does not detract so much from other features. Shading may be green-brown that gets deeper in tone in places that would have greatest shadow, assuming a low sun, usually from the west. Shading to give a general indication of slopes may be used where there are no contour lines. An impression of the general shape of hills and valleys may also be given where there are no contour lines, and without color, by *hatching*, which is a pattern of close ticks around raised ground. These treatments serve to tell you the land is not flat, but they do not give the accuracy of the area.

5

Geographic Coordinates

IF YOU HANDLE A MAP OF ANY AREA WITH WHICH YOU ARE FAMILIAR, THE presence on it of a town or other place you know helps you to identify the area covered by the map. If you make a sketch map to show someone the way, there is no doubt for them the part of the earth's surface with which you are dealing. If the map is part of a section of a country with which you are unfamiliar, you may have no difficulty in understanding which part it is from your general knowledge of the country. Difficulties arise when a distant, unfamiliar, comparatively small area is mapped. How do you find out where on the face of the earth the area is that's depicted on the map? Suppose a map of an area with which you are familiar is given to someone from the other side of the world. How does he discover where your well-known piece of land is?

There has to be a method of marking maps that show what they represent in relation to all other areas and maps. The map of one particular place has to be unique. There must be no risk of it being confused with a map of another area. If someone is given a map, he should be able to learn where it belongs even if he is in another country a considerable distance away. There are several schemes used to find map areas and precise positions on maps, but the oldest and most widely used employs latitude and longitude.

LATITUDE

The earth is an almost perfect sphere. If angles are measured from the center, they can be imagined as marked on the surface of the sphere in any direction. With the North and South Poles as fixed points at opposite sides of the sphere, a line drawn midway between becomes the *equator* (FIG. 5-1A). Angles are measured north and south of it; the North Pole is 90°N, and the South Pole is 90°S. Between the equator and the poles, other lines drawn around, called *parallels of latitude* (FIG. 5-1B), show divisions in degrees. On globes and maps of large areas, lines may come at 5° intervals. On large-scale maps of fairly small areas, there may be individual degrees that can be further broken down into minutes ($^1/_{60}$ of a degree) and seconds ($^1/_{60}$ of a minute).

Of course, every point on one parallel of latitude is at the same angle to the center of the earth. On the surface of earth, one degree of latitude is about 69 miles (110 kilometers). Because the earth is not quite a perfect sphere, the distances get slightly greater toward the poles, where there is a slight flattening.

Although parallels of latitude may be marked in whole degrees, some important ones are fractional. Above and below the equator are the *Tropic of Cancer* (23$^1/_2$°N)

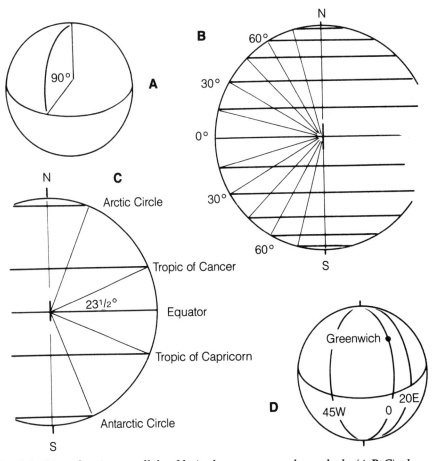

Fig. 5-1. *Lines forming parallels of latitude are measured angularly (A,B,C) above and below the equator. Meridians of longitude are measured the other way, from the prime meridian through Greenwich (D).*

and the *Tropic of Capricorn* (23$\frac{1}{2}$°S). These mark the furthest points north and south of the equator that the sun's rays fall vertically. At similar angular distances from the poles, there are the *Arctic Circle* (66$\frac{1}{2}$°N) and the *Antarctic Circle* (66$\frac{1}{2}$°S). These mark the limits north and south of the equator where the sun appears above the horizon every day of the year (FIG. 5-1C).

LONGITUDE

Knowing the latitude of a place on the map on which it is shown only tells how far north or south of the equator a place is. To locate the exact spot, a line drawn around the earth the other way is necessary. Such lines are *meridians of longitude*. Degrees can be used squarely to the direction for latitude, but there is no convenient starting point—like the poles for latitude.

The meridian of longitude almost universally used is the one through Greenwich Observatory, England. There have been others used by some countries, but if any of their maps and charts are marked differently they will usually show a conversion to Greenwich. Some American maps have been made showing the longitude based on Washington, D.C. Because this is exactly 77°W of Greenwich, the same meridian can be used and the conversion is simple arithmetic.

Greenwich (pronounced "Grennitch") was chosen because its observatory became the base in the great days of exploration when many of the explorers and navigators sailed from England. The observatory at Greenwich is still functioning, although observations of celestial bodies for the purpose of obtaining navigational information with precision are now taken in remote places away from interference by man-made things. Greenwich is on the south side of the River Thames (locally called London River), about 10 miles east of the center of London. An interesting ceremony still takes place daily; a large ball encircling a tall mast drops exactly at noon. In the days before radio, this allowed any shipmasters within view to set their chronometers.

With the meridian of Greenwich as 0°, other circles are drawn east and west of it through the poles. America has its longitudes described as west of Greenwich. The other way—across most of Europe and into Russia, India, and China—is east of Greenwich. This continues both ways until they meet at 180°; this is the *International Date Line* passing north to south through the Pacific Ocean. For purposes of navigation it is treated as a straight line. But where it passes through a few populated islands, it is deflected for date purposes.

As the lines of longitude converge on the poles, they cannot be used as measurements on the surface of the globe (like the lines of latitude). The distance between them is maximum at the equator and gets progressively less until it reaches zero at the poles. At the equator, 1° of longitude is the same as 1° of latitude (69 miles). At 40°N (New York), it is about 53 miles. At 50°N (Winnipeg), it is about 44 miles. At the Arctic Circle (66$\frac{1}{2}$°N), it is about 27 miles.

Ocean navigators out of sight of land depend on accurate computation of latitude and longitude to know where they are. The user of a map ashore may not need to use the mariner's methods, but a knowledge of the meaning of latitude and longitude allows him to locate places with precision. Some maps are indexed, and places are identified by their latitude and longitude. The lines crossing at about right angles to each other form quadrangles and these are convenient outlines for parts included in a map. According to the scale, a map may be designed to cover an area embraced by certain of these geographic coordinate lines in each direction.

INDICATIONS OF LATITUDE AND LONGITUDE

On many maps, the angular distances in both directions are shown in the margin at each corner. With the comparatively small size of the paper on which the map is printed—if it is to a fairly large scale—angles only in degrees would be much too coarse a calibration. These corner angles are marked in *degrees*, *minutes*, and *seconds*. For instance, a corner may be marked 77° 37' 30" and 39° 22' 30" (FIG. 5-2A). The first comes above the vertical edge and represents longitude. The other is the latitude of the horizontal edge at the corner.

There is no need to indicate north and west; it is assumed that the reader is sufficiently familiar with the subject to know he is looking at a map of part of the United States (the example shown in FIG. 5-2A is near Harper's Ferry, West Virginia). If other whole degrees can be positioned along the margin, they are shown. On a large scale, it may be just minutes—possibly at half-minute (30 seconds) intervals. Lines might not be taken across the map (FIG. 5-2B), but are marked on opposite sides; the map user will have to put a straightedge across if he wants to use the marks for location.

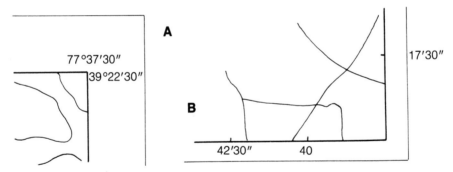

Fig. 5-2. *The locations of lines of latitude and longitude forming borders of a map may be marked at the corners, and other calibrations are marked along the edges.*

National topographical maps of the United States are made in quadrangles based on latitude and longitude. How much is contained in a chosen quadrangle depends on the scale, but maps of large scale have their outlines to degrees and minutes, while smaller scale maps are between lines representing whole degrees. Because latitude lines are parallel, the top and bottom of the map are parallel, and follow the appropriate lines. Longitude lines get closer towards the north. Convergence is very slight over the area of a map of large scale, so the longitude lines on edges of the map may be regarded as parallel with each other for practical purposes. When a small scale is used and the map covers a large area, making the map to longitude lines would result in it being narrower at the top to a noticeable extent. A map may then have its sides parallel and the longitude lines drawn or marked on the top and bottom border within this outline.

Because of the narrowing of the gaps between meridians of longitude further north, a map within certain lines of a part of the country near the Canadian border will be narrower than one contained within the same limits near the Gulf of Mexico. Some national topographic maps are known by the distances between parallels of latitude and meridians of longitude which contain them. See TABLE 5-1.

Table 5-1. Series and Scales of National Topographic Maps.

Series	Scale	Quadrangle Size (latitude)	(longitude)	Area Contained (square miles)
7¹/₂-minute	1:24,000	7¹/₂ min.	7¹/₂ min.	49 to 70
7¹/₂ × 15 minute	1:25,000	7¹/₂ min.	15 min.	98 to 140
15 minute	1:62,500	15 min.	15 min.	197 to 282
U.S. 1:250,000	1:250,000	1 deg.	2 or 3 deg.	4580 to 8669

Maps in the 7¹/₂-minute and 15-minute series do not each cover a very great area in relation to the whole United States or even a state, so there are a very large number of them available. They are known by the name of a town, city, or other prominent feature on that sheet. Index maps to small scale are issued showing all of the sheets available in the areas—usually a state.

Maps to smaller scales, with their larger area coverage, can be shown on more extensive index sheets. For instance, sheets of the 1:250,000 series can all be indexed on a map of the entire United States on moderate paper size. As with larger-scale maps, each sheet is given the name of somewhere prominent that is included on it.

IDENTIFYING LATITUDE AND LONGITUDE

If you want to find the latitude and longitude of a particular place, you have to discover what is already marked on the map and progress from that. If it is a large-scale map, you will probably find points along the border marked in degrees and minutes. At most scales, the calibrations will not be less than 30′ (half a degree or 30 minutes). If there are no lines already across the map, lightly pencil the straight lines between the border marks (FIG. 5-3A).

Draw lines parallel to them through the point you want to identify (FIG. 5-3B). Its latitude and longitude will have to be found by proportion. If the difference between two known marks is 5 minutes, you will have to measure at what proportion of the distance your new line comes and relate it to minutes. Suppose the distance in millimeters is 100 west of the nearest marked point of longitude, and the distance from one marked point to the next is 300 millimeters. From the figures at the marks, you might

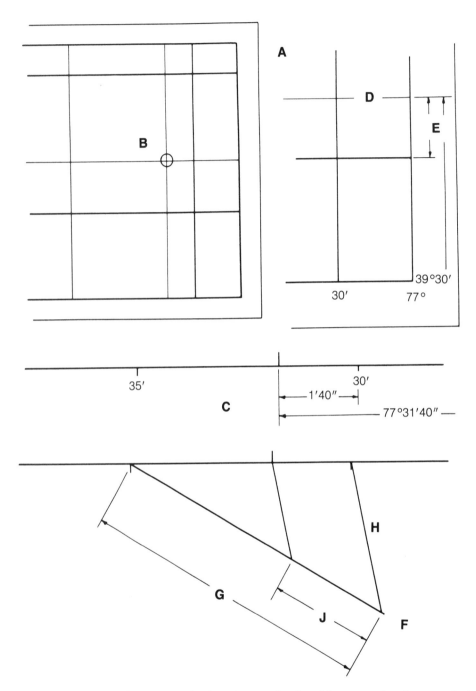

Fig. 5-3. *Latitude and longitude of a location can be found by measuring from marked lines. If a space has to be divided proportionately, it can be done geometrically.*

see that the difference is 5 minutes. To find how far west the place is, calculate proportionately: $^{100}/_{300} \times 5 = 1.66$ minutes. To bring that to minutes and seconds, multiply the decimal part by 60 to get 40, so the figure becomes 1′ 40″. That has to be added to the nearest reading to the east to get the longitude of the point. In this case, that is 77° 30′, so the longitude of the place is 77° 31′ 40″ (FIG. 5-3C). You may find that degrees are only marked at the corners of the map, while intermediate points are in minutes and seconds.

Latitude is found in the same way, but this time you are working north (FIG. 5-3D). Measure this distance north from the nearest marked point, find what the distance is between marked points and do the proportional calculation to get the minutes and seconds to add to the nearest marked reading to southward (FIG. 5-3E).

There is an alternative to the calculations. With measurements and proportions not coming in round figures, you could be working with rather involved calculations. You can lay out the distances geometrically. Draw a line at an angle to the map edge from one of the points. The angle is not important, but about 30° is suitable (FIG. 5-3F). Along that line, measure a distance that is easily divided by 60, if you are dealing with a gap of 1 minute, or 300 if it is a gap of 5 minutes (FIG. 5-3G). Accuracy is easier to obtain if the marked distance is not very much more or less than the distance along the map edge between points.

Join the mark on the line with the mark on the map edge (FIG. 5-3H). From the mark you want to measure, draw another line parallel to that and measure from one line to the other on the sloping line in the same units you used before (FIG. 5-3J). Each unit measured represents 1 second. If the distance is more than 60, convert it to minutes and seconds: a reading of 140 then becomes 2 minutes 20 seconds. This has to be added to the nearest eastward mark of longitude, or to the nearest mark southward for latitude, to get the reading for the particular position. If it is more convenient, subtract from the next reading further on to get the same result.

GRIDS

Locations in degrees, minutes, and seconds of latitude and longitude are precise and unique. You can pinpoint the place; nowhere else in the world will have the same combination of coordinates. This is, however, a rather cumbersome method if all you want to know is the general location of a place. It would be better to have a quick reference that would lead your eye to the immediate area when what you want should be obvious. On many maps a *grid* is provided for this purpose.

It is a common arrangement on motoring maps and street plans of towns to have an index that lists all the places with a reference to their grid position. A grid is an arrangement of vertical and horizontal lines superimposed on the map and bearing no particular relationship to parallels of latitude or meridians of longitude. Usually the lines form squares (FIG. 5-4A). The square sizes may match the scale of the map, but this is not necessarily so. In a motoring atlas, the squares (not the lines) might be numbered across the top and bottom of a map from left to right and lettered down the

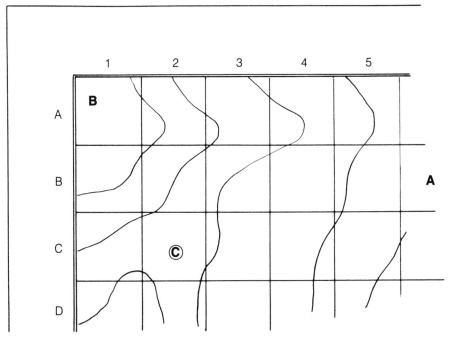

Fig. 5-4. *A grid may be drawn over a map to provide references for locating places.*

side, starting at the top (FIG. 5-4B). The atlas index then lists places with a page or map number followed by a square letter and number. For example, the place may be in square C2 (FIG. 5-4C). There is only one square C2 on the page, so your search is brought down to that and location should be easy. There is no standard way of arranging such a grid, but the arrangements should be obvious and will usually be explained in a commercially produced map, state map, or atlas.

There are military grids and other used for general purposes in other parts of the world. All are truly rectangular grids, superimposed on the geographically projected map, and they may be related to the scale of the map so that they can be used for measurement.

The *Universal Mercator Grid*, which may be called the *U. T. M. Grid*, is becoming increasingly popular. The world is divided into 60 zones with each 60° wide and covering most of the land areas of the world. Numbering within each zone is the same, but the zone has to be identified.

GRID REFERENCES

A user of any grid that employs measurements and numbers both ways can quite simply obtain a reference point that is very close. A common example has the map marked in 1 kilometer squares (about 5/8 mile). Along the top and bottom edges, the lines forming the squares are numbered from the left (west), but probably not starting at 1 because the sheet joins others in forming the overall pattern of the grid. The left and right edges of the map are similarly numbered at the grid lines, from the bottom to the top (FIG. 5-5A). Each group of grid numbers may be given a pair of index letters to show the large area in which they are contained. If you are only concerned with one sheet, the letters may be ignored.

As each square is 1 kilometer (1000 meters) each way, one tenth of a side will be 100 meters. If you can get as near as that on the ground, you are within shouting distance!

Grid reference numbers must be taken in a certain sequence; otherwise, they give a wrong reading or may even give you a point in space. They should be read first from left to right, then up a side—along the passage and up the stairs. That's one way to remember it. There are two figures opposite each line. If the figure is less than 10, there is 0 before it. In finding the grid reference of a place, identify the square. Then, estimate the number of tenths of the square width across the square and add that figure; you get three figures in that direction and can get three figures the other way in the same manner. For example, the point to be located may be in the square with the left-hand number 16, and we estimate it is 7 tenths across the square. The grid reference number that way is 167 (FIG. 5-5B). Up the side of the map it is the square that has the lower number 32, and we estimate it is 3 tenths further up. The number that way is 323 (FIG. 5-5C). Because the horizontal number has to be given before the vertical one, the grid reference for that point is 167 323.

As a further example, take the west edge of the kilometer square in which the point lies, and read the two-part figure opposite in the top or bottom margin (FIG. 5-5D). Estimate the number of tenths eastward from the line (FIG. 5-5E). Put the results

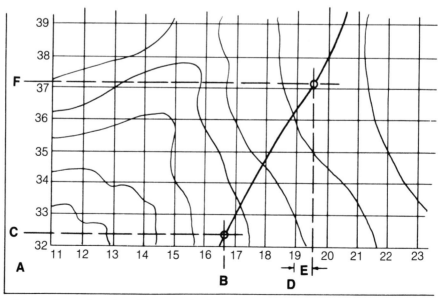

Fig. 5-5. *With numbered grid lines, a further figure can be found by estimating tenths of the distance across a square in both directions.*

together as a three-figure number—in this case 195. Take the south edge of the kilometer square in which the point is contained and read the two-part figure opposite it. Then estimate how many more tenths northward from this line (FIG. 5-5F). This gives us 371. Putting the three-figure numbers together in the correct order gives us 195 371.

If we are only concerned with a particular map sheet, this is probably all that is needed for a unique reference. However, the same grid reference applies to a point some distance away on other maps and other scales. In some cases, it helps to avoid confusion if the grid letters are also quoted. They should be found overprinted on the map or detailed in the margin. The full unique grid reference will then read, for instance: SR 195 371.

The final location within a square has been described by estimation. This should be sufficiently accurate and can be surprisingly close, but a little device can be bought or made to measure within the square. It may be called a *roamer* or a *template*. A different one is needed for each scale. In one version, there is a right angled triangle cut out of thin transparent plastic and calibrated along the square edges in a scale of tenths of 1 kilometer (FIG. 5-6A). It can be put over a square with its corner on the point and held with the calibrations parallel to the grid lines; distances can be read both ways (FIG. 5-6B). Making a roamer may present practical difficulties. An easier-to-make version is a right-angled corner of a piece of card marked in a scale of tenths of 1 kilometer from the corner both ways (FIG. 5-6C). That can be put over the square with its corner on the point and distance read each way (FIG. 5-6D). Although you cannot see through the card, there should be no difficulty in positioning a card roamer in most situations.

If a grid has been applied to a map, its crossing lines are at 90° to each other. Except at the equator, latitude and longitude lines do not cross squarely. This means that on most maps the grid lines cannot be treated as if they were comparable or matching in any way to the parallels of latitude or meridians of longitude.

For practical purposes, anyone setting a map with a compass would usually be wrong in assuming that the vertical grid lines were running either true or magnetic north and south. Using a compass to relate to the grid lines would result in setting the map in the general direction of north, but there could be an error of several degrees. To allow for that, the north indication in the margin of the map may be made up of three arrows (FIG. 5-6E) showing true north, magnetic north, and grid north. From the difference in angles between these, you can see what to allow if you want to relate your compass to grid lines.

PROJECTIONS

Only a globe can give a true representation of the earth's surface. We use flat maps, and even the area represented by a large-scale map is slightly distorted due to changing a surface with a slight double curvature to a flat one. The difference is so slight that for practical purposes it can be ignored. This may apply to a map covering a day's motoring distance, but for maps covering large areas of the earth's surface, the distortion of

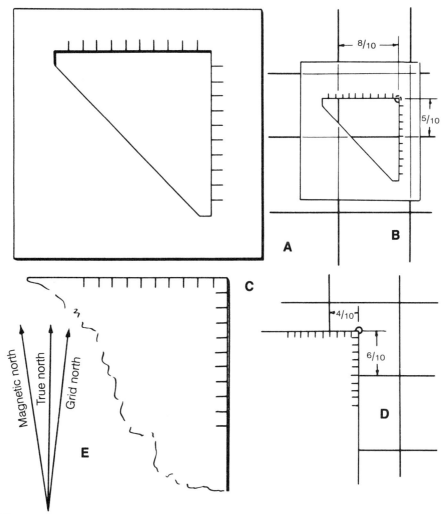

Fig. 5-6. *A template or roamer may be used to measure tenths of a grid square.*

what is being represented on a flat surface when it is actually part of a sphere is enough to result in errors. There is no way that all errors can be eliminated. A method of projection from round to flat has to be chosen that will eliminate such errors as are considered important for a particular purpose, while leaving others.

The majority of map users do not need to know much about the way flat maps are projected from the basic globe shape, but it helps in interpreting maps if the problems are appreciated. For instance, in some cases of worldwide maps, distances are not what they seem and countries may be in disproportionate sizes. If all you have in your hand is a sheet covering perhaps 50 miles each way, you can assume the distances and shapes on it are relatively correct. If you want to check the route you fly from New York to London, many flat maps will give you a false idea of direction.

The map of the world with which most of us are familiar is a rectangular sheet wider than it is high (FIG. 11-13) with the latitude lines drawn parallel across the map and all the meridians of longitude drawn vertically, so they cross squarely. Usually the map does not go much further south than 60°, nor north more than 80°; that takes in most of the major land masses.

The map is a *Mercator projection*. It is formed as an imaginary cylinder surrounding the globe, touching it at the equator; then opened out (FIG. 5-7A). The height of the cylinder matches the curve around the earth from pole to pole. At the equator, the scale of the flat map agrees with the globe. But on this projection, each parallel of latitude is drawn as if it were a great circle like the equator. Therefore, the scale increases as we go north and south from the equator. The latitude increases in the same proportion as the longitude, and we can read directions of one point in relation to another.

Because meridians of longitude actually meet at the poles, but are drawn parallel on this projection, widths are exaggerated the further we travel north and south from the equator. Greenland, for instance, seems much wider than it actually is, relative to countries nearer the equator. Because of this, there has to be a scale provided to allow measuring at different parallels of latitude (FIG. 5-7B).

As can be seen, there are great differences between the extremes of the scale. This shows how much has to be allowed when visualizing the size and shape of one country in relation to another.

Conic projection is another method, of which there are several named types. Basically, a hemisphere is enclosed by a cone, touching it at one parallel of latitude—40°N or S may be chosen (FIG. 5-7C). The cone is opened out and applied to a rectangular piece of paper (FIG. 5-7D). The curves representing latitude are all drawn about the apex of the cone. The one representing 40° has correct scale lengths along it, as it is the same as the globe, but the scale is distorted along lines parallel to it according to their distance away from it. Meridians of longitude all meet at the apex of the cone.

In another method of conic projection the cone is assumed to pass through two parallels of latitude—20°N and 60°N, in the example (FIG. 5-7E). On the opened-out projection the two parallels are drawn their actual distance apart around the curve of the globe (not straight along the chord represented by the slope of the cone). The advantage of this method over the previous one is that it lets the map coincide with the globe along two parallels, with correct distances along them and less distortion at places further from them (FIG. 5-7F).

Other projections have curved outlines. Within a circle, places on the globe may be all brought to the front half of the world. Half the world may be on a circle and the other half on another circle—in effect, two side views of a globe. To get something of the same effect, an outline may be elliptical, with latitude lines straight across and longitude lines drawn elliptically to meet at the poles (FIG. 11-12). This gives land mass areas relatively correctly. Other maps with curved outlines may be broken into parts to get more accurate representations of the great land masses.

Traditionally, most schemes for projecting flat maps from a globe have concen-

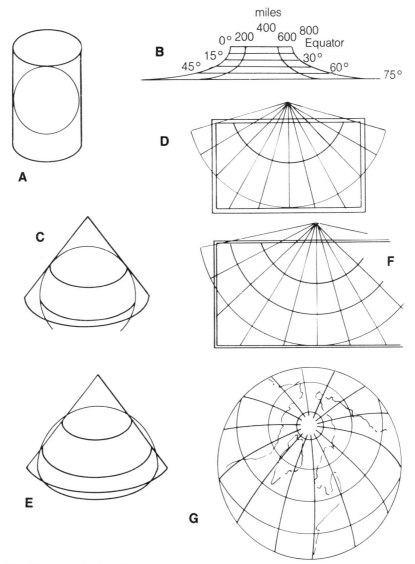

Fig. 5-7. *The spherical surface of the earth may be projected on to a cylinder (A) to be opened out. The resulting map needs a graduated scale (B). Conic representations of a hemisphere (C,D,E,F) give better representations of shapes. A round map is particularly appropriate for polar areas (G).*

trated on the middle areas north and south of the equator. With the increasing development of flights over the polar regions, there has come a need for maps more correctly portraying the north polar area in particular. Many of the methods of projection that we have become used to are either far from accurate at long distances from the equator or details there are so tightly packed compared with equatorial areas that they are difficult to read.

Maps on various projections are now made with the North Pole as the focal point instead of the equator (FIG. 11-14). Some round projections have the pole to one side of center and lines of latitude arranged about it and meridians of longitude through it. How much is contained depends on how far the map is to go. Parts within the immediate polar area can be somewhat accurately to scale, but distortion increases as distances away from the pole become greater (FIG. 5-7G). Other projections of this type are within elliptical outlines.

Only a globe can show places to their correct scale and correctly related to each other, but one of these polar projections gives a better idea than other flat maps of the routes between familiar air terminals. For instance, it can be seen that a straight line between New York and London goes over Newfoundland, while Fairbanks, Alaska, to Oslo, Norway, is almost directly over the North Pole. Other maps, that can be regarded as a sideways look at the world, would not tell you this in the way that a map of the top of the world does.

Geological survey maps of the United States are based on versions of the conic projection using two parallels of latitude, with a transverse Mercator adaption for the large-scale maps. The effect, as far as users are concerned, is for parallels of latitude to be treated as straight lines across the map parallel with the bottom margin, while meridians of longitude come slightly closer at the top of a map than at the bottom.

6

Setting a Map

A MAP IS A PICTURE OF PART OF THE EARTH'S SURFACE. USUALLY A MAP shows land mass, although surrounding sea may be included. If it is mainly sea, it is a *chart* and more likely to be intended for the navigation of shipping, and is employed in a different way. The map is produced to offer information at a small scale to a particular area of land, so it is important that we can locate places and directions on it.

The map is of little use if we cannot find where we are on it and directions to other places that interest us. Relating the map to the land and water it represents is called *setting*, *orienting* or *orientating*. Once we have established this relationship, we can begin to plan routes, locate places of interest, explore new territory, and generally discover information that is there to be read and interpreted.

Fortunately, there are many ways of setting a map in addition to using a compass. They vary according to circumstances and information available. Quite often it is possible and advantageous to use more than one method, so each confirms the findings of the other. Sometimes, as when travelling by car, road numbers and plentiful signs make matching the map to the route so simple that it is oriented unconsciously. Things may be very different at night in undeveloped country or in a maze of forest tracks.

Setting or orienting applies mainly when you are in the field, and the map has immediate use in relation to the terrain, but it is helpful to be able to visualize the application of information while studying a map at home, or some other place away from the actual country you will be travelling.

SETTING WITH A ROAD

On most roads you do not have to go far to find something marked on your map, which you can identify. It may be a junction with another road, cross roads, or a marked building beside the road. A railroad crossing is useful, as you then have two lines on the map, which have their counterparts positively identifiable on the ground. Whatever you use as your key marked position, you know where you are on the map and on the ground (FIG. 6-1A). You should now be able to turn the map so the marked road, and possibly the railroad, if there, are in the same relative directions as on the map (FIG. 6-1B).

It is still possible to be working in reverse, with the map 180° out, so next you must use another bit of information to make sure the map is the right way in relation to the ground. You have come from somewhere and that may be the best guide, particularly if there is a sign, or you passed one on the way. Turn the map so where you came from, as marked on it, matches the direction on the road.

Quite often there is something else that will confirm the setting. There might be a township not far away. There could be a church, fire lookout, or other marked feature. If the mapmaker regarded it as worth recording, it was because it was prominent. With the map set to the road, look in the direction where the feature is indicated (FIG. 6-1C). If you can see it, that confirms the map setting. If you cannot see it, do not assume, immediately, that you have oriented the map wrongly. There may be trees or some other obstruction to your view. Try something else.

If you are travelling by car and your job is to give directions to the driver, you may want to turn the map so it is set to the road, but if that means it is upside-down, you may have difficulty in reading words printed on it. In that case, it is better to have the map the right way up, even if it means the route on the map is from the upper to the

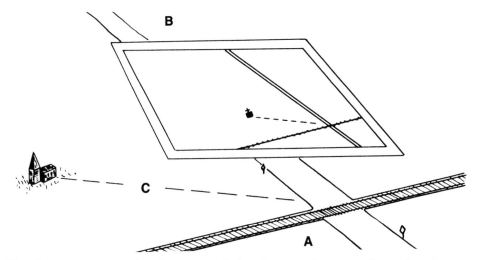

Fig. 6-1. *A map is set when features marked on it are in the same relative directions as what they represent on the ground.*

lower part of the map. You have to practice map reading from the right and left directions without turning the map around.

It may be better to turn the map around than to give a mistaken direction at a road fork or crossroads, but try to get used to reading left and right from the direction on the map you are travelling, rather than related to your body in the way you are sitting. Imagine you and the car following the road on the map. You would be facing the direction being travelled. Think of it in that manner, and give directions as in those circumstances. Your driver will not thank you for making him go the wrong way, nor for dithering as you approach a turning place. He may not be able to go slowly enough while you change your mind, so remember the scale of the map and think ahead to the next move. It is all there on the map, even if you have not arrived there yet.

SETTING BY LANDMARKS

If you have no doubt about where you are on the ground, and you can locate it on the map, this is a starting point for setting the map, even if you are uncertain of directions. You may be at a fork in tracks, outside a marked hut, below a lookout tower, or about to leave a paved road. In all cases, the spot can be identified (FIG. 6-2A). Look on the map for some sort of other landmark. Try to find it on the ground. The map scale will give you a clue to distance. It is not much use looking for a hut 10 miles away! If there is an identifiable object, turn the map so an imaginary line between you and the object on the map and on the ground coincide (FIG. 6-2B). The map is then set in relation to the ground and you should be able to plan your route in any direction.

Setting by one landmark may be satisfactory and the only way possible, but if there is another mark within view, use that as well. The two imaginary lines will confirm each other in orienting the map (FIG. 6-2C).

Sometimes there is no solitary object that you can use as an exact *fix*, but there may be some general feature that will serve as a guide. Suppose you can see traffic on a road in the distance. You may be able to estimate how far it is away. Look on the map for a road at about this distance and turn the map in that general direction. Does the road go squarely across your view? Does it appear from traffic movements to go away or towards you? If there is more than one road on the map that might agree, these things will help you to select the right one. A railroad track might be used in the same way. If the road includes a hill, that might be a useful guide. Much depends on the length of the hill and the frequency of contour lines on the map. Even if the road on the map does not cross two contour lines, their heights will help you check which way the road on the map should slope. You can see if it does so on the ground (FIG. 6-2D).

With solitary objects and the more general guide of a road or similar object, remember to use scale. Even if your estimation is not very good, you will avoid the errors that would come from assuming something is close when it is actually too far away to be seen. It helps to use distant objects that can be identified. When you turn the map towards them, the risk of error is less than it would be with a very near object, because the imaginary line on the map may then be very short and, therefore, difficult to line up accurately.

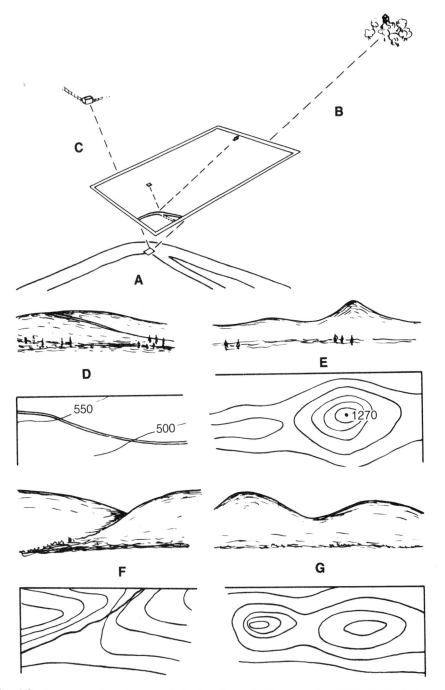

Fig. 6-2. *A map may be set to match the bearings of objects in view (A,B,C). With the map set you can interpret symbols and contour lines into what you expect to see (D,E,F,G).*

If there are no objects about which you can be certain, you might have to check the shape of the land and relate it to contours on the map. If there is a definite peak, much higher than the other land in view, it will probably be marked on the map with a spot height and contour lines close around it (FIG. 6-2E). You can set the map on that without much risk of error. It may be more difficult if the terrain is undulating and does not rise very high at one spot. If there is a river or stream from the hills, there may be enough of a gap to be seen by contour lines (FIG. 6-2F). You can set the map by the distant hollow on the skyline. If the hills are more moderate, they may still show a pattern that can be identified from contours. Remember that close contours indicate steeper slopes than those widely spaced. There could be two nearby hills with different profiles (FIG. 6-2G). If there is an isolated hill nearer, but in the same direction, that would confirm your identification. Look around on the map for contour line arrangements that could be seen on the ground as hillocks or valleys from your viewpoint.

Allow for complications due to trees, which may disguise the actual lay of the land. They are more of a nuisance with near hills, as they blend in more with the profile at a distance, so try to identify and orient on a distant range of hills or some natural feature.

Waterways are not so useful in setting a map, as they usually are in hollows and therefore not visible at much distance. However, if the waterway is large enough for you to see some of it from one point, the way its course takes may help you to match up the map with it. Falls or rapids may be marked on the map. In any case, the direction of flow gives you a guide. The water will flow from higher to lower contours on the map, so if you come across a known waterway, the map can be turned to match the direction of flow.

LOCATING POSITION

If you are uncertain of where you are, there are several things you can do to narrow down the choice of position on the map until you have a close approximation, if not an exact point where you are standing. A compass makes location easier, but there is much you can do with only a map. If the sun is visible and you know the time, you can arrive at a close estimate of compass directions. Similarly, on a clear night you can use the stars to find north. We will assume a dull day and only a map as a guide.

From your previous movements you should have some idea of the general area you are in, so you can reduce your examination of the map to that part. If you started from a known position, pinpoint that on the map. Allowing for the time you have been travelling and your probable speed, you can draw a circle, or estimate its position, showing the maximum you could have traveled. You may know the general direction you have moved, so there is no need for a complete circle. Quite a small arc may be all you have to consider (FIG. 6-3A). You are somewhere in that sector. A first limitation of area in this way avoids searching all over the map in unlikely places and helps to steady any tendency for anyone to panic in your party.

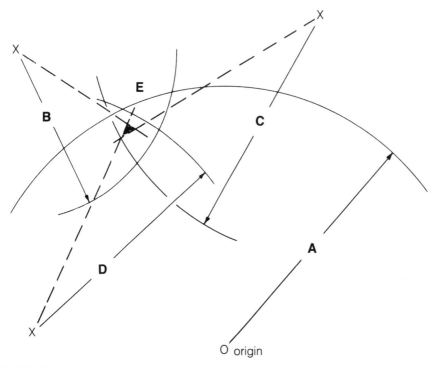

Fig. 6-3. *You can estimate your position on a map by drawing arcs of distances from land-marks you can identify (A,B,C,D) or by taking sights (E). You are within the overlapping arcs or crossings of sight lines.*

Unless you are in a flat desert with no features—and you should not be in that sort of place without a compass to use with the map—there should be man-made or natural features within view that can be matched with symbols on the map. Man-made features are easier to identify with certainty. There may be individual buildings, towers, or other projections above their surroundings. The presence of habitations may be indicated by rising smoke or the glow of light at night, even if you cannot see the buildings in a township. Overhead power lines are a help. Even if you cannot see them immediately, regular gaps cut through a forest may indicate them. A gap for a power line may be much straighter than one due to a trail or stream and may go over hills, where a track or trail would go around. A road of any importance is likely to be obvious by the traffic and roadside buildings. A road or railroad may be located by the poles supporting overhead lines, even if you cannot see the track on the surface.

Natural features that will guide you depend on your situation. A visible stream helps in orienting a map. If the country is a mixture of woodland and open fields or barren land, the pattern of groups of trees might be shown on the map and you may be able to match the drawing with the actual view. Check the date of the map. Revisions are not very frequent. If the map has not been corrected for 20 years, trees may have been felled or more may have grown outside the bounds originally drawn. If no man-made or natural feature can be positively located, contours may help. Even moderate changes in elevation can give you a clue, but look on the map for isolated rises, particularly those that are identifiably higher than their surroundings.

ESTIMATING POSITION

If you can identify a feature, estimate how far away it is. Draw or visualize a curve from it with this radius on your map (FIG. 6-3B). Do the same for another feature. If you can choose a feature that is nearly square to your view of the other, you will get a closer degree of accuracy than if it is at a finer angle (FIG. 6-3C). If possible, find a third feature, preferably at a wide angle to either of the others, and draw a curve at the estimated scale distance from it (FIG. 6-3D). Do not expect precision, as your estimates may not be very close, but the resulting crossing curves allow you to reduce the probable map area in which you are.

Move the map around so the chosen features are in the same relation to each other as they are on the ground. By trial and error, sight each of them across the map—preferably with the map on a flat surface—until the sightlines are as nearly correct for all three as you can get them. This should bring the lines on the map close to or actually crossing (FIG. 6-3E). If they cross in a small triangle (what the navigator at sea calls a "cocked hat"), you can assume you are within it.

The position obtained by sighting should come within the same area obtained by estimating distances. If it does, one method confirms the other, but if it does not, the sighting position is more likely to be accurate than the estimating position. Estimating distances over different terrain can often be misleading.

If the two methods give you widely different positions, it will be advisable to check back on each of them. If you can find a fourth point, it should confirm which of the earlier locatings is more correct. Even if the fourth position is just a minor hill or valley, which cannot be treated as a spot location, an estimate of its distance and a sight made in relation to the other three sightings will show if any of the earlier work contained errors.

Of course, you may not be in a position where you can find three or more positive points to work back from, or you may find them all in the same general direction, so sight lines are at an acute angle, and their crossing could be anywhere within a mile or so. Even such a vague location may help you to then check other features, such as your elevation in relation to surrounding country, or how you got to the point from a previous known one, so you can reduce your findings to a closer estimate. If the only result is to make you vow to have a compass with you next time, that too is a good thing.

ORIENTING WITH A COMPASS

Compass and map are complementary. Even if all you are doing is using a map in a built-up area, with paved roads and all the other attributes of civilization, a compass may prevent you turning the wrong way along a street, or going out of town on the wrong highway. If you plan to go into less developed country, a compass becomes increasingly necessary, while going into the mountains or other purely natural areas without a compass could be disastrous.

It is good practice to use a compass with your map, even in situations where you could find your way with the map only, so you become used to handling the compass. The fact that you already know where you are going and can confirm this on the map, provides a check on the way you use the compass. Then, when you eventually have to depend on known territory, you will feel confident in your actions.

Any compass can be used to set a map, but you are most likely to use a small portable one with a liquid-damped needle. For general map work, a compass with a transparent base and calibrations in degrees is convenient. Most have the north-pointing needle rotating and the calibrations on the rim or base. A rotating card, with the circle of calibrations turning with the needle is less common, but may be found in sighting and surveying compasses intended for precision work. This has the advantage of cutting out one action in using the compass, as the calibrations are always correct in relation to the needle. When setting a map, the additional action with the separately calibrated compass does not make much difference.

Check which way is north on the map from the compass arrows in the margin. Nearly all maps have their tops north, but it is unwise to assume this and always advisable to check. Some maps may have north in a different direction because that suits the shape of the area being illustrated or the feature is long and narrow, such as a river and its valley, which would fit better on to a sheet or page with a different north direction.

NOTING VARIATIONS

The compass arrows on the map may be two or three together. When there are three, the extra is *grid north*, meaning the way the grid over the map has been laid out for locating places in relation to an index or for military or other purposes. Ignore this when setting a map. If the grid lines are drawn across the map, it would usually be inadvisable to use them for positioning the compass, unless their variation from north is only a few degrees; then you may feel the error they induce would be so slight as to be ignored for practical purposes, when all you want is a general direction.

The angle between true north and magnetic north will vary in different parts of the country. On a small-scale map of a wide expanse of country it could be very different at opposite sides. On most maps, the variation shown in the margin is at the center of the side of true north. Fortunately, it is only a few degrees in most parts of America. For practical purposes, the difference can often be ignored, if all you want to do is decide which road to take. If you are going across unmarked country and want to arrive exactly at a certain point, the difference between true and magnetic north should be taken into account.

If your compass is the type with the degree calibrations on a rotating rim, or bezel, or in the base, turn the calibrations so north is truly in line with the base or the case (FIG. 6-4A). If the side of the map has been checked to represent true north and south, put the compass over the border and turn the map until the border and the north-south line on the compass agree (FIG. 6-4B). This assumes true north and mag-

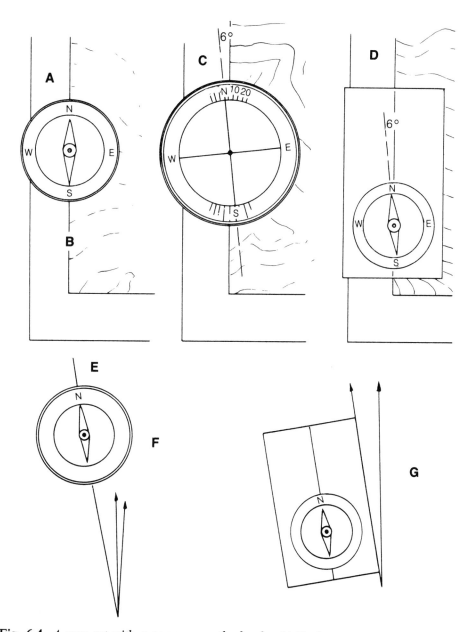

Fig. 6-4. *A map set with a compass on the border (A,B) does not allow for magnetic north, so it should be moved to suit this as indicated on the map (C to G).*

netic north are the same, which may be accurate enough. The map and the part of the earth's surface it represents will be set correctly in relation to each other, except for the error due to the difference between magnetic and true north at that point. In many cases, this is more accurate than you need for the setting, so nothing more has to be done.

If you want to allow for the magnetic difference, note what this is. As an example, suppose magnetic north is 6° west of true north. If the compass has a card rotating with the needle, set the map so the border line passes through 6° at the northern edge and 186° at the southern edge (FIG. 6-4C). The compass north end of the needle will then be pointing correctly and the map edge will be true north and south.

SETTING WITH A NEEDLE COMPASS

If the compass has the calibrations that do not turn with the needle, set the calibrations at 6° and 186° to the centerline of the compass; then position the compass over the border so its centerline matches. Turn the map with the compass on it until the needle points to the north mark (FIG. 6-4D). You will then have the map edge set to true north.

If it is a map where the north direction is not the same as the border of the map, you will have to use the north arrows themselves. On some maps the arrows are not very long; positioning a compass over them could result in slight inaccuracies. If you know in advance that you will have to use the arrows, it is worthwhile drawing a longer line through the magnetic north line before you leave home (FIG. 6-4E). That will allow you to position the compass over the line with certainty (FIG. 6-4F). If the compass you are using has a rectangular base, it could be put alongside the magnetic arrow (FIG. 6-4G). The direction, of course, is the same. If you are using the magnetic arrow, have the centerline of the base and the north point coinciding. When you turn the map to bring the needle to point correctly, you will have allowed for magnetic variation, and the map will be set correctly in relation to the ground and true north.

If you expect to be making much use of a map that does not have its border pointing north, it may help to discover the bearing represented by a border line; use this for setting the map with a compass. Extend the magnetic arrow line so it crosses the border. Measure the angle between the border and this line, either with a protractor or the compass calibrations used as a protractor. In the example, we find that the border is running 300° west and 120° east (FIG. 6-5A). Set the base of the compass to these bearings and position it in line with the border, then turn the map with the compass on it until the needle and north point coincide (FIG. 6-5B). The map will be set in relation to the ground. For frequent use of a large map, this may be more convenient than using the border arrow. Make a note of the bearing to use.

Depending on the shape of the map sheet, it may be more convenient to use the border the other way. In that case, you have to allow for the 90° corner. You could continue the magnetic arrow line until it crosses the other border and measure the angles, if it is conveniently located, or you can add 90° to the angles found for the other border. In the example, this gives us a line running 30° northward and 210° southward (FIG. 6-5C). If the compass base is turned to this and positioned on that border, the map may be set in the same way as before.

ORIENTING BY THE SUN

Finding compass directions by using the sun was described in chapter 3. Even if you have a compass, the sun may be sufficient for a casual setting, so you take note of its

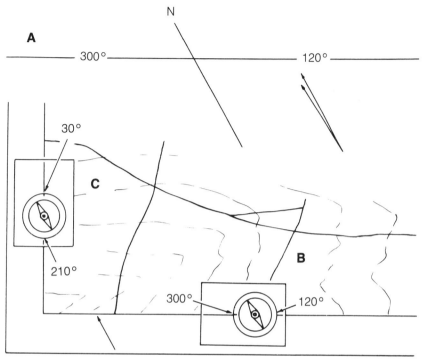

Fig. 6-5. *If the north direction indicated on a map is diagonal to the borders, that must be allowed for when setting a map.*

direction and use that. At its zenith at noon, the sun is south. You can turn the map in relation to the sun then and know it is generally in a reasonable relation to the land it represents. At 6 A.M. you can use the sun as east, and at 6 P.M. you can use it as west, so you can allow for other directions in relation to these and set your map accordingly.

If you want to be more precise, there is the method of using the sun in relation to the hands of a watch to find north. If you have a compass with you, that is unnecessary.

Rather similar to the use of a shadow from something across the dial of a watch, is the use of your own shadow. At noon, your own shadow is north. Allow for other times when you want to set the map quickly and approximately to check a reading. If you look at the map at 3 P.M., your shadow will be at about northeast, and you can turn the map so the shadow falls across it in that direction. You will know that the top of the map is approximately north.

ORIENTING BY THE STARS

If the sky is clear at night, the North Star gives you a clear guide to setting a map (see chapter 3). If your compass does not have luminous markings, you may have difficulty in reading it and the map at the same time. If you keep the north part of the map towards the North Star, the map will be set and you can concentrate on reading it in relation to the ground.

A further advantage of using the North Star is in avoiding the risk of deflecting the compass. If you use a flashlight close to a compass, the electrical field set up may cause an error in the way it points. Remember this when transferring bearings from map to compass, or compass to map, and keep the flashlight as far away as possible.

POSITIONING BY COMPASS

The methods already described for finding where you are in relation to identified objects is made much easier and more positive by using a compass with the map. As before, you may have a good general idea of where you are and can bring the location to a fairly small area of the map, but you may need to be able to get as close as possible to the exact spot.

It helps to identify two objects, preferably at something like 90° to each other in your view, but you may have to settle for landmarks at very different angles to that. A third object helps to confirm the position obtained from the other two, but with compass bearings there is not such a risk of appreciable error as there was in the earlier method without a compass.

Using compass bearings, you need to work with the compass over the map. It may be more convenient to put the map on the hood of a car or some other level place, which might not be convenient for taking sights. In wet weather, it may be better to have the map in a tent or hut, where you can interpret the readings taken outside, with more comfort and a better chance of accuracy.

Sight the object from your viewpoint with your compass. If it is a sighting compass with a prism, you can merely look across it and read the bearing when the object is in view. With a very simple needle compass, you may turn the rim or base to bring the north mark to match the needle; then look across the center and read the bearing at the far side. With a compass having a rectangular base, you still set the needle and north mark together; then, sight centrally, or along one edge, and read the bearing shown over the central line (FIG. 6-6A). Make a note of this bearing and go ahead with sighting another landmark and reading its bearing. Do the same with a third sighting, if one is available. Do not confuse your notes of bearings.

At the map, look for north-south lines in the vicinity that concerns you; they will be a help in plotting angles. If they are grid lines, check how far they are out of true with the north arrows in the border. Usually, they are within a few degrees of true and this may be ignored, particularly as your sighted bearings could be many degrees out if you are using a simple compass.

PLOTTING A POSITION

Plotting may be more easily done with a protractor, but the compass itself can be used as a protractor. Lightly pencil a north-south line through the symbol of the object you sighted (FIG. 6-6B). Put the center of the protractor over the symbol and mark from its rim the bearing, or the reciprocal of it (180° more or less) (FIG. 6-6C). Draw a line through the symbol and this point (FIG. 6-6D). Your location is somewhere on that line.

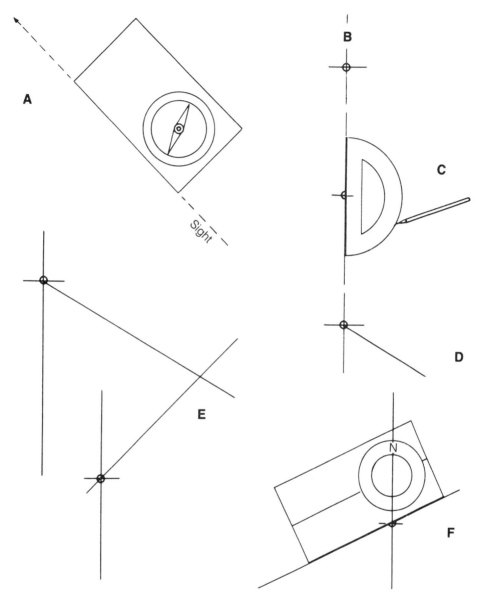

Fig. 6-6. *A sight may be taken across or along the edge of a compass (A) and bearings transferred to the map with a protractor related to north-south lines (B,C,D,E) or the compass can be used as a protractor (F), allowing for magnetic variations.*

Do the same at the symbol for another sighted object. That line will cross the first (FIG. 6-6E). If you have worked accurately, that is where you are on the map. To confirm it, plot a third bearing. In field conditions, it is very unlikely that the three lines will cross on one spot, but the smaller the "cocked hat" triangle, the better you can consider your sighting and the more accurate your location. Or maybe the better your luck!

A rectangular protractor that is also marked with a scale is useful in the field, if you know that you will want to transfer sighted bearings to a map. In addition to measuring angles, it can be used for measuring and drawing lines. Have a soft pencil, preferably with an eraser on its end, so anything you draw can be removed from the map and not stay there as a hard pencil or ballpoint pen line would.

If you are without a protractor and your only compass is a round one, you can put it over the symbol with its north mark correctly located in relation to the lines on the map; then, read and mark the degrees you want from its scale. You cannot achieve such accuracy as you would with a protractor.

If you have a compass on a rectangular base, greater accuracy is possible. Ignore the needle. Turn the rim of the compass so the bearing you want coincides with the centerline marking of the base. Put one edge of the base through the symbol and turn the whole compass until its north-south marking agrees with a meridian or other north-south line on the map (FIG. 6-6F). Keep the edge of the base through the symbol. When the north-south reading is correct, the edge of the base is at the bearing angle and you can draw a line through it. Repeat at the other one or two locations, and you will get a similar result to using a protractor.

All of the above methods of finding where you are have ignored magnetic variations and assumed that magnetic, true, and grid (if any) north are sufficiently near for differences to be ignored. If there is an appreciable difference, you must allow for the variation, as already described. It may be worthwhile practicing and plotting bearings in an area known to you, where you know the sighting location and the position of landmarks. This will allow you to check the accuracy of your working and enable you to make plots ignoring magnetic variations and others with it, to see the difference. In many cases, the variations have a cancelling effect and both sets of plots may arrive at the same spot; at other times, the differences may be enough to matter.

FOLDED AND CASED MAPS

In practice, most maps are used folded. Opening a map completely may be impractical, particularly in bad weather or strong winds. You should note how the map is folded. Nearly always the folds are north and south and east and west. For setting the map you can use a folded edge, without having to open the map. A vertical fold will also serve as a meridian when plotting directions on the map. So that you do not have to open the map to discover information, memorize the scale or make a note of that and anything else you may want to know while the map is folded. For outdoor work, it is best to keep the map in a transparent plastic case (see chapter 13).

7

Finding Your Way
with a Road Map

THE SORT OF MAP WITH WHICH MOST OF US ARE FAMILIAR IS A ROAD MAP
obtained from a filling station, the American Automobile Association, or a state
traveler's information station. We may have bought a Rand McNally, or other, road
atlas, to get maps of all the country within one cover. There are a great many of these
maps aimed at automobile users who want to get across considerable distances, usually by the most direct route and in the minimum time.

The map may serve just that purpose, or it may indicate the locations of places of
interest for the tourist or vacationer. If it is an oil-company map, there may be emphasis on the location of that company's filling stations. If it is a state map, there will
probably be information on places of civic and tourist interest. Some giveaway maps
may not be as reliable as they seem. They may have been produced as advertising,
with little regard for more recent alterations, new roads, or other features that could
affect where you want to go. Any map has some value, but it is worthwhile checking
the antecedents, or earlier editions of a map before placing too much reliance on it.
Maps used to illustrate such things as campground directories may have additional
information overprinted. If that did not register exactly in the second printing, there
could be important errors. In that case, a written description of a route may be more
reliable than a map.

If you intend to traverse a part of the country once and will be using freeways or
other major highways, it may not matter much what map you have, providing it shows
the more important places along the route. If there are errors, it is unlikely that they
will affect your travel. If you are more concerned with an area in which you can expect

to travel frequently, and not always by the same routes, it would be wiser to start with a map of known accuracy. Care is taken with official state maps. (The feedback resulting from an error would reflect badly on the state officials and legislature.) Commercially produced maps are in a similar position. Their publishers take care to keep them up-to-date. This means that, in both cases, you should get the most recent issues and not rely on one someone has passed to you after having had it for many years. The older map may be useful for preliminary planning, but you should pick up a new state map when you cross a border, or be prepared to buy the most recent edition of a commercially published map or atlas.

SCALE

Think about how you intend to use the map. If you want to travel coast-to-coast, the map that shows the whole route has to be quite a small scale to get it on the paper, so there cannot be much detail. It might well be at 100 miles per inch, and at that scale you cannot expect to find more than the main towns, state boundaries, a network of interstate highways, and some other of the more important roads. That may be all you want for preliminary planning. You can sort out the route you will take; you can note road numbers and estimate or measure probable distances between stopping places. If it is to be a dash by the most direct route, without any side trips or any interest in places along the way, you might just travel with the aid of this one map, but almost certainly maps of bigger scale for parts of the route will provide helpful information along the way. The countrywide map may take roads apparently through towns, where you can actually go around them. A larger-scale map will give you this information.

As the scale gets larger, a surprising amount of additional information can be included. At 20 miles or 25 miles per inch, most states go comfortably on to a piece of paper of reasonable size and it becomes possible to show all roads of any importance, with just about all towns and townships. Some road maps do not give much information on rivers. There may be lakes and sea inlets, but only the very large waterways may be drawn. Possibly rightly, the compilers of the maps think that a motorist is not concerned with water, but a bridge over a river can be a useful landmark, allowing you to pinpoint where you are on a road. Many road maps of medium-scale do not show railroads, probably as a result of the same reasoning that leaves out rivers. However, the presence of a railroad nearby or its crossing of a road, over, under, or on the level, can be another useful guide to exactly where you are on a road.

The choice of a suitable scale for a road map depends largely on the density of population. If there are more people, there are more roads. For instance, most of what matters to the automobile driver in Pennsylvania might be put on a map with a scale of 10 miles per inch, but in the Philadelphia vicinity this would not show much besides the major highways. However, if that area was enlarged to about 2 miles per inch, there might be space for every road of any use to motorists, so the driver could cross the area or go to places of importance or special interest.

This map would still not tell you how to get about the city center itself. For that to be in sufficient detail, the map would have to be drawn with each mile represented by several inches. Quite often such a map may be inset into the border of the main map of a more moderate scale. The problem with that arrangement is that it will overlap part of the main map. It is usually placed so what is hidden is unimportant or part of another state, but it may be better if several of these very large scale plans are grouped separately. This is quite often done on the back of the main map; that makes it difficult to relate what is on one map with the other, as you cannot look at them side by side—unless you obtain a second map.

The scale shown in the border of a road map is often quite insignificant, hidden among other things in the margin—possibly just a line representing 1 mile, 10 miles, or whatever the compilers thought would be convenient. If there is no statement that the map is drawn to "5 miles per inch" or whatever it is, you should convert the inadequate little scale reference to something more easily understood. For convenience in fitting the map to an atlas page, the scale may be an odd amount. Most of us are used to thinking in inches, so see how many miles on the map are represented by one inch, even if it is an odd amount like $4^3/4$ miles. That might be more easily remembered as 19 miles per 4 inches. If you are not too certain about your powers of estimation, check the scale length of your first thumb joint. In this case it might represent 6 miles. If you are sitting beside the driver and reading the map, you can move your thumb along a road to measure distances. It would also be helpful to draw your own longer scale in a vacant space along a margin.

On many maps, distances along roads are marked, so you do not have to rely on measuring or estimating them. Somewhere in the margin, or at the front of a road atlas, you should find an explanation of how the distances are indicated. They vary between makers of maps. One method uses arrows or *ticks* pointing at the road, usually at a town or road crossing (FIG. 7-1A). If the arrows are colored, the distance is a figure in the same color between them. A more complicated method uses dots and arrows with distances in one color, with others in another color giving longer cumulative distances. You should then be able to read an overall mileage as well as intermediate ones that give you a guide to distances between smaller places or road junctions. With simple arithmetic, you can add short distances to overall distances to get accurate mileages between places some way apart.

Where interchanges are marked on a road and numbered, the numbers may indicate distances in miles from the state border or some other key point. In that case, subtract one number from the other to get the distance between them (FIG. 7-1B). If the interchange numbers do not indicate mileage, there should also be a figure showing distance.

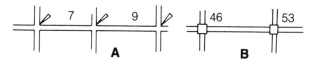

Fig. 7-1. *Distances may be shown between marked points on a road map (A) or exit numbers may indicate mileages (B).*

On most road maps, there is a grid marked along the edges to use with an index for finding places on the map. The grid divisions may be related to scale. If so, it is worthwhile remembering the scale distances between marks, so you can use this as a guide when estimating distances between points.

ELEVATIONS

It is very unusual to find contour lines on a road map. For anyone with a little experience of mapping in wilderness or undeveloped country, this can be disconcerting. You can easily get the impression that the state shown on the map is flat, when actually heights are very different in some parts of it.

Fortunately, freeways and other through highways are built so that slopes are never more than an automobile can climb without difficulty. Even then it may be annoying to find you will be climbing steadily among slow-moving trucks for 50 miles or so, when you assumed that even if the road was not level, elevations along it would not vary much, and you would be dealing only with modest rising and falling.

Even without contour lines, there are some clues to the state of the terrain. If most roads are straight and cross each other with a regular pattern, and show no or few curves, the land surface must be fairly level. If the roads twist about on the map, that is usually because they had to be built to get up and around hills using reasonable gradients. If the names of places on the map include "gap," "summit," "pass," or other indication of height in their name, the road there must be higher than it was further back, so be prepared for hills. Both types of roads can be seen on a map of South Dakota, where there is a mostly straight geometric arrangement of roads in the east, but towards the southwest corner of the state, roads and names show there must be some high country.

Road maps often give spot heights of hills or mountains that stand above the surrounding country. Often, if the whole area is high, there may be no general height indication. The spot height is more of a landmark than a clue to the gradient of a road near it. Where a road climbs through a mountain pass, there may be a spot height marking the summit of the pass. If there is a height near the road some place else, the two figures give you an idea of how much you have to climb in a particular distance, but that could mean a steep slope at one end of an otherwise gentle slope, rather than an even gradient.

If a road skirts a large lake, its general elevation must be fairly static, because water remains level. That does not mean the road will be without short rises and falls on lakeside cliffs and other land variations. You cannot expect, however, to be making any big climbs while by the lake. If there is a river on the map, you can ascertain its direction of flow from high to low. Unless it is a rapid river, the fall of a road near it may only be slight.

The compilers of maps without contour lines assume that any modern car is capable of negotiating any road drawn on the map. That is probably so, but it would be useful to know more about elevations along the road you are travelling. Sometimes, the elevations of towns are given in the index. If there are places of interest along the road, guide books and leaflets about them may tell you heights. If you expect to travel to an area you do not know, a contour map is worth consulting in advance, even if it does not show roads and may just be a school atlas of the whole country. This will give you an idea of general elevations in that part of the country, compared with your starting and intermediate places. You will then know if you will be slowed by hills or may gain in speed and fuel consumption by going down hills.

ROADS

How roads are marked depends largely on how many colors the mapmaker has available. Consult the information in the legend or margin. There could be ten different ways of showing roads. Freeways are usually most prominent; they could be dark blue with a red border. The comparable toll road might be almost as prominent dark green with a black border. In both cases, if the road was under construction at the time the map was compiled or revised, it might be shown broken. Other four-lane divided highways have their own colors, possibly orange with a red border (FIG. 7-2A). All of these almost shout at you from the page. The makers of the map assume, probably rightly, that most users want to know about these through routes before anything else.

Other roads may not be so easy to differentiate. A principal highway that is not four-lane and divided may be a broad red line, while other almost similar highways are also red, but narrower (FIG. 7-2B). You may have to look closely to decide which is which. Lesser roads may be grey or another less prominent color (FIG. 7-2C) and at the bottom of the scale are close parallel lines. Usually it would be unwise to use an unimportant road without local knowledge, even if it appears to save a few miles compared with one that is obviously in motoring condition.

The signs that you expect to see along a highway, indicating its class and number, are reproduced on most maps in a reduced form, so the symbol can be identified in the shape you expect, although there may be some simplification to suit the small reproduction (FIG. 7-2D). The actual style used will vary a little between mapmakers, so check the sample symbols shown in the margin or legend. For instance, an interstate sign may be yellow with a black top and number, or it may be all black with a white number. Where there is a business loop or spur, green may be used instead of black. U.S. Highway signs are usually drawn as open shields, in black or red line, with the number the same. State and county roads may be more simply marked, if the scale is large enough to have space for their identification. With smaller scale maps and areas with many roads, it is more likely that only interstate and U.S. Highways will be marked by symbols.

If your map includes part of Canada, the Trans-Canada Highway will be marked with a stylized maple leaf on a shield (FIG. 7-2E), while other Canadian Autoroutes have a simpler numbered shield. If the map takes you over the Mexican border, their principal highways will have their own numbers in an arrowhead-type of shield (FIG. 7-2F).

Road markings on the map will have fairly obvious meanings, but always check the legend. Variations in shape and color may tell you more than you expected.

With many maps having insets of larger scale portions to illustrate particular or

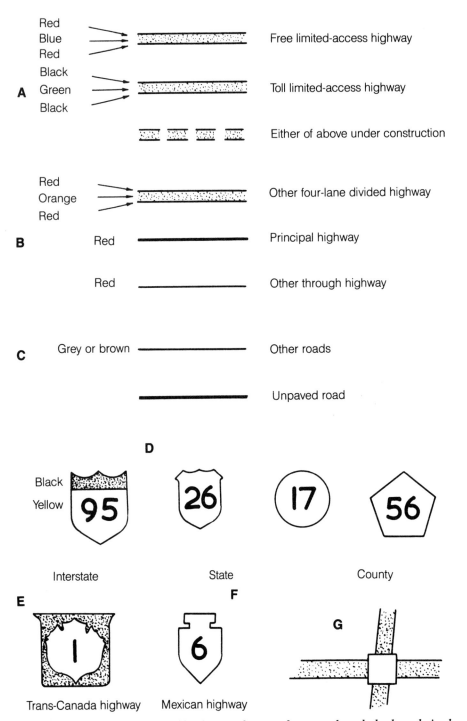

Red
Blue
Red
→→→ [====] Free limited-access highway

Black
A Green
Black
→→→ [====] Toll limited-access highway

[= = = =] Either of above under construction

Red
Orange
Red
→→→ [====] Other four-lane divided highway

B   Red   ▬▬▬▬ Principal highway

Red   ───── Other through highway

C   Grey or brown   ───── Other roads

───── Unpaved road

D

Black
Yellow   **95** (Interstate)   **26** (State)   **17**   **56** (County)

Interstate   State   County

E   **1** (Trans-Canada highway)   F   **6** (Mexican highway)   G

Trans-Canada highway   Mexican highway

Fig. 7-2. *Road types are indicated by the way they are drawn and symbols show their classifications.*

congested areas, the road markings are generally similar to those on the main map, but there could be additional information shown by variations in the width a road is drawn, the color used, or the type of its borderline. A special legend nearby should explain this. There may be arrows indicating one-way systems. You may find that where two roads appear to join on the smaller scale map, they actually cross by one going under the other, as shown on the inset larger scale map, and there may be no facility for interchange.

If you need to get past a city, there will probably be a route that takes you around. Quite often this leaves the main highway well outside the city limits, so check your map in advance. The shortest route may be straight through the city center, but it will be quicker on most days to go a few miles further around the marked bypassing route. If you have to go into the city to find a particular place, the inset map may guide you there. Examine this in advance for names of streets, any one-way streets, and the turns you have to take. It may help to list these on a separate sheet. In busy streets, there may be little time to pause and read your map, but a list prepared in advance, that gives turn directions as well as street names, may allow you to keep moving.

If a limited-access highway crosses the map, you will need to know where you can join it or leave it. There may be symbols to show interchanges—a square at the junction is common (FIG. 7-2G)—but there could be more you need to know that cannot be shown at the small scale. At some places, you can leave, but not join the freeway. There may be other peculiarities.

For more detailed information in these circumstances, some maps carry an additional diagrammatic representation with every interchange shown very much as it is actually laid out. Although this is a map, it is not intended to show how the road runs. Refer to the general map for that.

Instead, the road is artificially brought to a straight line on the drawing, which may then be divided into many sections to fit on the paper, probably on the reverse side of the main map. There is no scale.

To read such a diagrammatic map, first look for its legend, so you know what is indicated. On the map (FIG. 7-3) you can see the main highway, usually in color. Where other roads cross, you can see immediately which goes over the other by the way one road has been cut away. River bridges are also shown. It is unusual for a waterway to go over a road, but that is not impossible, as a canal may cross on an aqueduct.

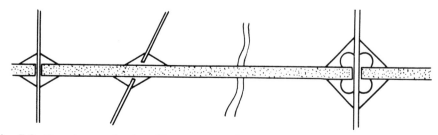

Fig. 7-3. *Crossings and exits of interstate roads are shown diagrammatically.*

At each interchange you get a pattern showing the various linking roads, so you know in advance how you will travel from one road to the other. If the other road is of sufficient importance to have a number, that is shown. Remember that all of this is diagrammatic. Once you have left the interstate highway, refer to the general map. The direction of that and the other road may be very different from what you are imagining while working on the straightline diagram; therefore, you will have to orient yourself again to more realistic directions.

Do not try to estimate distances along the road diagram. You can do that on the general map, but if you want to read distances on the diagram, the legend will tell you how miles are marked. The interchange exit numbers are prominently shown, possibly with the number boxed. Other numbers alongside the road give distances between interchanges, usually taken to one place of decimals, such as 5.1, 1.5, 10.2, and 0.6. Note the last one—if the distance is less than 1 mile, the zero sign goes in the unit position, so you do not overlook the decimal point. Distances are almost certainly marked in miles, but remember that the metric system is coming, and you may find distances in kilometers. There should be a prominent note on the map to say so. In Canada or Mexico, you will find kilometers rather than miles.

Remember that the diagram of the limited-access highway is just to show you how to get on and off, with distances along it and some brief information about where linking roads go. Use it only to get that information. If you are travelling far, refer occasionally to the general map, which shows the actual directions and turns of the road and where places really are in relation to it. Then you will have a much better idea of the situation and can position yourself on the map in relation to the surroundings, rather than feel like some sort of automaton directed along a straight channel on which you are having difficulty in keeping awake.

LEGEND INFORMATION

Road atlases and state highway maps try to provide motorists with more special information than would be found on a topographic map of the area. If it is a state with plenty of recreational areas, campgrounds, leisure centers, and other things to attract the touring motorist, there will be symbols showing the positions of all these. They will also tell you the sizes of towns, and may show county boundaries. How all this special information is indicated varies between maps, so you need to consult the legend or margin information.

The size of a town could be important to you. If it is small, you can expect to get through without meeting traffic congestion, but you may not find may facilities there. There may be nowhere to eat or sleep, and the stores may not have much to offer. A place with a larger population could provide more services, but it may be difficult to get through. A really large place may be what you want if there is much shopping to be done or you want a selection of motels to choose from for the night. Unless there is a through route shown, it may be better to take a bypass road, if there is one, and you only want to get past the town quickly.

There are two possible ways of showing the size of a town. Different dots or symbols can be used, or all markings can be the same. The size type used for the name may also show the population. For instance, a range of symbols may go from a light open circle up to a fairly heavy circled dot (FIG. 7-4A). If size is indicated by type, similar population groups start with quite small and light type, with the size and heaviness increasing to very prominent letters. A snag with the letter sizes comes in densely populated areas, with other city centers besides the prominently marked one. The heavy lettering may obscure some place else.

Instead of the dot, the actual area covered by a larger town may be shown, usually with shading taken to the approximate portions covered by houses or to the city limits. The state capital usually has a symbol incorporating a star (FIG. 7-4B). A county seat may have its name in a different color.

The symbols used for parks and recreation areas vary between maps, but green is the preferred color. If it is a state with varied recreation facilities, there may be many indications of what is available. For instance, state forest land may be overall green, while state park land may have white diagonal lines across the green. A state park may be shown by a symbolic tree. If there are historic sites, they have their own symbols.

An airport is marked by an airplane, as might be expected, but on many maps you can tell what sort of airport it is, either by the type of airplane drawn or the way it is arranged. An airline service airport may have a plane in a circle, while a general service airport is without the circle, and a military airport has a more warlike plane outline (FIG. 7-4C).

Inset maps of local areas to a larger scale may have additional symbols. Look for their own special legend. Within the vicinity of large cities you may find special markings for passenger railroads, park-and-ride areas, and bus terminals that are of use to commuters.

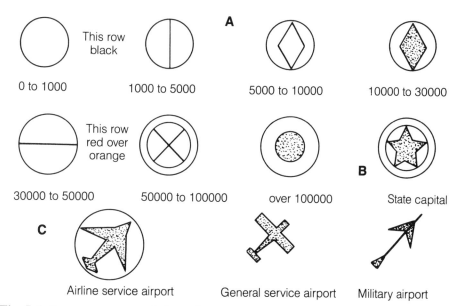

Fig. 7-4. *Some maps use symbols to show populations of towns and other symbols for different types of airfields and airports.*

On the insets and the main map there may be markings to show places of interest. These are usually numbers on colored backgrounds so they are easily seen. From the number, refer to lists giving details of museums, historic sites, and other places worth visiting. Such lists give plenty of information without crowding the map with detail.

Most maps have grids with reference letters and numbers along the borders, but there may not be lines across the map. Somewhere alongside the map or on the other side of the sheet is a comprehensive index of all the towns, cities, and other communities named on the map, with their grid reference alongside.

To find a place on the map, you may be able to run your eye across from the margin grid markings in both directions and spot what you are looking for. That may not always work, particularly if there are many names in the area and the one you want is not very prominent. Then you need a straight edge to put across in both directions. The edge of another map or a newspaper will do. With luck a straight edge in one direction and an estimated line the other way will get you to the place you want, but if necessary, lightly pencil along the edge in one direction and move the straight edge to the other reference to locate the exact square in which your place is. Sometimes, you can drop upon the place name if you have just a vague idea of where it comes in the grid crossings. On another occasion, you may get to the stage of penciling in the outline of the square and thinking the mapmaker forgot to put in the name. Such is map reading!

Welcome stations are important places for anyone travelling across states. They should be marked near border crossings. There you can get state maps and a considerable amount of information, accompanied by local maps. Obviously, the greatest demand is for tourist information, but for business interests you should be able to find maps there to suit your needs, not necessarily on display in a rack. Get street plans of the larger communities in the state. Arrange to enter a state where there is a welcome station so as to get complete, up-to-date maps and other information.

Margin information usually includes a *mileage chart*, showing the distances between prominent places on the map. This may be arranged squarely, with names along two edges. Follow down the line from a place name until it crosses the line from another place name. The figure given is the distance between them (FIG. 7-5A). In another chart arrangement, the names are placed diagonally, but you still follow down from the higher name until the line crosses a line coming from the other name (FIG. 7-5B). With this arrangement, be careful that the names exactly match their lines, or you could work along a wrong column.

It is best to treat the distance you obtain in this way as a general guide. Obviously, the figure is very close, but when you make the journey your distance may be slightly more or less. The listed distance will be the most direct, but not necessarily the quickest, if it passes through congested areas that you choose to go around. There could be more than one way in any case, with different distances. The listed route may include a ferry or tunnel, which you prefer to avoid. The compiler of the chart will have worked from a map. Some roads shown reasonably straight may actually include many twists and turns too small to show on the map, but which can add a few miles to the total distance between points. Another problem is deciding from where to mea-

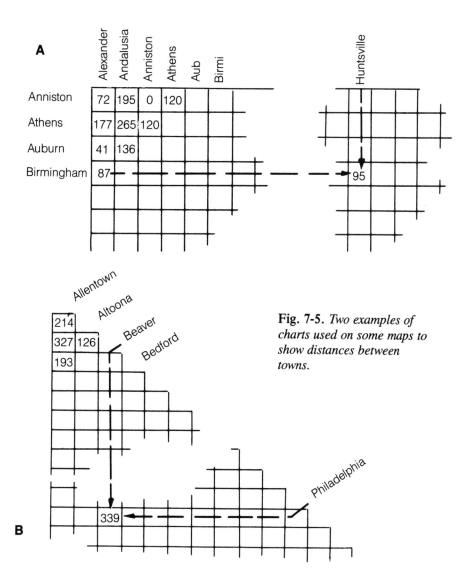

Fig. 7-5. *Two examples of charts used on some maps to show distances between towns.*

sure. The point in a town that you decide is your destination may not be the one the chart compiler used.

As a final check on margin information, look for an arrow or symbol that represents north. Sometimes it is a fairly elaborate symbol instead of a plain arrow. Sometimes it is not there at all. In that case you must assume that the top of the map is north. The map compiler may be confident that everyone knows the shape and direction of his state, and he need not provide a compass direction. Even then, you will probably find latitude and longitude figures along the edge of the map. If the height of latitude markings on opposite sides of the map from the bottom margin are the same, that edge is running east and west, and the side edges are north and south. Do not expect longitude markings on top and bottom edges to give you the same result. They are converging towards the top, and the distance along the border to a longitude mark on the top edge will be greater than to the matching marking on the bottom border from the side of the map.

SIMPLE ROUTE FINDING

The main use of a road map is for finding your way when travelling in some form of vehicle. The type of vehicle has some bearing on the choice of road. There are places where you would happily go in a compact car, but would hesitate to take a large truck or even a motor home. If your vehicle is large, take particular note of the method of indicating types of road. The shortest way on the map may not be for you. Instead of a minor narrow road, you would get there quicker and with less trouble if you took a longer route with larger roads.

Even with a straightforward single road between your start and finish, there is more information you can extract from a map than appears at first glance. Suppose you have spent the night at a motel just off the I-95 and will get back on to it at the same interchange, somewhere near the South Carolina-North Carolina border. You intend to get across the South Carolina-Georgia border before your next stop on your way south.

You could just get on the interstate and keep going, but you can start off with greater knowledge if you do some preliminary map reading. You could scale the road to see how far you have to go. In South Carolina, the distance from the southern border is shown on the map at each interchange, so you discover that border to border is about 200 miles. Then the general direction you will travel is between south and southwest (FIG. 7-6). In the morning, the sun will be too far to the east to affect you, but by the afternoon you can expect to be wearing sunglasses.

You will want to stop occasionally. There is one rest area marked about 30 miles down the road, and that may come earlier than you need one, but another is shown where the road crosses Lake Marion, about 100 miles on your way. That looks like a pleasant spot, so you settle on that for a mid-day break. You feel you will have gone far enough when you cross into Georgia, so what can the map tell you about accommodations? Motels are not marked, but about 10 miles into Georgia, the I-16 crosses the interstate not far from Savannah. This is an obvious place for several motels, so you will make for that area with confidence that you will find a bed for the night.

ALTERNATIVE ROUTES

The ability to interpret information on a map can make route planning simpler when there is a choice of roads to follow. Suppose we are travelling southwest on the I-65 in Alabama, between Montgomery and Mobile, but have to go off the interstate to see someone at Blacksher.

We are strangers to the area and do not even know the whereabouts of Blacksher, so we consult the map index, which gives us the grid reference. We locate Blacksher. The type used to print the name is the smallest used for place names, so the population

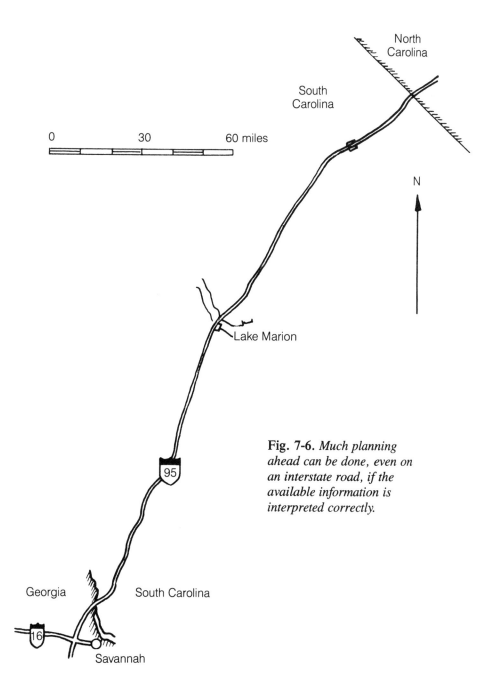

North
Carolina

South
Carolina

0   30   60 miles

N

Lake Marion

95

Fig. 7-6. *Much planning
ahead can be done, even on
an interstate road, if the
available information is
interpreted correctly.*

Georgia   South Carolina

16

Savannah

is less than 1,000. It is situated where County Route 61 meets State Route 59. At this
point, Route 59 is almost north and south, while Route 61 joins it from the east.
Already we know quite a lot about this township (FIG. 7-7A). We also discover that
Blacksher is in Baldwin County, a few miles south of its border with Monroe county.

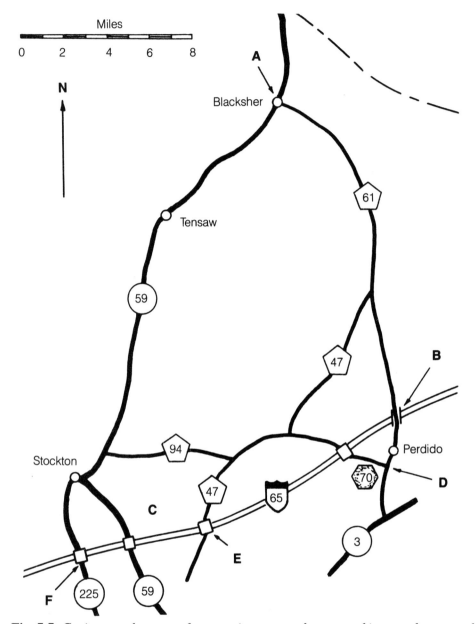

Fig. 7-7. *Getting to a place away from a main route can be managed in several ways, and the suitability of possible roads have to be assessed.*

There are numerous possible ways of getting to Blacksher, but can the map tell us the preferable way? The map shows County Route 61 going over the I-65 without an interchange (FIG. 7-7B). A few miles further on, County Route 47 crosses over, and the square symbol on the interstate indicates there is an interchange. More interchanges that have possibilities come within 15 miles (FIG. 7-7C).

Suppose we go off at the first Route 47 interchange? There is a choice of direction. We can go west to a junction and turn north, but there is a short piece of road going east to join the County Route 61 that will allow us to turn north over the interstate and get to Blacksher that way (FIG. 7-7D). The way the roads are drawn on the map indicates that they are two-lane and paved, so with a car or small truck there should be no problem either way. This is almost a toss-of-a-coin situation, but what does the number in a red hexagon mean? That refers us to a list of attractions. In this case it is a vineyard and winery. If that interests us, it may settle which direction we choose.

From Blacksher, we want to get back to the I-65 and continue to Mobile. If we went back down Route 61 and turned on to Route 47, we could continue to join the I-65 further west than we left it (FIG. 7-7E). However, State Route 59 seems more direct, particularly if we turn on to State Route 225 at Stockton, and follow it to its meeting with the I-65 (FIG. 7-7F). Unless we have a good reason for going the other way, this is the obvious route because State Route 59 is shown to be a larger road than the others.

If our vehicle is larger, we shall have to decide if County Routes 47 and 61 are suitable for it. They probably are, but it may be advisable to go off I-65 and look at them. The diagrammatic map of the interstate shows that it is possible to get off and on again if we decide not to use these roads. If we want to be certain of a larger road for our vehicle we can go on to State Route 59 and exit there, then on the return journey go back to the same place, or use the fork of the State Route 225 to save two or three miles.

On the Alabama highway map of about 8 miles per inch, that is as much as can be shown. It is possible to find out quite a lot from what is presented. For anyone with a car or truck wishing to find their way to a small township, all they need is on the map. That is the object of this particular map, but some people may need to know much more about a small area. In that case, it is possible to get maps on larger scales, showing counties or even smaller areas, with much more information included. A topographic map would also show elevations by contour lines.

CHOICE OF ROUTE

If you wish to travel far in anything but the more remote areas, and there is no obvious through route to your destination, you will probably be faced with deciding on an alternative. This often applies when your destination has several possible converging routes. You have to weigh up the advantages of maybe three possible routes, all of which involve changing roads and directions many times. For instance, suppose you want to go by car from town A to town B (FIG. 7-8). There is no direct road. The map shows a controlled-access, divided highway crossing between you and the destination, while there are two multi-lane undivided highways. The other roads shown indicate that they are two-lane paved roads. You are satisfied that your car could be used without trouble on any of the roads shown. So far as you know, the elevation of town A is not very much above town B on the coast, and you do not expect to meet more than a slight rise or fall on any of the roads.

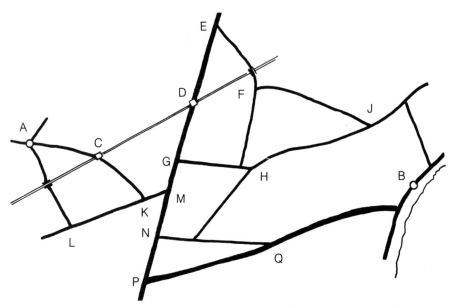

Fig. 7-8. *A map allows you to plan in advance which of many roads you will use to get between two points.*

There is always an attraction about large divided highways. If you want to travel fast without interruption, is the one shown of any use? Interchanges are possible at C and D. Two other roads that cross it and might have been more use, do not connect with it. If we join the road at C, we have to leave it at D; then, travel either way some distance without getting any nearer our destination. Will that be worthwhile? If we go north, we must turn east at E and cross the divided highway to F. If we go south, we can turn east at G to reach H. From either of these points we can go to J and so to town B.

Without knowing more of road conditions and traffic problems, it is difficult to decide which of these routes is better. Distances do not seem very different. The only way to decide may be to use a map measure along the roads.

There are, however, other ways. You can get there by using roads further south and ignore the divided highway, which you can cross at C to reach K. You may go under the divided highway to L, then to K, and on to M. It would be possible to go north to G, across to H, and so to J. In total distance, it is probably less than either of the other routes, although you spend slightly more time on the poorer roads. But there is another alternative. You can turn south to N and then east, or you can continue to P and turn east. Much depends on the quality of the road going from N to Q. If you prefer the better roads, you continue to P, and go back through Q towards the coast and town B. It will be a little further, but you should gain in speed and ease of travel.

If you are keen on exploring back roads, there are other possible ways of getting from town A to town B. The object of the trip may not be to get there with the minimum mileage. You may be interested in seeing more of the country in a particular area, and that will settle which route you take. It could be that you need to visit a place on the way. It may be that you have been between town A and town B before, and you want to try a different route. If you have to return to town A, you can go one way and back another. Unless the signs are good at road junctions, this is not a journey to start on without a map. Even then you should not expect to find directions to town B given at early interchanges.

Another choice comes when there is an interstate or other limited-access multi-lane highway, cutting across the states in broad sweeping curves when it is not a straight line. It allows traffic to move smoothly and steadily, but it was not always there. Before it was built, there were other roads going the same general direction. In some cases, the new road has taken over the bed of the previous one, so there are no roads running close to its direction any more, but in many places the old road is nearby.

If you want to travel far and fast, you use the interstate highway. There are occasions when you must, but many of the older roads are more interesting and surprisingly less crowded. The interstate has taken the large trucks and automobiles that need to get somewhere quickly. At one time, all of that traffic went on the other road, but now most traffic is local and not much of it is fast. Your map will show you if there is still a good road that will get you at least partly in the same direction as the interstate (FIG. 7-9).

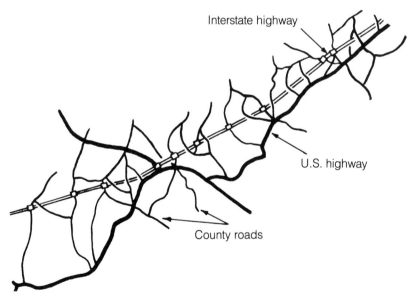

Fig. 7-9. *Besides interstates there are often other roads which can provide alternative routes.*

Of course, such roads pass through towns, but if any of these are large, there may be bypass roads. The roads may wander, and between points that match on both roads, you may find the second road is several miles further.

Sometimes the old road goes some way from the new road, but there are interchanges at nearby points. You can leave the old road for the new one and stay with it until you are attracted by the new one again. In many cases, you can be sure the old road is fairly large and in good condition if it has a U.S. route number. In some cases, it is a named highway.

Even if you do not have time to travel more leisurely on the old road, it is worthwhile noting places where short roads can provide interchange between the two. If you need a store or a fill-up of gas, you may go off the interstate and follow the old road through towns. You may shop more cheaply in a small town than where all the other motorists in a hurry shop. You can rejoin the interstate at another interchange.

An advantage of the old road is that it has more links with other roads in all directions. With the limited access of the interstate, you may not be able to join the road you want directly. It may only go over or under, without any link roads. If you check in advance, you can get on to the old road in time and make a turn where you want to, without having to go past on the interstate to an interchange that lets you off to return by back roads to the road you wanted.

An interstate highway is fine if the place you are heading for is close to it, but if it is some way off and you stay with the interstate until a sign for the town leads you off, you could find yourself in line with large numbers of other vehicles all going to the town, in the same direction. Quite often it is possible to find other roads off the old road beside the interstate that do not carry directions to the town because the roads are unsuitable for heavy traffic. Your map reading may allow you to leave the interstate earlier and go along the nearby older road. You can approach the town on another road to avoid the congestion on the major approach.

DISTANT ROUTE PLANNING

In flatter areas, more roads were laid down north and south, or east and west, than in other directions. In more hilly country, the roads have to follow terrain to keep the gradients moderate. Road patterns on the map are then far from geometric. In places that have long been settled, and particularly those with a great population density, roads may not conform to any pattern. They may have followed around a person's property or followed tracks that the first settlers found were easiest going for mules or oxen.

The north-south and east-west grids of roads are fine if you want to go in any of these directions, but if you need to go diagonally, you have to work out a zigzag course. Even with the other road patterns, there are many times when there is no obvious route across them to your intended destination. If there is a free or toll multi-lane limited-access highway in the right general direction, that will probably be your choice and other roads will be chosen to link with that at suitable points. If you have to travel hundreds of miles, such a road is easier, unless you have the time and inclination to travel more leisurely on the other roads.

If your intended journey, however, seems to be always crossing roads instead of going along them, you will have to work out a more or less complex route. Start your planning with a map that shows you both your start and finish on one sheet, even if that is quite a small scale and there is not much detail. The advantage is that you can see what part of the country you have to cross and pick out key places on the way. You will need maps of a larger scale for greater detail of parts of the journey, but if you try to plan on them you may find yourself deviating considerably from the shortest route.

Good planning maps are produced by the American Automobile Association (AAA), or you may find them in atlases. You need a guide to the free and toll limited-access highways, with other principal highways, and the main towns they serve. Along the eastern seaboard and for many hundreds of miles inland, you may find a maze of through routes already there. You will have little difficulty in choosing the best way to go. If you want to go north or south near the western coast, the choice is obvious, but there are many parts of the greater continental areas where you will have to discover roads that can be used for part of their lengths to get you to your destination.

Lay a straight edge between your intended start and finish. Lightly pencil along it (FIG. 7-10A). If you were flying, you might follow that line, but on the ground we have to follow man-made roads.

On our imaginary route, the first road that is of any use to us goes some way off a straight line, so we shall have to take it. That first straight line is no longer any use to us, so we go on the first road to the next convenient point and draw another straight line (FIG. 7-10B). Find a road that will take us a reasonable distance in the right direction and follow it until it deviates too much; then put down another straight line to the destination (FIG. 7-10C).

As you progress in this way, there are other things to consider. How far do you hope to travel in a day? You may have to find a motel or campground each night. It may be better to make a small diversion from a straight line to find what you want. In

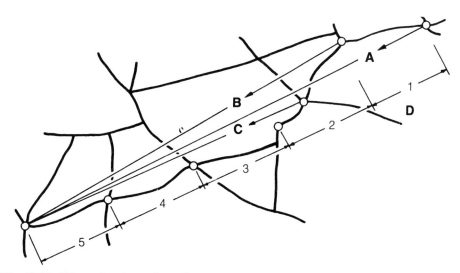

Fig. 7-10. *When planning a long-distance trip, any necessary deviations from a straight line have to be arranged as if from a new starting point.*

the preliminary planning, note these requirements, but this first survey is only very provisional. There may be places of interest on the way and your route can deviate to suit them. Remember that once you have gone off a previous straight line, there is nothing to be gained by returning to it. What you need is a new straight line to work from, starting where you find yourself at that time. Unless, of course, it is a minor deviation, and you could be getting back to a better road.

In this preliminary survey, try to settle on some key places that are close to the route, preferably marking daily distances (FIG. 7-10D). Now turn to the larger-scale maps and use them to plan how to get from one key place to the next. In this way you will not be tempted to choose what seems a better road, but which gets you over to the next map some way off the best route. The larger-scale maps will show you if your original ideas are feasible.

To travel long distances it is best to avoid back roads as far as possible, but there are places where a state or county road may provide a link between two useful highways. Consider such roads for short distances as connections, but otherwise it is better to always choose roads on which you can hope to maintain a good speed. Your study of large-scale maps may give you ideas that were not obvious on the small-scale planning map. If necessary, go back to it and revise your key places or daily distances.

Use guide books, campground guides, and motel directories. You may have to look for some accommodations on the way, but the more you know in advance, the better is the planning and probably the easier your state of mind.

When you have plotted the route and divided it into daily sections, make notes to guide you. Divide your notes into daily sections, with the names of places, road numbers, and distances, which you can get from the maps. There is little point in planning if you do not set out with the intention of keeping to the planned route, but do remain flexible. As you progress, you may want to make variations. You may travel more or less in a day. You may discover information on a place you ought to visit, that delays or puts you off the intended route. If something like that happens, there is usually no value in going back on the originally planned route. Instead, study your maps again and plan how to get to your destination from the new position.

On such a lengthy traverse of the country, it is worthwhile taking along a straight-edge, preferably marked with scales of your maps. A pair of dividers or a map measure are useful for stepping off distances on the maps. You may find little real need for a compass, when you are travelling long-distance highways, particularly if you have the sun to guide you, but a compass may confirm what you work out by other means. There may well be such an occasional occurrence as a thick fog or a black night and no signs at a crossroad, when it helps to know north.

FINDING YOURSELF

A navigator tries to know where he is at all times. Even in the midst of an ocean, the ship navigator uses various aids to locate his position as precisely as possible. Frequent position locating is important if he is to eventually reach the correct destination. Ashore, we have solid objects with known locations, so identifying positions should not be very difficult, but we all know of occasions when our sense of direction has gone completely astray and, for the moment, we are very uncertain of where we are.

A simple problem is "How far have we travelled?" If we are on a road without landmarks, and it seems to go on interminably across a desert or other featureless terrain, or even in country with landmarks obscured by darkness and heavy rain, we begin to think we ought to have reached the end by now. Maybe we should have noted the mileage shown on the odometer when we started, but it is too late now. We can borrow the ocean navigator's method of dead reckoning. He knows his speed and direction and the time elapsed since last "getting a fix." If none of his other methods of locating his position are possible, that gives him something to work on. If another method is also possible, the two can be checked against each other. If we noted the mileage reading and the time at the start, we know how far we have travelled and can measure on a map or estimate how much further we have to go. If we want to, we can put a spot on the road map to mark our present position.

Suppose we noted the time, but did not read the starting mileage. We can make a reasonable estimate of our speed and from our watch, we can discover the time elapsed since we started. A simple calculation will tell us approximately how far we have travelled, and how much more of the road is before us.

If the navigator is sitting beside the driver, he or she can usually keep map reading in step with the actual roads traversed. However, if the driver is alone and has to do his own navigation, it often happens that he has gone further than he last planned. That, and the position when he stops, are separated by an unknown amount. Even with a separate navigator, there are occasions where you make several turnings, roads fork unexpectedly, and you take one on chance. Or the road doubles back and crosses one you were on previously; you overshoot an intended turning and take a further one in the hope of regaining the intended route, but do not. Or a landmark that you expected on the right is on the left. We all do it occasionally, so do not panic.

It helps to first orient your map. If you have a compass, take it and the map away from the car so you are not troubled by deflection. Determine north and set the map to agree. Without a compass you can set the map by using sun or stars or by locating and sighting landmarks, as described in chapter 3. Consider how far you have travelled since the last known mark. By a combination of methods you should be able to arrive at a fair approximation of your position.

Finding landmarks may be too much to expect, if you are temporarily lost and visibility is poor. You know where you started from. Even if you did not note the time and mileage reading, you can make a fairly accurate guess of both. From this you can determine the general area on the map where you must be. You know the road you started on. You must have stayed with it at least until there was a fork or crossing. Which way did you go then? Somewhere further you confused turnings, or you would not be lost. What are the possibilities? If you had gone one route, where would you expect to be now? If you had gone a different way, where might you be? There may even be a third possibility. From those projections you will have to allow some tolerance, due to speed or time not being quite what you thought. However, you can put one, two, or three marks on the map as possible positions.

Check the location of other things on the map. If you are at one marked spot, there may be a group of houses farther along the road. If you are at another spot, there may be a fork in the road soon. Identify as many likely places as possible. Think back to your more recent movements. Did you join the road you are on from another? Maybe the map shows such a turning in relation to one of your marks, but not to others. Was the last mile or so of road straight or curved? How does that compare with the map? If none of these guides give you a positive position, you may have to continue, but you now know what to expect to find from any of the marked possible locations. If you find that group of houses or forked road, you are back on course with your confidence improved, if not fully restored.

Once you have established a position without any doubt, it will probably be best to stop and decide your best route from there. You could be some way from where you originally intended to go, and you may have to work out a new way to your destination. So that nothing goes wrong this time, look at alternatives; then, if you take a wrong turning, you should know where you are, even if it is the wrong place. You can get out of it without getting lost.

It is natural for human beings to look ahead, rather than upwards or behind. There may be little need to look upwards when map reading, but we should look back more than we do. A direction opposite to the way we intend to go is a reciprocal bearing, 180° different from it. We may not be working in degrees, but it is useful sometimes to get oriented to things behind us. You can look back and locate towns and landmarks you have passed more easily than some you have yet to come to. With their aid you can orient your map and then check on places ahead of you. Distances behind you may be known or more accurately estimated. If you are uncertain exactly how far you are along a road, those distances taken with others estimated by comparison ahead will better determine the spot you are on—both on the ground and on the map.

INTERPRETING TOWN PLANS

A street map of a town or city is usually on quite a large scale. You may find 3 inches or more representing 1 mile. After the small scale, by comparison, of a state or other expanse of land covering many miles, you have to turn your thoughts to distances between points in hundreds of feet, rather than miles. This means that, if you drive into the town without appreciating the scale you are using, you may overshoot the turn you want by many streets before you realize it. Getting back may not be easy.

The very large scale allows for considerable detail. You can expect to find churches, museums, halls, and other prominent buildings marked. Even if you are not visiting them, they are good landmarks. If you stop and ask the way, a local person will often tell you to turn right by the Methodist church, continue to the post office, and the address you want is just past there. Such places are often more easily identified as you approach them than a sign saying "NE 50th St." beside one of them. Before entering a city by car, it helps to list landmarks, as well as street and avenue numbers, so you do not find you have to make a panic turn across the traffic because you have just seen the street number you want at the last moment.

Town plans do not always give you the right impression of a town. The business districts of older cities may be a maze of towering concrete canyons, with little space for parking. A map dealing with a newer midwestern town of considerable size may represent something much more spacious, where there are gardens around buildings and the streets are broader. You have to consider the age of the place. It is helpful to obtain a brochure or book with photographs, so you can visualize what you will be driving into. Even then, allow for publicity photographs being flattering, without an indication that the pleasant view you are shown is due more to the careful angling of the camera than to the appearance of a vast area.

If the town plan shows park-and-drive or commuter railroad stations, you can be sure it is a town where a visitor might be unwise to drive. Even if you do, you may have to park some way from your destination and pay well for the privilege. If you go into a city by bus or subway, it is very easy to emerge on the streets completely disoriented. The sun may be hidden by buildings. You could use a compass, but probably the best way of finding directions is to get to a crossing and discover the names or numbers of the streets both ways. Even then, be careful not to be the wrong way around, if the names are the same both ways and the streets cross squarely. Usually there is some other feature that will help you to turn the map the right way, such as a marked church on a corner or a marked building further along one way. If you are still uncertain, and cannot find anyone to give you directions, you may have to walk a block to another crossing; then, the two considered together will positively show you how the map should be in relation to the surroundings.

In a large city, it is very easy to waste a lot of time going by wrong ways to places of interest. Plan ahead. If you are using a car, that is very important because you may not have time to stop. You will have to settle for instant directions. If you are on your feet, you will not want to walk unnecessarily, but you will have time to stop and study the map. In many cities, places of interest are surprisingly close—remember the very large scale.

If city streets and avenues are numbered and cross squarely, planning where you want to go is not difficult, even in such large places as Chicago. Most places have other roads going diagonally, and you should check ahead where these come in relation to the other crossings, you can orient with them. If there are thruways, and you are using a car, you need to plan ahead where to leave for your intown destination, or you may go miles further before you can get off again.

If you are driving, check on the map for one-way streets. There may be arrowheads on the mapped roads or small arrows beside them. Make sure your map is the most recent one. Of the many features in a town, the one-way systems seem to change most often. An old map may show you a two-way street where it is now one-way, probably with the flow opposite to what you want.

If your main interest in a town plan is in finding your way through because there is no suitable bypass, you may have to follow regular streets that everyone else seems to be using. If you have no particular reason for going into a business district, it is often possible to plan a way via streets further out from the center and get through quicker, even if the distance is slightly greater.

Of course, in many towns and cities you can find an interstate or turnpike that will get you through quickly. Remember, these are limited-access highways. The map will show you where to get on and off.

The town plan may show you other principal roads that are intended for through traffic. Not all of these are without forks or crossings; plan ahead so you know where you have to turn. There should be signs ahead along the roads, but among all the other signs, advertisements, and other attributes of urban life, they are not always easy to see. It is wise to know how you intend to negotiate the town from your previous study of the map.

If there is a river passing through the town, pay attention to the location of bridges. A river tends to divide the network of roads into two groups. You will have to decide where it will be best for you to cross the river and change from one group to another, especially if you have to change from one limited-access highway to another.

8

Finding Your Way in the Wilderness

WHEN YOU ARE TRAVELLING ON ROADS, MAPS ARE WORTH HAVING AND you might find a use for a compass. If you travel without them, the result could be inconvenient—although not disastrous. If you get away from roads and start to explore undeveloped country, a map and compass may be essential and going without them could have serious consequences. When there are no man-made signs to finding your way, you have to depend on natural features and your ability to interpret a map to make use of them. With map and compass you can enjoy walking, horse riding, or canoeing in unknown and unspoiled country. Without them you could lose yourself and, if nothing worse befalls, involve search parties in a lot of unnecessary work rescuing you. Using map and compass in country that is undeveloped and rarely travelled by man brings home the value of these aids. Finding your way is for real—if you go wrong there is unlikely to be anyone you can ask. If you come to a halt there will not be a passing motorist to stop and help, as there might be on a road. You depend on your own resources, and these include your map and compass, with your knowledge of how to use them.

Obviously, the free, or inexpensive, road maps you pick up at filling stations are no use in the wilderness, except perhaps for access to your starting point. They may show you places around the perimeter of your chosen area, where you might come out and find transport. They can help you to orient in relation to nearby man-made features, the location of townships and similar things. If you see aircraft landing and taking off outside your area, such a map may show you the probable airfield. Even if you are going into the wild to get away from civilization, you cannot avoid seeing aircraft.

The knowledge of where they are heading might be useful in settling your directions or confirming directions found by other means.

TOPOGRAPHIC MAPS

The maps you are most likely to find useful are the 7^1/$_2$-minute series national topographic maps. These are 1:24,000 scale, so 1 inch on the map represents 2000 feet. The actual area covered varies because it covers an area between any points of 7^1/$_2$° latitude and 7^1/$_2$° longitude. Longitude meridian lines come closer together as the area represented is taken further north. But as a rough guide in deciding on the choice of map, estimate each as covering about 8 miles each way. Very similar in relative coverage, but twice as wide, are the 7^1/$_2$ × 15-minute series to a scale of 1:25,000, where 1 inch on the map represents about 2083 feet.

Either of these maps gives the greatest amount of detail, but if you are planning to be in the wilderness for long and to travel some way, you may find you need a very large number of these maps and carrying all of them may be a problem. There are 15-minute series maps to a scale of 1:62,500 which makes 1 inch represent nearly 1 mile. As the name indicates, the quadrangle is enclosed within 15° of latitude and 15° of longitude. As a rough guide in choosing these maps, estimate each as covering about 20 miles each way. As a further rough guide, the distance you walk in the wild in a day is unlikely to go right across such a map, so even for travel near a straight line, two maps should at least cover three days travel. As you will not usually travel straight and may actually be moving about in a closer area, the number of maps you need to this scale may be very few.

See the index sheets of maps at the chosen scale and get enough. Make sure the maps you have when you set out cover more than the area you intend to travel. It is always unwise to assume that there is nothing of importance just over the edge of a map and not bother with the next one, although you intend going that way. A trail that leaves the map and comes back again a little further along, may actually go in a long loop on the next map and include some hazards you should know about. You may have decided on the route you intend to take and have maps to cover it, but something may arise that necessitates you getting out to civilization another way, and you should make sure your maps will cover such emergencies.

The 7^1/$_2$-minute series maps certainly provide considerable detail. If there is one area where you will concentrate your exploration and such a map contains it, that may be worth having, even if you decide not to have that scale for other maps and use 15-minute series maps for the rest of the area.

COMPASSES

Your compass will be needed for setting the map and for plotting courses, and there will be occasions when you have to steer by it as you constantly refer to it to keep on course—like a ship, although you may be pushing through trees and undergrowth.

Because of this, be sure to have a compass that can be used for sighting with a good degree of accuracy. It could be a sighting compass where you can read the bearing at the same time as you sight it, or one of the cheaper and popular compasses with a rectangular base, as described in chapter 3. A plain compass, in a round case and with an undamped needle, would not be useless, but results obtained from it might be some way from the precise bearings obtained with one of the other compasses.

It is unlikely that a compass will become damaged, but it is always possible. It might be lost, or it could be crushed in an accident. If you are without a compass, it is always possible to get a reasonably accurate direction using the sun or stars, but a compass is much more accurate. If you are going into the wilderness, it is advisable to have a second compass, preferably carried by someone else. This is not a book on planning wilderness travel, but it is always safer to be with at least one other person. Both ought to have compasses and know how to use them with the maps. One person may be incapacitated. There should always be another who can still navigate to safety, in the same way that a reserve compass is desirable.

For security, a compass should be on a strap or cord around your neck, but do not just let it swing as you walk. Put it in a shirt pocket or inside your shirt. It could have its own case, but you need to be able to refer to it without trouble, so do not use a complicated way of packing it. You may prefer a compass on a wrist strap.

If your planned trip into wild country is your first, do not wait until you get there to practice how to use your map and compass. You can learn to set a map with a compass and plot a course anywhere, providing that you have a local map. It need not be a topographic map. You could use a town plan or a road map, providing you can get somewhere to see enough of the area it represents. There may be a hill or the top of a building, where you can orient the map and use the compass with it. With these man-made fixed things you can check the accuracy of your work. People who wear glasses sometimes have difficulty in getting accurate sights with a compass. If this is your trouble and you find your readings are always a degree or so left or right, now is the time to discover it, instead of when you are actually hiking miles through unmarked terrain. With advance discovery of the flaw, you can allow for it when in the airfield.

A useful exercise in taking bearings is a compass walk. In its simplest form you check how accurately you can walk around an equilateral triangle. Set your compass to any bearing that will get your triangle within the available ground—say 30° (FIG. 8-1A). Mark your starting place on the ground with a coin, stone, or peg. Walk in the direction you have set your compass for any convenient distance, counting your steps. At this point, add 120° to the original bearing (this is the outside angle of a triangle with equal sides and angles). With the new setting (FIG. 8-1B), walk the same number of steps on that course (in this case 150°) to another corner of the triangle. Add 120° to get the third course (in this case now 270°), and walk in this direction (FIG. 8-1C). If you have kept an even steady pace and have walked exactly on your compass courses, you should finish at your starting point. Getting it exactly right may be too much to expect, but if you are very far out, try again with a different first angle. Of course, the longer the sides of the triangle, the more risk there is of variation, so try your skill on larger triangles.

It is more complicated to have triangles with different sides and angles. You could set out one with a rule and compass on paper; then, treat that as a map and repeat the

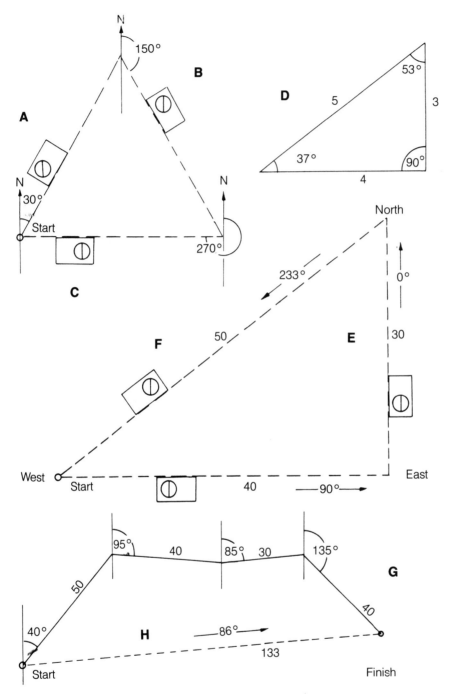

Fig. 8-1. *Practice in setting and following a compass direction by testing on triangular and other courses.*

course to any convenient number of paces on the ground. This will give you practice in maintaining courses at odd angles, using intermediate settings on the compass. If you do not want to set out a triangle on paper, you can use a triangle with the sides in the proportion of 3:4:5. A triangle set out in that proportion has 90° between the two short sides, but the other two angles are 37° and 53° (FIG. 8-1D). You can pace a base line (in this case east and west), say 40 steps; then turn north and go 30 steps (FIG. 8-1E). Turn there and go 50 steps on a course of 233°, which is 53° west of south (FIG. 8-1F). That should bring you to your starting point. Try other arrangements. Start with a different corner. Use the 50 steps side as a base and see if courses from each end meet at 90°.

You can draw courses to scale on paper, using a protractor for the angles. Set one another on tests to see who can get nearest to the intended destination on the ground (FIG. 8-1G). This could be just a matter of a few paces in each direction in your yard or you could make it a treasure hunt with longer distances between points over a field or larger expanse of land. Work out a check bearing and distance on your drawing between the start and finish (FIG. 8-1H) so you can confirm the nearest competitor with a check on this straight course.

FIELD WORK

We may talk of going into the wilderness, but it is difficult for most of us to find a part of the country where man has not left his mark in some way. There may be forest tracks left from earlier tree fellings, overhead power lines, or fire lookouts. Compared with the country most of us know, however, that this is wilderness and those pieces of evidence of man's work might be useful landmarks when we start finding our way.

The simplest exercise in navigation comes when it is possible to see the destination from the start and the terrain between is fairly flat and unobstructed—the sort of situation in a desert or a large expanse of flat cleared land. Suppose you have left your car and the last road behind you and are about to hike into undeveloped country. Amid the mostly open land, your map shows you a group of trees a few miles away in the direction you wish to go. You may spot the group of trees with no further guidance from the map, but if there are other trees breaking the skyline, you may be unsure for which group to aim.

Orient the map with your compass. Locate where you are on the map and sight through that point and the trees on the map. You should then be able to identify your group of trees and not confuse them with others (FIG. 8-2A). Another way is to use the compass as a protractor on the map in your car or at home before you start. Draw a line between your start and the group of trees, then put the compass, or a protractor, on the line and read the bearing from the north direction of the map (FIG. 8-2B). At your start, set the compass to this bearing and sight across it to see the trees (FIG. 8-2C).

Once you have located the group of trees, you can probably just walk to them without bothering about the course, but land which is apparently flat when viewed from a distance may have undulations across it. If the hollows are more than 6 feet

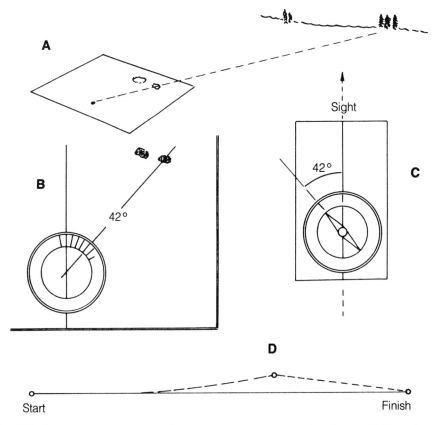

Fig. 8-2. *A sight across a map can be converted to a compass bearing and followed as you travel.*

deep, you can be out of sight of your destination when in one, so it will help to know the bearing to follow until you are high enough to see the trees again.

You may think you will have no difficulty in walking in a straight line. You probably will keep straight if you have a target in front of you, but when walking with nothing particular in view, most of us follow a curved course. We have heard of people who have been lost, coming back on their own tracks, showing they have walked in a large circle when they thought they were keeping straight. If you have to walk some way out of sight of your destination and then come high enough to see it again, you may find you have strayed from your original course. If that has happened, take a new bearing of the group of trees (FIG. 8-2D) and discard the old one from now on.

INTERMEDIATE LANDMARKS

Suppose your destination is too far away to see, or it is hidden by trees or unevenness in the ground. The way you expect to walk seems reasonably flat and you do not anticipate any obstructions that would prevent you walking directly in a straight line. Obtain the bearing of your destination from your map and compass. Sight in that direction. With luck, you will see something that will serve as a landmark for the first stage of your journey. It may be an isolated tree almost on your line of sight. It could be a crag or projecting rock. The tree may not be marked on your map, but contour lines may show the crag if it is of sufficient size (FIG. 8-3A).

The first landmark need not be exactly on your line of travel, providing you can see it as you approach; then pass at what you estimate is the right distance from it. If it is marked on the map, you can find how far away it is. If it is not marked, you will have to estimate its distance. Estimation is something that improves with practice. When you are walking it is very difficult to estimate speed and distance. Usually you do not travel as fast as you expect when on rough ground amid trees, undergrowth, and rocks. Distances you have to travel may be thought of in time as well as feet or miles. You might manage 4 miles per hour on flat, level, open ground, but in wilder conditions 2 miles per hour is a more likely speed. So, estimate how far to the first landmark and how long you expect to take to reach it. If it is not obvious after the elapsed time, look around for it. If you have been walking with frequent reference to the compass, you should find it easily.

Having arrived that far in the right direction, you have to decide how to carry on. If the destination is visible, your route is easy. Most probably, it is not. Is there another intermediate landmark? If it is easily seen, that is fine. But if you are now in a hollow or surrounded by trees, you will not see anything very far away.

There may be a feature on the way that is shown on the map and can be easily identified, such as a stream (FIG. 8-3B). Streams are usually far from straight, so if you visualize its meanderings, you may be able to identify a particular place on it when you reach it. Again, estimate your probable distance and time to the stream. Suppose the general flow of the stream follows a sweeping curve. When you get to it, you can check the direction of the part you have reached with your compass and refer to the map. Be careful not to be misled by minor twists in the course of the stream. The bearing of the stream will then give you a clue to where you are on it (FIG. 8-3C). It might be worthwhile exploring the stream a short distance each way to see if there are any sharp changes of course that can be identified on your map.

From here you may be able to set a course to your destination, or you may have to find some other landmark to use as a guide. If there are no landmarks on or very near your route, it is still possible to make use of things far away, but likely to be seen while you are walking. Suppose there is a pointed hill away to the right of your route, easily seen and identifiable on your map (FIG. 8-3D). You can take a bearing on it and check that this agrees with a bearing between your location and it on your map. This is not essential, but it confirms you are not mistaking the hill.

There may be a gap in the trees along your route. If you travel on a compass course and come to a gap where you can see the hill, take a bearing on it and plot the line on your map. This should cross your course where you are (FIG. 8-3E). You will not have walked in an absolutely straight line, so treat this as approximate, but it should indicate the immediate area you are in, and show if you are going the right way.

If the hill is visible most of the time you are walking (on what you hope is the right course), you can take bearings on it at intervals. These sight lines crossing your

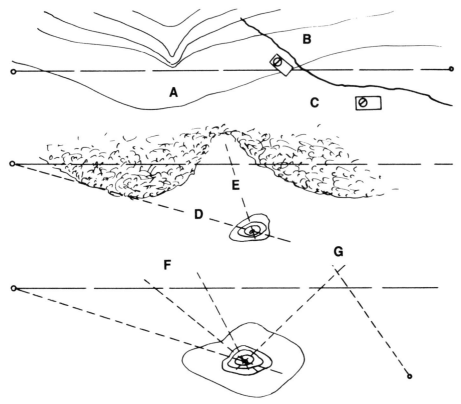

Fig. 8-3. *Natural features may be sighted and plotted to act as guides to your position as you progress across terrain and map.*

course line will show how you are progressing (FIG. 8-3F). If another identifiable object comes into view as you progress, take its bearing as well. The line on the map which crosses the one from the hill is more likely to be your exact location than where either of the sight lines crosses your route line (FIG. 8-3G); this is so because your line of travel may have deviated. If you have walked several miles through rough country, even with frequent reference to the compass, you could now be some way off course.

Whenever any calculated position puts you off course you will have to check all you can over again. If it is something identifiable on the map, there will be no doubt. If you do not know the place, and bearings do not agree, you will have to weigh up the factors and decide which are most probably right. If you are not where you expected to be, it is of no use to spend time saying "At X we should have gone straight on instead of turning right, then at Y . . ." You must get from where you are now to your destination. Discard details of what led up to your present position. Later, you may work out what went wrong and learn by experience, but what you have to do now is set a new course from the spot you are on to your destination.

OFFSET COURSES

Soon you discover that theory and practice do not always agree. It is possible to set a course on a map and decide that if you keep going in that direction for several miles you will get exactly where you want. The course may be worked out on the map to the nearest single degree, but when you start walking with the compass, you can only refer to it occasionally. Your reading may be regarded as good if you are within 5° of the plotted course. You may cover the distance and arrive in the general vicinity of your destination, but you may not be able to find it. You might spend a lot of time searching fruitlessly.

Suppose the destination is a hut on a forest track. It could be a position on a stream or a rock on an escarpment. If there is something identifiable crossing our general direction, that can be used as a *lead*, or *saver*, to get you correctly placed at the end of the hike. In the case of the hut on a track, you might arrive at the track and be unable to see the hut, so you have to explore along it. If you choose the wrong direction first, you could waste a lot of time walking before deciding to turn back and check the other way.

That can be avoided by deliberately *offsetting* the course, so you hit the track knowing on which side of the hut you are. Suppose the direct course shown on the map is 265°. The route is through trees for 2 miles, with nothing on the way to check the accuracy of the course (FIG. 8-4A). Even if you are very careful to check the bearing frequently, you could finish up on the track maybe up to 1/4 mile either side of the hut.

Instead of using a direct route, the course is set 10° to whichever side you choose. The terrain or the windings of the track may influence the choice of bearing, but as an example, try to follow a course of 275°. If you travel exactly on course, you arrive at the track knowing which way to go to the hut (FIG. 8-4B). This arrangement allows you up to 10° error—good enough for your course reading—and it will still get you there.

Much depends on your ability to maintain travel on a bearing. For a short distance you may choose a lesser offset, or you may have to use a larger one for a greater distance or awkward terrain. However, if the distance is great, you will probably use intermediate landmarks. You can maintain course as directly as possible until you reach the landmark between your last landmark and your destination. You offset that enough to allow for any errors you may make.

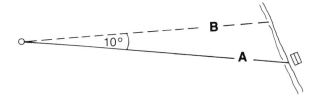

Fig. 8-4. *Planning a route to one side of the intended destination ensures you knowing which way to go when you reach the path.*

DETOURS

Usually we go into wilderness country for pleasure and not just to go between two points by the shortest and quickest route. This means that we want to move about in various directions and, we may prefer easier, and more pleasant routes than might be followed in straight lines. Obviously, we need to know where we are and how to get to certain places, but our travels are not just mapping exercises.

If we leave a straight line, there have to be safeguards to avoid getting lost. If there are enough landmarks that we can get bearings on, it should be possible to wander freely and pinpoint our position on the map when we need it. Freedom to move about without constant checks is dependent on the terrain and your experience.

You might depart from a straight line where the direct route goes over some impassable, or at least undesirable, obstruction, and you need to go around it. It may be just a high ridge of land that would be laborious to climb over, when contours on the map show there is an easier route possible by going around (FIG. 8-5A). There are several possibilities, particularly if the obstructing hill represents only a small part of the distance you want to go.

You could maintain the direct route until quite near the hill, then go around it until you can resume the direct route again (FIG. 8-5B). You could aim immediately for a point that would get you around the hill on fairly level ground, and then take a course straight from there to your destination (FIG. 8-5C). You may prefer to follow a more curved route (FIG. 8-5D), or you could combine methods, such as taking the first half-way and then going straight to your destination.

It helps to have landmarks, or steering marks, in addition to the hill, which may be prominent enough to be seen from your start. If there is something on the side of the hill where you will make the detour, use it for sighting.

Even if it is off the route you hope to take, you might be able to take a bearing of it. If the hill itself has a sufficiently prominent top, that can be used for bearings, but usually such a hill is rounded and you cannot determine a spot that is visible all around. There may be a tree or other object that you judge to be visible from both sides. That could be used for checking a direct course (FIG. 8-5E) before and after your detour.

Suppose the straight line course is 190°. Get as near as the course will get you to the foot of the hill, so you can still see the chosen tree. Take its bearing. If it comes exactly on 190°, you are lucky, but tree positions may not be like that. Suppose the bearing is 180° (FIG. 8-5F), which is 10° less than the course. Go around the hill until the bearing of the tree is 20° (FIG. 8-5G). That is 10° less than the back, or reciprocal, bearing of your route line. When you have reached that point you know you are in a position to resume course on 190° to your destination. This would be correct if the distance from the tree is the same on both sides of the hill. It will probably not be, but the error will be slight and the course correction will be as close an approximation as the rest of your navigation.

If the straight line route goes through the tree or other marker, all you have to do

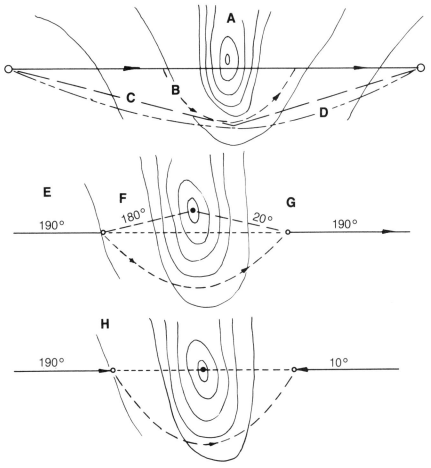

Fig. 8-5. *To pass an obstruction you can go around in several ways, while using a compass to keep on course.*

is go around the hill until the tree is the route bearing (+ or − 180°)—in this case 10° (FIG. 8-5H) then get back on your foreward course.

It might be possible to get by with a detour to one (FIG. 8-6A) or two points. If there is a landmark, use it. If not, you can get fairly accurate results by estimating distances or counting steps. When you get to a suitable point, alter the course by 60° and go a definite distance in that direction (FIG. 8-6B). You will have to judge the distance travelled to put you about square to the line of the direct route, and with enough clearance on the other side of the hill to get back to your direct route, without climbing.

Alter the course so you return at 60° to the direct course in the other way. Travel the same distance on this leg (FIG. 8-6C). Then, resume the direct course to your destination. Detouring to a point may take you further off course than you wish. If the hill

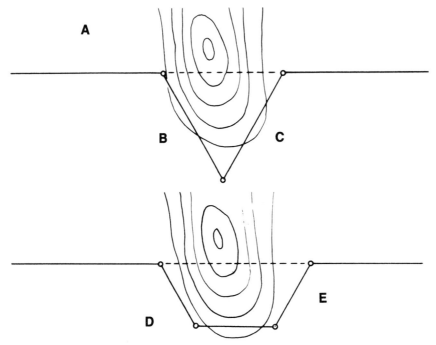

Fig. 8-6. *An obstruction can be passed in two or more legs.*

allows, you can go off a measured distance at a known angle, until you can see that the route would now be easy if you went about parallel to the original way (FIG. 8-6D). There is no need to measure that part. When you judge that you can get back on the original route, make the change at the same angle to it as originally, and go the same distance as the first angled leg, to the new departure point (FIG. 8-6E).

Alternatively, start on a course that will clear the hill. If there is a landmark, use it as a guide, but otherwise set a course that appears to go to a point at the foot of the hill at about square to the direct route (FIG. 8-7A). Until you get there, you may be uncertain of the terrain, and you may find you can go closer to the hill or get further away. Continue until you judge you are about square to the hill top. A bearing of it 90° more or less than the course you have taken, will serve as a guide, but precision is not important.

As close as possible, find your position on the map. Estimate how far you are from the top of the hill. You may get a bearing and distance from some other identifiable object. Pick your new route from that point (FIG. 8-7B). In the particular circumstances it might be better to swing out from the start. You may have to estimate distances and bearings, but it helps to have at least one mark that you can find both on the ground and on the map. Without this, the alternative is to decide to go a certain distance on one bearing, then change to another, and so on, to get around the obstruction (FIG. 8-7C).

In any of these detours, do not neglect to look behind you. You should be more

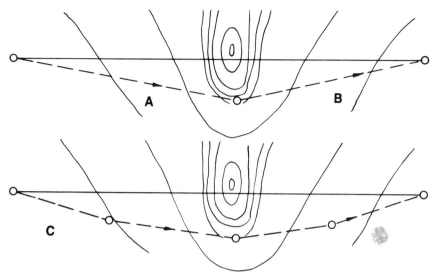

Fig. 8-7. *A diversion can be plotted ahead to use known positions to change direction.*

familiar with what you have passed than with what you have yet to reach. Use reciprocal bearings to check progress and to see what course you are on. If you stop somewhere and decide that the course should be 340°, go a short distance on that bearing and look back. There may be a particular formation of rocks or pattern of trees at the place you have just left. If you expect to have them in view behind you for some time, occasionally look back and check their bearing. If you are travelling correctly on course, it should be 180° more or less than your course bearing (in this case 160°). Obviously, you cannot be walking facing backwards, but an occasional check behind will confirm how you are moving, and it may be the only check possible on direction.

SIMPLE EXPEDITION PLANNING

If you plan to travel for several days, you should have an overall idea of how your routes will be arranged, even if you change your plans later when you know more about the terrain, discover parts in which you want to spend more time, or the weather causes alterations. If you have a plan and know the area from the map, there is no need to stick rigidly to advance ideas, providing you take care not to just wander haphazardly and get lost.

It helps to spend some time learning all you can from a map *before* moving off. If you discover all you can, you will be better able to visualize the country and know what to expect as you walk across it. Pauses for map reading will be mainly for checking what you expect, rather than surprising you with some information you had not noticed before. As an example, suppose you are planning a fairly leisurely two days in an area you do not know, except from the map. You can get to the bridge on the trail in the southeastern corner of the map (FIG. 8-8). You think it would be interesting to go

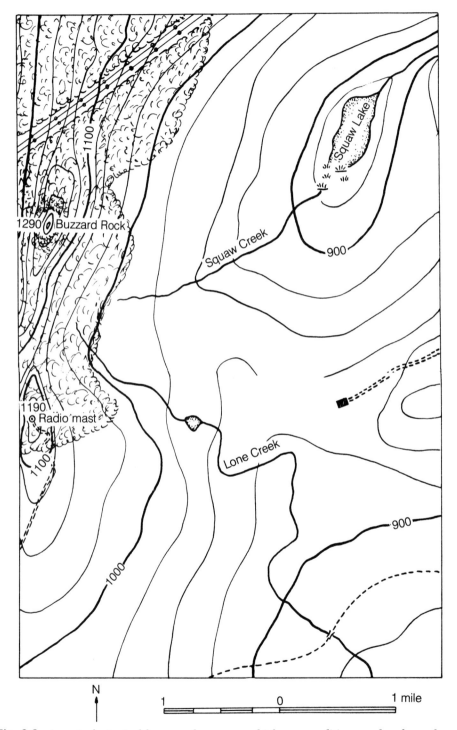

Fig. 8-8. *A part of a typical large-scale map on which an expedition can be planned.*

up to Buzzard Rock, then down to camp near Squaw Lake, and return next day via the hut shown near the eastern side of the map.

You note that a straight line from the bridge to Buzzard Rock is about 4 miles and from there to the lake is 3 miles. It seems probable that the walking distance may be up to twice this. Is your party capable of walking 14 miles? Suppose you get to Buzzard Rock, but fatigue makes you decide to shorten the distance to camp? You could still find water if you camped near the higher part of Squaw Creek. If you camp near Squaw Lake, a straight line from there back to the bridge is about 5 miles. You might walk 10 miles. Having established what seems feasible and made plans for a shortened alternative, you can study the map to visualize the country.

The trail bridge over Lone Creek is at an elevation of about 880 feet. You should be able to see the radio mast at 1190 feet. From the map you discover the bearing on that is 306°. A check helps to orient the map. From the map, you check that Buzzard Rock is on a bearing of 325°. Use your compass to sight in that direction. Can you see it? Trees may obscure the actual rock, but the outline of the trees should give you a good idea of where it is.

What about the hut, 2 miles north of you? It is higher than you and the country is apparently open, so you may see it, but it could be hidden by an outcrop of rock, a slight rise in the ground, or some trees or bushes. A hut no more than 10 feet high is easily hidden.

The map shows the forested part of the mountain. Check the date the map was made. It could be ten years old. Firs, pines, and other softwood trees can grow appreciably in that time; so much so that they may have been felled. Young trees may have grown outside the marked tree line. Hardwood trees do not grow as rapidly, but you may find young trees outside the marked line, particularly if it is a natural, mixed forest. From the bridge you should be able to check much of the shape of the forest and see if it agrees with the map.

Look at the contour lines. They are drawn at height differences of 25 feet, with every fourth one marked. Towards the northwest corner of the map they are much closer than in other parts. Therefore, the land there is quite steep, but elsewhere the wide spacing indicates fairly flat country with only slight ups and downs.

Neither of the creeks falls very much, so they are quite placid streams. Even where they rise within half a mile of each other, they do not start to drop very much. There may be occasional slight falls, but you would not expect to find rapids. The small pond on Lone Creek may be due to rock obstructions, an accumulation of driftwood and soil, or just because there was a hollow there that the stream had to fill before it could flow on.

Squaw Creek appears to have found a hollow to fill and make the small Squaw Lake, but the ground was obviously soft and porous near the upper end, which has left it marshy. It will be interesting to check the actual lake formation when you get there. The marshy end may have some different wild life.

The approach to Buzzard Rock could use Lone Creek as a guide for much of the way, but which side of it? We do not want to wade it frequently. If you follow the east side of the creek, there is a large sweep of it to push you off direction and, in any case, you will be coming back that way, so it will be better to keep to the west side of the creek, at least as far as the pond. A bearing from the bridge to the pond is 330°. If you follow the creek until you note that it begins to sweep east, you can then leave it and go on a compass bearing to the pond. Your route touches the stream again before you get there, so that provides a check on direction.

A direct approach to Buzzard Rock from the pond could involve some steep climbing towards the end. Without going very far off the straight line, you can go south of it to get on to the ridge about half a mile south of the rock and walk along the more gentle slope to it. Much depends on the density of the trees once you get among them. You can probably notice when you get to the top of the ridge, but as you enter the trees, note the distance and bearing to the ridge. When you have gotten that far, note the distance and bearing to walk to reach the rock.

If the rock gives you a high enough viewpoint over the trees, you may be able to see Squaw Lake. Even if you cannot see the water, the different vegetation may indicate marsh. The lake is about 300 feet lower than where you are and about 3 miles away. Its bearing is 75°. If you are unsure of where the lake is, sight on that bearing. Something in the vicinity should give you a clue. There could be willows or other water-loving trees that are not present elsewhere.

The map shows some close contour lines east of the rock. If you want a scramble down through the trees, this may be the way to go, but if you want an easier descent, go north along the ridge about half a mile, maybe as far as the power lines. Turn east down the easier slope shown by the more widely spaced contour lines. Once you have broken through the trees, your route is less than 2 miles of gentle slope, and you should see the lake some time before you reach it. Because the south end of the lake is marshy, your best camp site will probably be near the north end, or even a short distance down the outfall stream.

Next day, your journey back to the bridge is in two parts: first to the hut, then from there to the bridge. The contour lines show that the hut is slightly higher than the lake and the bridge, but the difference is not much. The widely spaced contour lines show that slopes are very slight and elevations should not affect the ease of walking, unless there are outcrops of rock or other obstructions not high enough to affect contour lines.

If you have camped on the north side of the lake, and you find that the creek below the lake cannot be crossed, you will have to follow the west side of the lake and probably sweep further west to avoid the swamp. Estimate your position and take a bearing of the hut on the map. If you sight on that bearing with your compass, you will probably see the hut 2 miles away—if not the actual hut, maybe some indication of it or the unimproved road to it.

If you can cross the stream where it runs out of the lake, you can set a more direct route and avoid going back partly over country you were on yesterday. It is about 3 miles and slightly uphill to the hut, so you may not see it, but take a bearing and check if any evidence of the hut is visible. If you are uncertain of what you see, walk along the bearing. You should see the hut before you have gone very far.

From the hut to the bridge is almost due south about 2 miles and slightly downhill in general. In fact, you will probably go up and down small undulations many times. That could be the way you choose to go, but it may be more interesting to go about 220° to the creek and follow its eastern bank to the bridge. From there, we assume it is an easy walk along the trail to your car parked just off the edge of the map.

This guided exercise shows what can be read by an intelligent interpretation of the map. Do not assume too many details of the terrain; be prepared to expect variations. Unmarked things may impede your progress. The map shows where there is forest and where there is not. The part without forest is not necessarily clear and easily passed land. Plan ahead with the aid of the map, but be prepared to accept the need to modify your plans when you get into the area illustrated.

EXTENDED EXPEDITION PLANNING

If you intend to go into undeveloped country for several days, it is advisable to procure all the necessary maps well in advance so you can familiarize yourself with features on them. In particular, you should know all the symbols and be able to get the most from them. Most maps do not carry a comprehensive legend. It is assumed that users will be familiar with standard symbols and any information provided as a legend or in the margin of the map will refer to things peculiar to that map. Sheets of standard topographic symbols are available; learn the relevant ones so you can recognize them on any map. It may be annoying or even disastrous to discover a symbol you do not know when you are in the middle of wild country.

If the area you will be covering is fairly extensive, it will be helpful to have one map that embraces all of it, although you may want several maps of larger scale to use when you are in the field, as suggested in the previous section. The single map gives you an overall picture of your probable routes and how they will link. Take that map with you or leave it behind, depending on circumstances. By the time you start, you may be so familiar with the routes on the larger scale maps that the wider coverage small-scale map will be unnecessary.

How you plan an extensive trip depends on what you want to do. If you are canoeing, you are obviously confined to water. If you are walking, you should be able to go almost anywhere. If you are on horseback, parts may be impassable for you. You must decide on your objects. If you want to cover as much as possible, you will be thinking of the maximum mileage each day. If you are more interested in fishing, you may intend to be static, or inactive, by a lake for a day or two, the only distances are those involved in getting to and from or between fishing lakes or rivers. If you are a naturalist, you may need to pause occasionally for periods you cannot forecast. There could be other reasons for going into the wilderness. Consider them as they affect times and distances, which have to be taken into account as you work with map and compass.

As with the shorter expedition in the last section, make an assessment of what seems a reasonable distance to travel each day. How long will you allow for being on the move each day? How do you expect the terrain to affect progress? What is an honest assessment of the ability of your party? As a result of balancing these partial unknowns, you arrive at a figure you can regard as the distance that may be covered in a day, when nothing interferes. It may be that something of interest will warrant a delay. If so, estimate how long you will stop there and take it out of the daily estimated time and distance. Suppose, as a result of all this, you decide 15 miles in a day is reasonable. You know that, if you had to extend its efforts, your party might manage 20 miles, but for preliminary planning 15 miles is the figure to work on. When you get down to daily planning on the map, daily distances will have to vary to suit the locations of intended stopping places. The preliminary thinking guides you towards planning distances that are possible, and prevents you coming up with ideas that will not work out in practice.

If it is country where you have been before, you may already have ideas about navigating within it. If not, look on the map for landmarks that could be of use to you. Ideally, there will be somewhere or something, always within sight that you can take a bearing on; then you progress from one sighted landmark to another. That may not always be so, but you can check in advance where to expect landmarks. If there is one, or more, that you can use every day, you should be able to travel in the certainty that you can say where you are within acceptable limits.

The landmark may be something prominent, like a mountain peak, or it may be something lower on the ground, such as a stream, a cliff, or a marked trail. If you come to it or can see it and take a bearing on it, your map and compass work will be confirmed. There are less definite things to use. If you find you are consistently going up or down hill, you should find contour lines that confirm this. If the rise or fall is only slight or not continued for a great distance, it may be all between contour lines and not indicated on the map. You can judge relative steepness from the closeness of contour lines on the map. These lines give you a general indication of position, although not an exact spot. A forest designation on the map also helps in locating, but the edge of forest areas on the map may not actually be abrupt changes on the ground, unless it is fenced. There could be a sudden change from densely packed trees to open ground, but it is more likely to be a gradual tailing off into scrub and smaller trees. There could still be plenty of isolated trees in what the map appears to indicate as open country. Do not put too much reliance on the boundaries of forest being exactly as shown on your map. Allow for the age of the map. In ten years trees may have grown, others have been established or some have been felled.

SPOT POSITIONING

At all times, try to know where you are—perhaps not the exact spot, but a general area that is not too big for you to get back on course before too long. If you know that after passing through a gap between the hills, you will eventually see the top of a distant mountain, it does not matter for the moment where you are, within several miles, as far as navigation is concerned. When you see the mountain, you can get a bearing. If you are travelling through dense forest without landmarks, it would be better to follow a compass course and keep a record of time and estimated distances. You will then know where you are within perhaps 1/2 mile after walking for 1 hour. If you are in open country and can see two landmarks and want to wander about looking at things or finding your way by a circuitous route around obstacles, you know that you can always take bearings of the two objects and plot the bearing lines on your map. You are where the lines cross, within a margin of error depending on the accuracy of your work, but near enough to give you the general direction of travel. If you find one landmark will be out of view, it may be helpful to make one last plot before you lose it.

In most country that you plan to traverse, there should be enough natural features for you to identify. There may even be some man-made ones, such as power lines, trails, and rangers' huts. Hilltops are useful, because they can be seen from a distance, but if they are rounded and extended instead of pointed, they do not give you a very trustworthy bearing. Use them, but try to get a bearing on something else as well.

DEAD RECKONING

If part of your journey takes you through forest with no apparent features to guide you, you will have to use *dead reckoning*. Although this improves with practice, it is unlikely to give you exact results. You have to use your compass combined with estimates of distance covered in certain times. For a short distance, the error may not be much, but if you have to travel all day in that way, it is almost impossible to prevent small errors compounding to a big one. If there is a feature ahead that you will identify when you reach it, you may have to scout in several directions to find it.

Be careful not to get lost. Suppose you are certain you have travelled far enough, but cannot see the hut you expected to be there. If you start wandering to look for it among trees, you could soon be far from your dead reckoning position and have no idea of your position. Go out on a bearing a certain number of paces from a marked position; then, use a reciprocal bearing to get back if you do not find the hut. Try many more similar moves until you find it (FIG. 8-9A).

If it is a stream flowing from among the trees, and you want to get to it where it reaches open ground, it will be wiser to aim to reach it upstream of the point you want and follow it down (FIG. 8-9B), than to aim direct and finish some way from the stream (FIG. 8-9C). Similar reasoning applies to a forest trail which forks. If you aim directly at the fork and eventually come to a trail without a fork, you do not know which way to go to get to the fork (FIG. 8-9D). If you aim to one side of the fork (FIG. 8-9E), you know which way to go to it if your navigation is not very far out.

Faults in dead reckoning may become serious if you have to use the method for several days. This is unlikely, but an understanding of the problem helps in making corrections when you are in more navigable country. You have to employ reckoning when there are no landmarks to use for getting bearings. This could occur in a desert. It might occur in dense forest, but most forest is on uneven ground, so you may be able to identify rises and falls with contour lines on the map, as information to supplement your dead reckoning.

Consider that you are travelling with dead reckoning as your only guide, and your course is 100° (FIG. 8-10A). After 1 hour, you estimate you have walked 3½ miles. You feel confident that you have kept on course, so you draw a line to the scale length

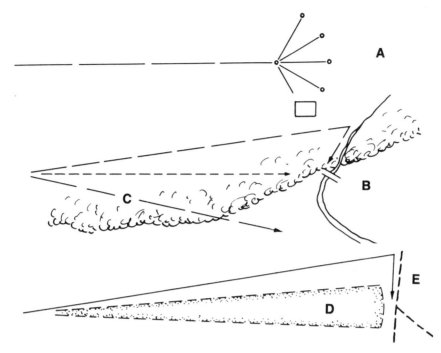

Fig. 8-9. *You may have to search in many directions to correct an error (A,B), or you can aim to one side and know which way to go when you reach an identifiable feature (D,E).*

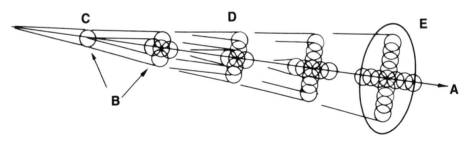

Fig. 8-10. *The possible errors become magnified, as seen by the circles, if you plot again at several positions without landmarks to confirm where you are.*

in the right direction. At hourly intervals you make similar plots (FIG. 8-10B). You have to trust this as your only guide, but if you stop after 5 hours you could be some way from your plotted position.

It is not easy to keep exactly on course, or to estimate distances precisely. If you actually wandered off course by a few degrees or went slightly more or less distance, your exact position at the end of an hour might be anywhere within a small circle (FIG. 8-10C). At the end of that hour you could still be close enough to where you intended. As you go on making similar errors, the position you are in after the second hour could be within any number of circles, depending on where the actual departure point was at the first hour circle (FIG. 8-10D). By the time you have travelled 5 hours, the possible area in which you finish could be quite large (FIG. 8-10E).

Fortunately, some errors tend to cancel out. If you underestimate distance in one hour, you may overestimate in the next. If you go off course one way during one hour, you may go off course the other way in the second hour. Do not, however, count on having that luck. Continue to navigate as accurately as you can.

When you are using dead reckoning, look for other possible aids, even if they are rather vague. There may be a very distant range of hills. Try to identify the skyline appearance and get a bearing, even if you know it cannot be very accurate. The surface is rarely exactly horizontal. If you can see a slope, check with contour lines. They are usually at quite close elevation intervals in that type of country. If you can see the sun, check its direction in relation to the time. The line of sight of it will cross your track. The North Star does not appear to move, as the sun does, but checking it in relation to your compass helps your confidence.

It is very unlikely that you will have to navigate by dead reckoning for long periods without being able to get a sight of something that will enable you to fix your position. Use all the landmarks you can, but dead reckoning is useful as a navigation aid that supplements other findings and as a means of keeping a record of progress. If you are logging your journey, corrected dead reckoning results will make your log book entries.

If you must navigate by dead reckoning in open country, do not forget to look behind you. You may see footprints or hoof marks in sand or snow for quite a long way. You think you are travelling straight. The view behind may surprise you. Your trail could be curved or wandering. Take a bearing of the average direction. If it is very far off a reciprocal bearing of your intended course, you will have to correct your course ahead. If this shows that you are not navigating as accurately as you expected, take back bearings more often.

VEHICLE NAVIGATION

In desert conditions you may be using a vehicle. A compass inside a vehicle is notoriously inaccurate, and the deviation may vary considerably on different headings. Do not depend on a car compass without checking and correcting.

The best way to get a vehicle on a correct course is to start by taking a bearing of the direction you want to go with a hand-held compass some way from the car or other vehicle. Stand ahead of the vehicle and sight in the direction you want to go. Get the driver to position the vehicle behind you (FIG. 8-11A). Walk in the bearing direction far enough for the driver to see the way, possibly by your footprints. If the surface is so hard that footprints do not show well enough, put a marker where you start walking and another where you finish, probably 300 feet or so ahead (FIG. 8-11B).

Get the driver to line up with the marks you have given him. Get back into the vehicle and sit in the position you will travel. Have the engine running. If you will be using radio or any other electrical gear, have that switched on as well. Hold the compass as

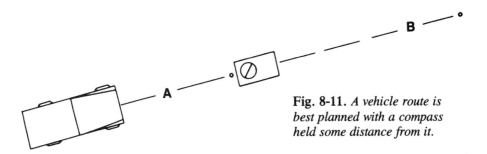

Fig. 8-11. *A vehicle route is best planned with a compass held some distance from it.*

you will for navigating the vehicle. Note the vehicle heading on your compass. Because of all the interference due to the vehicle and its equipment, that reading could be very different from the course you read while standing clear, but it is the course to follow while you are in the vehicle. If there is another compass mounted in the vehicle, note the reading on that. The driver can follow the course shown on that, which may not be the same as your hand-held compass, but providing both of you use your own courses, that does not matter. Obviously, you should not bring the compasses close enough together to deflect each other.

Theoretically, if the driver keeps on course you cannot go wrong, but it is worthwhile stopping occasionally and taking a reading away from the vehicle as a check. You can look behind you and see if the wheel tracks are straight. It may be advisable to make a check soon after starting, as the moving vehicle may have caused a slightly different deviation from when it was stationary.

FINDING YOUR WAY OUT

So you got lost? If you still have a map and compass, you are not really lost. Do not panic. There must be a definite point where you knew you were not so long ago. Working from that you can settle on an area you must be in. Already it is not so bad.

Orient the map with the aid of your compass. You know that you are not just anywhere on the map, but in a fairly small area of it. Concentrate on that area. Think back to your last known position, even if it was only a dead reckoning one and may be represented by a circle. That gives you a starting place. You probably left it with a definite aim, even if things went wrong on the way, so allow for leaving that point (FIG. 8-12A). How long ago was that? Do you think you were walking straight? In broken country the furthest you are likely to have gone in 2 hours is 6 miles. Draw or estimate a curve of that distance from the start (FIG. 8-12B). It is unlikely if you were not on a definite course that you would have travelled that far, so you are probably somewhere inside the circumference and maybe a long way back if your course has been erratic.

Try to get into a position where you can see some way. Does the map show anything that would serve as a landmark? The highest point of a distant range of hills may be marked (FIG. 8-12C). Take a bearing of it and believe your compass. When you are lost, there is a temptation to think other things are mistaken besides you. If you have a definite bearing and no doubt about the object sighted, you must be somewhere on the line plotted in that direction. Try estimating how far away the hill is and that will give you a clue to the scale distance to it on the map.

Ideally, find another landmark and take a bearing on that. Your location is where the two sight lines cross, and you are no longer lost. That may be too much to expect in rather undistinguished natural country, so we must look for other signs. Contour lines can be helpful. If there are close ones in another direction and the slope is towards you (FIG. 8-12D), you may spot a piece of land that matches. Contour lines showing a distant slope away from you are not likely to be of much use as the ground falling away will not show (FIG. 8-12E).

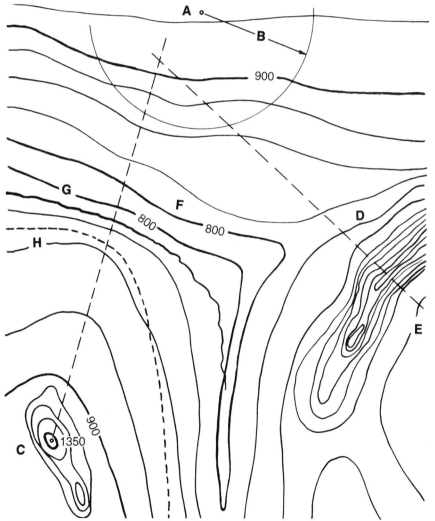

Fig. 8-12. *Finding your position may be by taking sights to cross within the area you expect to be, while noting slopes, streams and other features to compare land and map.*

What about the land formation in your immediate area? Suppose the land is sloping towards the south, into a valley (FIG. 8-12F). Look for contour lines indicating this in the vicinity of the sight line drawn from the hill. You are on that line—or at least somewhere close, allowing for errors.

Water is useful for identifying a position. Having gotten yourself almost certainly at a point on a south-facing slope, is there any water shown on the map that should be within sight or easy reach? Perhaps there is a blue line in the valley. Many valleys have a stream or creek through them. If yours does, that is your next mark. Now that you are expecting it, you may be able to sight water, typical waterside foliage, or trees in the direction you expect (FIG. 8-12G). If not, you can go into the valley and look for water. If conditions are very dry, there may not be any water, but you might see the stream bed. In either case, you have further confirmation of where you are.

Having gotten yourself located in a very small area, the next thing is to decide where to go. You may be finding your way out, or you may be going on to the next campsite, but there is still a slight doubt in your mind that having got lost once, you may do it again. Look for something positive on the map, in the general direction you want to go. Even if it takes you slightly off your route, getting to it will confirm that you know what you are doing. There could be a cliff, marked by contour lines running together. There may be something man-made like a quarry or a dirt road. A power line or a trail may be of more use than one of the single points, as they could be missed, but you are almost certainly going to find some part of a trail or power line.

From your estimated position, set out for this marker (FIG. 8-12H). If you find it not too far from where you expect, up goes your confidence. If you do not strike it as you expect, go back to first principles again. Reorient your map with your compass. Look for something to get a sight on. Look for something else to give you a cross bearing. If nothing is forthcoming, check on the lay of the land, maybe marked forestry, the possible nearness of water, and anything else marked in the vicinity on your map. By a process of elimination, you should be able to settle on a new position. With luck, it may not be far from the trail or other landmark and you can carry on to reach it. If not, look for another positive point that you can reach from your new estimated position.

WITHOUT MAP OR COMPASS

Suppose you have lost your map and compass in an accident—your canoe capsized and they sank, or your horse bolted with them. There is no great difficulty in using the sun or stars to find north, but you will have to rely on what you remember of map details for topographic information. If you still have a watch, correctly timed, you can use it with the sun to find a north-south line. Even without a watch, you will have some idea of how far the day has passed. When the sun is at its highest, it is south.

If you have anything to write on, it will be worthwhile to make a sketch map of what you remember from the lost map. You may be able to backtrack to your last known point, but things that were familiar when you travelled one way have a habit of looking very different the other way. However, they will be taking you to country that ought to be familiar. You should be able to identify landmarks you used for taking bearings. Knowing north and south, you can estimate bearings again.

Slopes are good guides. If you are on the side of a hill or mountain, there is not usually much reason for going higher, unless you are certain a place you know is on the other side. Trails and roads will usually be lower down and probably in the bottoms of valleys. If you have no good reason for doing otherwise, go downhill rather than up. Similarly, if you come to a creek, it is usually more useful to follow its flow than to go upstream. The stream may run into a river. Even if you cannot remember the stream on your map, you will probably remember the river and something about it that will help you find your way.

Keep to open country if you can. If you become closed in by trees, you may wander erratically, but in the open there are things to see that will help you keep going in one direction. If you feel that you must go in one direction for a long way, it helps to get two things in transit so you can use them, instead of the compass that has gone, to keep you on course. Suppose there is a peak and a prominent tree that are in line with your route (FIG. 8-13A). Keep them like that as you progress and you know you are going straight. Even if they are not exactly in line with your course, keep them in the same relative position and they will serve your purpose. If you cannot find anything in transit far enough away, choose nearer markers; then, when you have reached one, look for more to continue the same way (FIG. 8-13B).

Even if you cannot remember enough to take you back to your starting point or on to your destination, the way to help will almost certainly be downwards. If you follow

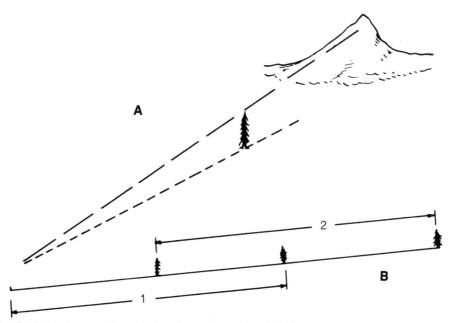

Fig. 8-13. *An intermediate landmark can be used to help keep on a long course; then you change to another mark when you pass it.*

a creek or a valley downwards, it will probably broaden. If there is a track, trail, or road, leading to civilization, that is probably where you will find it.

Of course, the moral is to make sure you do not lose your map and compass. Your compass should be on your person, preferably attached to a cord around your neck. If a companion has a second compass, at least one instrument should survive an accident. It is worthwhile having a duplicate map kept separately. With a map and a compass and enough knowledge to use them, you should never be really lost. You may not know where you are at the time, but you have the means of putting things right. A brief period of not knowing where you are then becomes an interesting episode and not the disaster it might be.

Sketch mapping is a useful and interesting secondary activity when going into wild country. You can draw a map of your route, partly based on the original map and partly on the terrain as you find it. You can put in many things that were not originally mapped, but which you found useful marks, such as prominent trees, rock outcrops, falls in creeks, trails made by animals, marks left by other explorers, and anything that would be useful if you went that way again.

This increases your powers of observation. If you ever reached the stage of being without your map and compass, your better observation may stand you in good stead, and if you still have a sketch map, that might take over as your navigation aid. More about sketch mapping follows in chapter 10.

9

Orienteering

ORIENTEERING IS AN ACTIVITY THAT COMBINES CROSS-COUNTRY RUNNING or walking with the use of a map and compass. As a sport, it has reached international status, with local, national, and international competitions and championships. As a recreation, it provides a purpose for walking or running in interesting surroundings, with a chance to exercise your skills in finding your way. There is something in orienteering for everyone, from a beginner to the enthusiast aiming at championship results. There is no age limit. Children can tackle simple courses, while older people, not concerned with speed, can tackle more advanced courses at their own pace.

An orienteering course is arranged to take participants between marked positions where they have to report. The area selected may be natural woodland or partly open country with hazards. It is unusual to include built-up areas or roads, except where they cannot be separated from a mainly natural setting. Competitors use marked maps, but they choose their own routes with the aid of their compasses and the way they interpret the maps. Starts are staggered, so each person is on his own and has to find his own way.

Orienteering had its origins in Sweden and other Scandinavian countries, where there are large tracts of forested country with little evidence of man's involvement. Major Ernst Killander first organized the sport in Sweden, as a form of cross-country racing in which the competitor had to pick his own route from a map. In 1946, it was given the name "orienteering" by Bjorn Kjellström.

The invention of the *Silva protractor-type compass* made map reading in orienteering conditions more practical. It is that compass, or similar compasses by other makers, that is used universally in orienteering events. More suitable large-scale maps have become available, and they have helped make the sport more accurate, with a reduced reliance on luck. Orienteering depends now almost completely on physical fitness and skill in interpreting map and compass.

The International Orienteering Federation (I.O.F.) has a membership of upwards of 20 countries, including the United States Orienteering Federation and the Canadian Orienteering Federation. There is now considerable standardization of details and procedures, but, obviously, local conditions must have some effect on the arrangement of orienteering events. The information contained in this chapter is based on common practices, but the reader may find some variations at the local level. There is, however, agreement on the general factors involved. Much of the lead and some of the equipment still comes from Sweden.

EQUIPMENT

A participant in orienteering can expect to be running over natural country and must contend with all that involves, such as trees, undergrowth, varied vegetation, and uneven ground, possibly to the extent of having to scramble on hands and knees in some places. With almost anything that nature can offer (including streams to cross), clothing should allow freedom of movement, but also provide protection. For most conditions, bare legs and arms are discouraged and usually inadvisable. Footwear should suit running over uneven ground. Specialist suppliers provide shoes designed for the sport, with soles intended to grip any surface.

For beginners, there may be someone at a control point to help and advise as well as record the participant's visit there. For most events, the control point is a three-sided fabric marker, divided diagonally in red or other distinctive color, and white (FIG. 9-1A), supported where it can be seen. Also with it is a pin punch (FIG. 9-1B), that will pierce a card with a pattern of holes special to that position. Each person arriving at the control point carries a card and punches it in the appropriate position to prove he has been there. The card could be hand drawn for the event or in printed form (FIG. 9-1C). Visits to control points should be in numerical order.

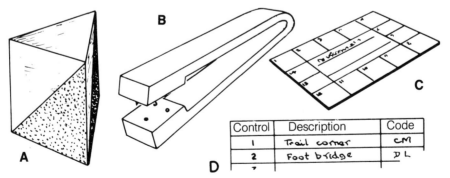

Control	Description	Code
1	Trail corner	CM
2	Foot bridge	DL
7		

Fig. 9-1. *An orienteering control point is marked with a white and colored marker (A). A special punch (B) is used to mark a card (C). A competitor carries a list of controls (D).*

Besides his map, a participant carries a list of control points with their sequence, a brief description, and a location (FIG. 9-1D). This may be carried in a special transparent map case or a plastic bag. Some protection is needed if the paperwork is to survive the rough conditions encountered.

For use in emergency, each competitor is expected to carry a whistle. Special plastic types are available, although obviously any whistle could be used. The whistle, compass, and map case may all be on cords around the neck, but there are occasions when any one of them is better in your hand. Participation in a few orienteering events will show you, from your own experience and from observation of others, how best to handle equipment.

COMPASSES

Although it would be possible to use any hand compass for recreational orienteering, the type used by almost everyone for this and competitive events is the protractor compass pioneered by Silva (FIG. 9-2). Besides these compasses, which are also suitable for many other purposes, some are made especially for orienteering. Magnifiers in several sizes may be included for reading fine details on maps. There are types with extra stable needles. Edge scales may suit orienteering maps. A compass may have a strap to go over a thumb, so you can hold the map with the compass resting on the surface and set the map to the compass in one action.

Parallel lines in the transparent base of the circular part of the compass turn with it, so you can line up the needle when you are not looking directly over it. You can see if the needle and lines are parallel even when holding the compass to one side, so

Fig. 9-2. *A compass held in front of you can be pointed towards an object and set to read its bearing.*

avoiding *errors of parallax*. The graduations on the rotatable rim are at 2° intervals. So a compass can be used at night, there may be luminous paint on the north end of the needle, on the rim and the end of the bearing line on the base. Some orienteering compasses have extra lines parallel with the main sighting line on the base.

MAPS

Much early orienteering was accomplished with existing maps of the largest scale available. Additional information was added by hand, including control points and features not already printed. This is still done, but many maps produced for general purposes do not carry (anywhere near) enough detail for orienteering. There are characteristics and features important in orienteering competitions that would not be of much interest to other users. A suitable general map can be used as a base, but considerable additional information has to be provided. If copies have to be reproduced, they will be in black and white, but experience has shown that color can be of the greatest value to anyone referring to a map while travelling on foot in a hurry through the sort of country chosen for orienteering competitions.

Where maps of sufficient orienteering value are already available, they can be adapted, and this may be conveniently done for simple beginners' competitions. For more advanced events, it is becoming common practice to produce special maps, even to the extent of making special surveys, so the map starts from first principles and is not affected by details on existing maps which may no longer be correct. This has resulted in maps of areas regularly used for orienteering, which are of ample scale and contain information on features denoted by symbols peculiar to the sport, as well as a plentiful use of color.

SCALES

There is an advantage in having a map to as large a scale as possible. Details on it are not crowded and can be easily read, with little risk of confusing or misinterpreting them. A large scale means that all that is shown is larger, so the size of paper needed has to be considered. The sheet has to be easy to handle and not have to be folded too many times. For the amount of land to be illustrated to cover many orienteering courses, a scale of 1:15,000 is favored (about 4 inches to 1 mile). About 6 miles in each direction can go on a sheet that is easily handled when folded into four parts.

Other scales could be used, but 1:15,000 is finding general acceptance. For a map prepared for orienteering, a 5-meter (about 16 feet) elevation interval is the standard, according to the International Orienteering Federation. This marking suits most terrain. In mountainous areas, it may be sufficient to use 10-meter intervals, while an area with little difference in height could have 2-meter or 2.5-meter intervals. Elevation differences should be the same all over a map, but *auxiliary contours* (*form lines*) could be put in if needed. This should be made clear in the legend.

An orienteer is using a compass that points to magnetic north (as they all do) and is concerned with a fairly small area. There is no need for him to adjust to true north. Special orienteering maps are made so they have their tops at magnetic north, instead of true north, and any bearings made on them are read as magnetic, without any further action. If the map is set with the compass over a side margin, the needle and border matching will be correct. If an orienteering map is ever related to a general map, this should be remembered—the orienteering map north-south and east-west lines will be angled to those of the other map by the amount shown as the difference between the true and magnetic arrows.

SYMBOLS

An orienteering map usually covers an area with very few man-made features. A large number of the conventional signs and symbols used on most general maps are for those things. The number of general symbols for natural features are comparatively few. The orienteer may use the symbols normally accepted where the objects occur, but for most of his needs he requires symbols for things not usually illustrated. He wants guidance on the density of scrub, whether there are crags or boulders, where the limits of vegetation are, and if he can get across a stream. He only needs to know about paved roads and power lines as possible landmarks.

At the large scale of an orienteering map, these things can have their own symbols. If color is used, it is easy to distinguish one from the other. Where the map is black and white, there may have to be a more limited range of symbols. Although orienteering map symbols are becoming standardized, there is still a possibility of differences, so it is usual to provide a legend with individual maps.

How well colors can be used on a map depends on their number. If there are only one or two in addition to black and white, the arrangement of symbols may have to be modified, but the meanings should be made clear by the legend.

Where there is a full range of colors available, there are standard International Orienteering Federation symbols. The orienteer planning his route is most interested in the terrain in relation to his progress, whether he can walk, run, or perhaps fight his way through. Overall colors are used to show the condition of the ground and how other conditions may be for the competitor. There may also be a need to show any private land that should not be entered.

Symbols for water are blue, as on other maps, but more information is given. The competitor can judge how best to deal with water courses if they come in his path. Roads, trails, and some other things will be recognized by anyone familiar with symbols on other maps, but many natural features that concern the orienteer are drawn in the same brown or red-brown as contours.

Recommended I.O.F. symbols are shown (FIG. 9-3), but they may be different if fewer colors are available.

SETTING A MAP

Setting a map with a compass has already been described, but in orienteering it is made simpler because all directions are related to magnetic north. Suppose you have a line between two control points. Put the long edge of the base on the line (FIG. 9-4A). Keep the base in place, but turn the compass housing around until the red lines in its

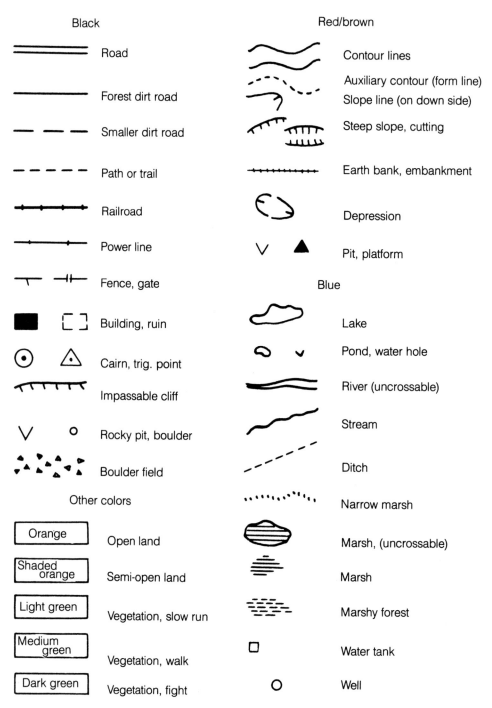

Black

Road

Forest dirt road

Smaller dirt road

Path or trail

Railroad

Power line

Fence, gate

Building, ruin

Cairn, trig. point

Impassable cliff

Rocky pit, boulder

Boulder field

Other colors

Orange — Open land

Shaded orange — Semi-open land

Light green — Vegetation, slow run

Medium green — Vegetation, walk

Dark green — Vegetation, fight

Red/brown

Contour lines

Auxiliary contour (form line)
Slope line (on down side)

Steep slope, cutting

Earth bank, embankment

Depression

Pit, platform

Blue

Lake

Pond, water hole

River (uncrossable)

Stream

Ditch

Narrow marsh

Marsh, (uncrossable)

Marsh

Marshy forest

Water tank

Well

Fig. 9-3. *Special map symbols are used to suit orienteering needs.*

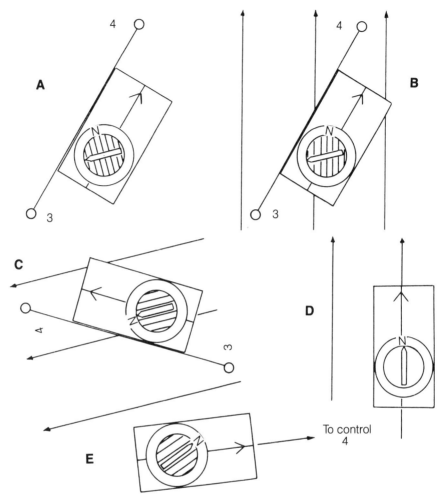

Fig. 9-4. *The compass is set from the map in stages to obtain the heading on a leg of the course.*

base are north and south in relation to lines on the map (FIG. 9-4B). In both actions, see that you are working the right way—the basic direction arrow pointing the way you will go and the norths of compass and map coinciding. Either could be inadvertently 180° out!

If you want to set the map the same way as the terrain, turn map and compass so the needle settles pointing at north on the rim (FIG. 9-4C). If you are only concerned with setting the map, and not with a route line as well, have the compass set with the north point on the rim over the sight line. Put this over a north-south line on the map and turn map and compass until the needle lines up (FIG. 9-4D). This may be necessary if, for general positioning, you want to be able to locate landmarks on the ground with their symbols on the map. If all you want to do is go quickly on your way to the next control point, remove the compass from the map (at position FIG. 9-4B) and hold it in your hand. Move around until the needle settles pointing north on the rim (FIG. 9-4E). If you look along the sighting line, you are facing in the direction of the next control point, so that is the way you go.

An advantage of setting in this way is that at no point do you have to bother wih bearings in degrees. By three steps you have found the way to go. When you are hurrying from point to point, that is all the immediate information you need. It helps, however, to keep your map set reasonably accurately to the land. Keep in touch with landmarks and the terrain, particularly contour lines that will indicate if you should be going up or down, of if you are coming to a rise or hollow that it would be better to go around. It takes practice to run with a map in your hand and set it so a glance relates the map to what is around you. Some runners find it confusing to read the map when the route to follow puts markings on the map upside-down. There is a tendency to expect to look at a map with the north always towards the top, but if you are going from somewhere northerly to somewhere southerly, look at the line on the map that way; otherwise, you may confuse turning left and right.

DISTANCES

To get from one control point to another, you need to have some idea of distance as well as direction. You may have a good sense of distance and can estimate how far you travel, but it is safer to pace the distance. Orienteers are counting paces most of the time they are competing. When you are running, it is simpler to count double paces—count for one foot only: every time your left foot goes down, count one more. As we all have different strides, we have to do our own preliminary measuring. Orienteering distances are usually metric. By the most accurate means you have, mark out a distance of 100 meters on a flat surface. Run between the points several times at the speed you anticipate using in competition. Count your double paces each time and average them. They will probably be between 35 and 45.

Remember how many of your double paces equal 100 meters. Some compasses have an indicator you can set to remind you. Alternatively, tape a note of the number on the compass or something else that you always take with you. From your 100-meter base, you can quickly convert to other distances.

Many of the techniques described for general map use have applications in orienteering. If there is high ground between the point you are leaving and the one you are aiming at, a straight line route might be difficult or impossible. Although that appears to be the short way, it might be quicker to go around (FIG. 9-5A). You may be able to go around on a contour level, or there may be a trail or some other feature you can follow.

If an orienteer makes use of a marked feature as a guide, he talks of using it as a *handrail*. The safest way to get to your destination without getting lost may be to make for a fence or stream that you can follow, until your pacing shows that you should turn away from it (FIG. 9-5B).

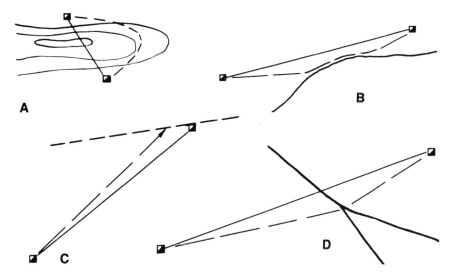

Fig. 9-5. *Skill comes in selecting a direction that avoids or uses features marked to permit the best speed between controls.*

Another technique is to aim off to one side of your destination. If you aim directly at a control point on a trail or beside a stream, and arrive at the trail or stream without seeing it, you may not know which way to go and may waste time going the wrong way first. It is better to aim to one side; then follow along until you find the control point (FIG. 9-5C).

The surest way to get to a control point may not be in a straight line. There may be a positive landmark nearer your destination and not far off a direct route, such as a fork in a trail. If you can get there easily, you can then take a bearing from that place. There is little risk of error in the shorter distance (FIG. 9-5D).

EVENTS

Orienteering events are laid out by experienced orienteers. Usually there are alternative courses arranged, depending on ability and the distance you are prepared to go. These may be color-coded or separated in some other way. How the courses are laid out depends on the terrain. It is convenient if the finish can be close to the start; then clothing and vehicles do not have to be moved. The course takes you around points that offer varied conditions, but follows a generally circular direction, and that has attractions.

A master map will be available at the start, from which you extract the information you need and transfer it to your own map. Alternatively, there may be premarked maps available. You will also collect or copy a list of control points. Obviously, this first collection of information is very important and your only guide to where to go once you have left the start. Draw a circle around each control point on the map and draw lines between circles.

The start is from a taped area and you will be timed from your starting whistle, with competitors spaced at regular time intervals. The last control point is usually not very far from the finishing point, and you will be guided there by tapes. Your time is taken as you cross the line. At every control point you must punch your card. It is your total time that counts. If you miss any controls, there are penalties or disqualification. A maximum time is usually allowed and you lose points if you take longer.

TYPICAL EVENT

Competitors arriving to take part in an event can see a master map and transfer details to their own maps, or they may be given premarked maps. The map of the layout for an imaginary event (FIG. 9-6) is black and white, as it might be for a small event, but added color would be justified for a larger or more advanced event and would simplify map reading. The start (triangle) and finish (circle) are close together and not far from a surface road, which will provide access.

The first thing to do is get a general picture in your mind of the layout of the area, without bothering very much about how the control points are laid out. The highest part is amid the fairly close vegetation, probably including trees, between points 1 and 2. The only part with closer vegetation is on the downward slope north of this. Man-made features in the area are an unpaved forest road around the higher ground and a trail leading north from it. The only water is a stream which passes near two control points, but does not appear to be big enough to cause difficulty.

From the contour lines, you expect that you can see the higher rise ahead of you at the start without difficulty. Slightly west of north from your starting viewpoint, you ought to be able to see the denser vegetation around point 5. Much depends on if there are trees and how sharply defined are the edges of the close vegetation. It is unlikely that the stream will be visible, but there may be signs of trees and other vegetation that favor water.

This broad visualizing of the whole area involved in the event lets you orient yourself. If anything goes wrong, you have a much better chance of knowing where you are than if you merely concentrated on point-to-point details.

Next you have to decide on how you will tackle each leg of the event. It is your skill in reading all that the map has to tell you that decides how well you perform in the navigation part of the event—the rest is physical. Only you can decide which way you will go. Sometimes there are two or three alternatives. You have to weigh up the advantages and disadvantages. Usually, it is a case of easier travel and a longer route, or a direct route and harder going. Of course, the map does not tell you everything. When you see the relative density of trees or vegetation you may change your mind.

On the event map (FIG. 9-6), from the start to control point 1 is straightforward. You have to determine your course and keep on it for the necessary distance. When you make the sight for your first bearing, look for a tree or other mark in the right direction and as far on your way as possible; then make for it. By then the vegetation will have gotten denser and you may not be able to use marks very far ahead. You will have to rely on the compass. At control point 1, punch your card.

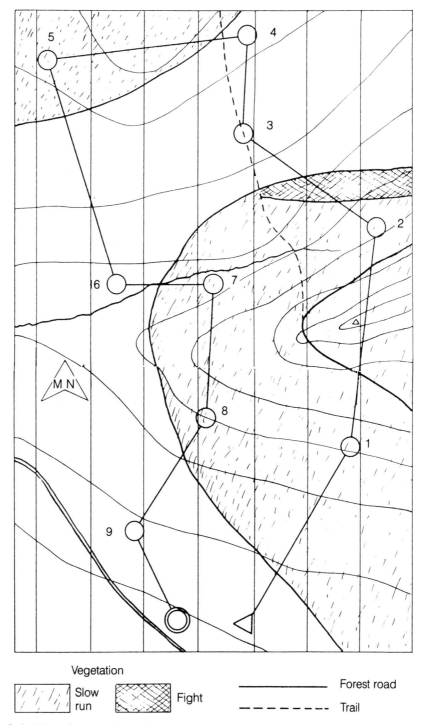

Fig. 9-6. *Map of a typical simple orienteering event.*

Vegetation

Slow run

Fight

Forest road

Trail

The next leg is the one that may require most thought. The straight line goes over a hill that has a surveying trig point on it. The way is tempting because the trig point gives you a definite check that you are keeping on course. How steep, however, are the slopes? A section on the line provides a picture of what may be involved (FIG. 9-7A). The height scale is exaggerated, but the slopes may be enough to make progress slow. Much depends on the vegetation, but the map classes it as a slow run.

You could leave point 1 on a direct course until you reach the forest road. If you then decide the straight route would be hard going, you can follow the road around, with not much slope and probably a good running surface. You will have to estimate where to leave the road for point 2, but the trail forking will show you when you are about halfway (FIG. 9-7B). If you decide at point 1 that you will use the road, it may be quicker to set a course for the curve of the road (FIG. 9-7C). You could leave the road diagonally towards point 2, but that would put you on a slower surface. It will probably be quicker to stay on the road until you are nearer to point 2.

From point 2 to point 3 is moderately downhill; although you have to go through dense vegetation if you keep to a straight line. The fight through it is not far. If you decide to try to keep to a straight line, there is a risk of missing point 3 if there is an error, and you could waste a lot of time looking for it. This is a place where it would be better to aim to one side, to the nearer angled part of the trail; then when you hit the trail, you know you have to go northwards along it to the point (FIG. 9-7D).

The path is tempting. Suppose you ignore the straight line—would it be better to skirt around the denser vegetation and go west until you meet the trail? That might be faster, as the trail should give you a good running surface. You have to judge if it would be more successful going fairly straight or making this detour.

From control point 3 to control point 4 is straightforward and not very long. There are no alternatives to a straight line, unless you decide to use the trail part of the way, for the sake of speed; then branch off.

Control points 4 and 5 are at about the same elevation, and there is a rise between them. The rise is not much, but a straight line takes you over it. Most of the way is vegetation classed as a *slow run*. It could be that going straight is reasonable, but you might consider *contouring*. If you can keep at the same level on a curved course, you will go further, but for a much greater part of the distance you will be on ground that allows a faster run (FIG. 9-7E). Accuracy depends mainly on maintaining the same level, as you cannot use the compass on a curved route. The alternative, if you want to use compass bearings, is to plan the route as a series of straight lines, with bearing distances scaled and noted.

From control point 5 to control point 6 is straightforward and a matter of keeping on course. You have a *catching feature* in the stream (FIG. 9-7F). If you reach the stream, you know you have gone slightly too far and will have to backtrack to look for the marker.

From control point 6 to control point 7 you can make use of the stream. You cannot tell from the map how easy it will be to follow the stream closely, but you can almost certainly keep it in view. You will have to find a suitable place to cross it. On the map, a straight line crosses about midway between the points. Be aware of the

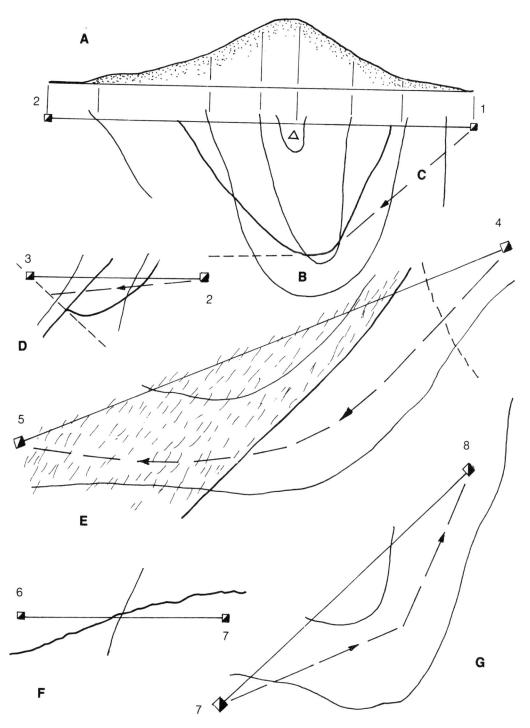

Fig. 9-7. *Details of possible ways between controls in an event.*

direction according to your compass, but careful use of the stream should get you there.

From control point 7 to control point 8, there is a rise on a straight course. It may not be enough to matter, but conditions are not always as smooth as contour lines signify. If you decide to get around at about the same elevation, you could follow a curved course. This may be a suitable place to do it in just two straight legs (FIG. 9-7G). Plot a course and distance that takes you out to a point you estimate to be suitable, then alter course for the marker. In addition to keeping to your course, this also needs careful pacing of distances.

From control point 8, it is a simple and short course to point 9. As you go slightly downhill you will probably see the paved road or its fences. If this is an event large enough for tents and many vehicles, you will probably also see them at the finish. These are guides. You still have to find point 9 and punch your card, so continue to work on course and distance.

At point 9 there may be tapes or other guides to the finish. If not, you will have to set a course, and travel on it until you come to the lead-in to the finish line. Remember, you have not finished until you cross the line, so keep up your pace until then, and record the best time you can make.

After an event, it is useful to compare notes with other participants. Besides laughing over errors and hazards, compare navigational differences. Apart from physical fitness, it is skill in navigation which is important. Did someone who put up a better time go a different way between points? If you had to search for a marker, why did someone else find it immediately? Compare the way you marked your maps. Has someone a better way than you of reading courses? This may be a time to check your paces. In event conditions you may not use the same number of paces over a set distance as you did in your trial runs.

Orienteering uses mapping methods in a more compressed form than most other map usages. Reading a map with more detail of a small area is good training for using maps of larger tracts or for cross-country travel.

OTHER EVENTS

Most orienteering events are as just described, but there are variations, which may be used over the same course on the day or on special occasions.

In a *relay event*, teams of three take part. The first runners make a mass start and obviously aim to get around the course as quickly as possible. Start and finish are at the same place, so the first member of each team returns and touches off the second, who does the same, ending eventually with number 3. This is the only form of orienteering that spectators can understand without the need for time references. Not all terrains are suitable, particularly if numbers are large. To avoid crowding, it is possible to arrange the course so runners have different routes—what the first man in one team does, may have to be done by the third man in another team.

In a *score event*, a large number of control points are arranged and given values according to their distance away from the start-finish or difficulty of access. The object is to visit the largest number of points in a set time and amass the maximum number of points. Getting between the points is up to the competitor, in any sequence he wishes, but timing and routes have to be arranged to allow for returning on time.

Night orienteering may not be suitable for beginners, but anyone with a little experience will find it fascinating. Courses are normally short and in reasonably open country. An event could be in a city park that would not be considered for a day event. Arrangements are the same as for a cross-country day event, but competitors use flashlights or headlights for map and compass reading, as well as for finding their way and identifying control points.

A *map memory* event is good training. Competitors are shown a map of one leg of the course, which they have to memorize and act on. At the next control point, they can see another map to the next point, but cannot take the map with them. Being able to memorize map details makes for speed over a course. Stops for map reading may then be a normal event.

For beginners, practice can be given in following a course by having a line event. The course on the ground is a straight line and there are markers at intervals. How far apart depends on conditions, but they should not be visible from very far ahead. Participants punch their cards or note some feature, such as a combination of letters, at each marker.

Although orienteering is particularly suitable for participants on foot, it can be adapted to some other means of progress. In some places it would be possible to arrange an event for horse riders. In areas where snow settles enough for skiing, orienteering is possible, providing an interesting objective for skiers. This variation is popular in the Scandinavian countries that gave birth to orienteering.

10

Mapmaking

$\mathbf{S}$OMEONE STOPS AND ASKS YOU THE WAY TO A PLACE ACROSS TOWN THAT you know well. While giving them directions, you doodle a sketch map on the back of an envelope. It may not be a very advanced example of cartography, but nevertheless, you have made a map. Such a map may have no scale and no indication of north, but it shows where the turns are, maybe some key landmarks, and a dotted line or arrows showing the best route (FIG. 10-1A). When it has served its purpose, the paper will be thrown away.

Suppose someone intends to visit you, and he or she has asked you to send a diagram of how to find your house. On this occasion, you have more time to prepare a map, but there is still no need for anything elaborate or absolutely correct in proportions or scale, providing your drawing gets your visitor from where he comes into the town to your home. It can all be done freehand, but names, particularly if they are unusual, should be printed rather than written, so there can be no confusion. You may be able to read your writing, but the person at the other end may have difficulty in deciphering it. Make his task easier by printing words.

Take the route from the last point that the visitor can reach without your aid—probably where he enters the town. Draw the streets he needs, but don't draw streets far off the route, unless there are some where he may go wrong and have to get back to the route. Give all the important street names; then think of the more prominent buildings that may guide him. A notation of traffic lights will help. You may draw the streets wide enough to put the names inside (FIG. 10-1B), or make the lines closer and put the names outside (FIG. 10-1C). If it has to be a fairly elaborate map, it is neater and clearer to draw the roads narrow and put the road names alongside.

Make the start and finish obvious, probably by saying where the starting road comes from, then indicate your home prominently. It is often difficult to get all the information you want to provide on the part of the map concerned. Print details away from the part of the map and take an arrow in (FIG. 10-1D). This is much clearer and gives you more scope than if you try to squeeze words at the actual position. This particularly applies to buildings you are using as landmarks. Unless the route is obvious, put arrows to show direction, either alongside the roads or between the lines (FIG. 10-1E).

Although the sketch is freehand, try to keep proportions reasonably correct. If you shorten the distance between turnings after keeping to a rather larger scale further back, your visitor may overshoot. When you have sketched the whole map, think of it in relation to actual distances. You might just put a dimension line between start and finish, indicating the approximate distance involved (FIG. 10-1F), or it may be better to provide a simple scale, possibly just indicating 1 mile (FIG. 10-1G). There may be little need for an indication of north, but it is advisable to get into the habit of providing a north arrow on every map you make. Estimate its direction and put one in (FIG. 10-1H).

If you have a printed map of the area, use that as a guide. It may be a smaller scale than you have to sketch and not have enough detail, but it helps you to get the features in correct proportions and directions quite accurately. It is very easy when sketching

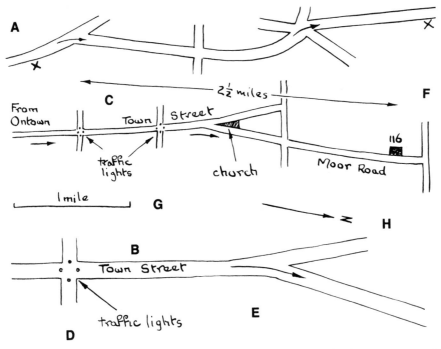

Fig. 10-1. *A sketch map should be based on the elements of standard mapping practices.*

streets across a large distance of town to find that the direction of some of them can finish up perhaps 90°) out of relation to other streets drawn earlier, if you are not careful or have nothing to guide you. It might be an interesting exercise to go out into some of your familiar streets with a compass and check their directions.

DETAIL SKETCH MAPS

Suppose you need to tell someone how to get from an address in one town to an address in another town 10 miles away. You need a fairly large scale for the details at each end of the journey, but the part between is on one highway with no complications and could be drawn to a smaller scale. Actually, there may be no need of a map between the towns, providing there is no doubt about how to get on and leave the highway.

Such a map may be sketched to a sufficiently large scale for the first town (FIG. 10-2A), as far as access to the highway to the other town. You can put a note about distance between and draw the map of the second town to the same scale as the first (FIG. 10-2B). Make sure the user will have no doubt about where he gets on to the part of the highway not drawn and where he has to leave it. In this sort of mapping, you can use the names of filling stations, shops, churches, and even billboards, if they are likely to be seen ahead by the map user. If he will be arriving after dark, think of illuminated signs that might help to tell the motorist that he is going the right way or where he has to turn. Information of that sort is always best printed away from the place concerned and led to it with an arrow. Do not put your notes so far away that the map reader might not notice them.

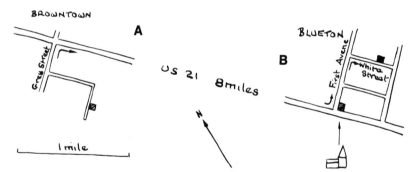

Fig. 10-2. *A sketch map of distant places may only need details at the ends.*

Provide an approximate scale. That obviously applies to the town details only. The distance between towns is taken care of by the note in the gap in the drawn highway. Add a north arrow. If you are a sufficiently good artist, you might use a simple sketch of a building or other mark your reader could use as a guide. All that is needed is the outline he will see in the distance.

The sketch map may be made with a ball point pen or pencil, but it helps to use some color. Arrows showing the route drawn in a second color will not be confused with map details. Pencil shading on a map may show parts that are built over. Do not get carried away with the artistic possibilities of your mapmaking. Remember, the object of the sketch map is to show someone how to get from one place to another. Additional information and elaborate coloring of nonessential details may only confuse.

Sketch maps may be needed for other purposes besides giving route instructions. Information may be needed on a plot of land that would not justify a proper measured survey. In addition, you may have to make the map from memory, but trying to visualize a piece of land that you think you know well can sometimes lead to errors. If at all possible, stand and view the land, then walk around it if you need more details. As with street maps, it is very easy to get relative directions some way out, so start with a few lightly drawn key lines, in what appear to be the right directions and proportions (FIG. 10-3A). You can then put in details over them and know that the general arrangement is right (FIG. 10-3B).

There is a temptation to work on details, perhaps starting in one corner and going off from that point with another detail. By doing this, you might find that you have "wandered" in the wrong relative direction when you get to the other side of the map, causing your map to be out of proportion. This is where the key lines are important. Certainly put in as much detail as you can *after* the main framework has been established. If it is to quite a large scale and you put in individual trees and other items that

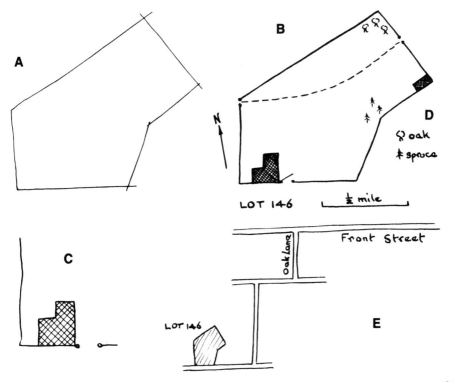

Fig. 10-3. *A sketch map or plan of a small area should be as accurate as possible (A,B,C,D) and may include an access map (E).*

would not be on most maps, you may have to add your own legend showing what symbols mean (FIG. 10-3D). Although it is freehand and approximate, add a scale and a north arrow. There should be a title, so anyone using your sketch map will have no doubt about the land it represents.

Suppose what you have drawn is a piece of land that others will want to visit. It would help if you can also provide a map showing access. That could be to quite a small scale if access is simple, although it would be better to a more accommodating scale if you need to show details of a more involved route. A simple map might be tucked into a corner of the large-scale map or drawn elsewhere on the same sheet (FIG. 10-3E).

ESTIMATION AIDS

Those who are not regularly concerned with measurements may have difficulty in getting proportions right on a freehand map. Of course, a rule can be used, but a quickly drawn map, when the need arises, is better done without mechanical aids. The ability to produce sketch maps in reasonable proportions is a worthwhile accomplishment. One aid to proportions is paper already marked with a pattern of squares, like that used for making graphs and scientific drawings. It does not matter much what the sizes of squares are. Usually every tenth line is darker, so you may have a pattern of 1 millimeter squares and a darker one every 1 centimeter. Usually the printing is in a light neutral shade, so ink or pencil will show over it.

For a map drawn on graph paper, decide that a certain number of large squares represent a mile; then get your map details in proportion to that. The squares also help you to keep north-south and east-west properly related. If you have difficulty in drawing straight freehand lines, the background lines will help you. A pad of squared paper on a stiff card backing is useful for field work.

If you need to discover moderate distances, you can pace them. It is worthwhile knowing what your average pace is. Walk a measured distance and count your paces. A proportion calculation may then give you a pace taken to many places of decimals, but convert that to the nearest round figure. Besides individual pace lengths, note how far you go in 100 paces or any other convenient figure. You may find it is useful to know how many paces you make to cover a distance that could be the basis for your mapping. For instance, 41 of your paces may cover 100 feet. That is a more useful piece of information than knowing that one pace is 29 inches.

There are a few artists' ideas that can help when making a sketch map. If you hold a pencil at arm's length, with its blunt end projecting about square to your view, you can compare lengths that come across your line of sight. For instance, you want to know how much longer one length of fence is than another (FIG. 10-4A). If you extend enough pencil to cover the short fence as you sight with one eye, you can swing across and see how many times the pencil goes into the view of the other fence. Of course, you must keep your arm extended the same amount and sight with only one eye. If you need to know a more exact length, you can pace across 100 feet, or whatever seems a reasonable amount, then mark it with posts. You can now sight how many times that goes into the total length (FIG. 10-4B).

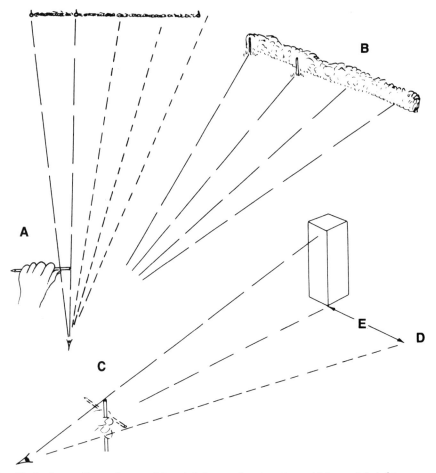

Fig. 10-4. *A pencil may be used for sighting and estimating widths and heights.*

If you need to make a fairly close estimate of the height of a building, adapt the pencil sighting method. Have an assistant move outwards from the building, square to your line of sight. Use the pencil to cover the building (FIG. 10-4C); then turn it horizontal. With your thumb at the foot of the building, get your assistant to move until you sight him at the end of the pencil (FIG. 10-4D). If you measure by pacing or other means from the building to where he is standing, that will be the same as the height of the building (FIG. 10-4E). If you cannot measure from vertically under the top you sighted, make allowance for how far out you had to start measuring on the ground.

Suppose you need to obtain the width across a river, a small canyon, or anything that cannot be paced directly. There is a simple geometric way of tackling this. Find something, such as a tree, that will serve as a landmark on the opposite side. Find a position where you can look squarely across at it and put a pole there (FIG. 10-5A). Walk squarely from this a certain number of paces and place another pole, then walk the same amount in the same direction again (FIG. 10-5B). If the total distance is about

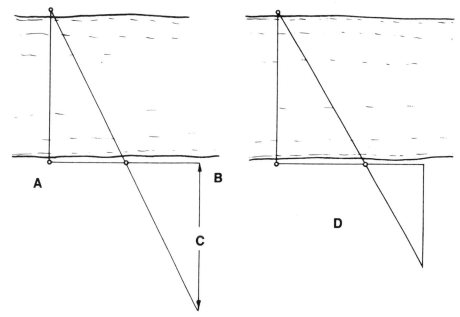

Fig. 10-5. *A distance that cannot be paced may be measured by relating similar triangles.*

the same as your estimate of the width you want to measure, that is about right. The exact number of paces each time is not important, so long as they are the same.

Turn squarely away from the river and walk until you can sight the intermediate pole with the tree. The distance you have walked is then the same as the distance from your first pole to the tree, assuming you walked straight and squarely (FIG. 10-5C). Obviously, there is a margin of error, but you can obtain quite a close estimate. Deduct the distances of the tree and pole from the river edge to get the river width.

If there is not much space to do this on the river bank, you can get a similar result by using proportional triangles instead of two of the same size. If you walked along the bank 20 paces to the intermediate pole and only 10 paces after that, when you walk from the bank and sight the intermediate pole, the distance will be half the width of the river (FIG. 10-5D). Other proportions could be used, but do not make the second triangle too small, as possible errors are magnified if this gets relatively much smaller.

LINE SURVEY

Suppose you want to make a map of reasonable accuracy of a path or trail. A freehand sketch may serve as a guide, but you would like to know the directions the winding path takes and the lengths of its parts, as well as the overall length. This could be part of the preparation of some new development or just to obtain sizes for paving materials or the lengths of fencing required.

Measuring may be sufficiently accurate by pacing, or you may actually go along the path with a tape measure. Even if you do not have a long marked tape measure it may be possible to measure a length of rope accurately and use that in stages along the path. If the rope is longer than the distance you want, it can be knotted, with the correct distance between knots, leaving some ends for handling.

Bearings along the path may be taken with a proper sighting compass, or you can get quite good results with the type having a rectangular base by sighting along an edge or across the central line. Have an assistant with a few straight poles. You could map as you go, but it may be better to use a notebook to list bearings and distances; then plot the whole thing later.

Place a stone or pole at the start. Get your assistant to hold a pole upright at the end of the first straight part of the path. Sight it and read its bearing. Pace or measure the distance to the pole and enter the details in your notebook (FIG. 10-6A). Go to that pole position and mark it with a stone. Stand over the stone and sight the pole held at the end of the next straight stretch (FIG. 10-6B). Note this bearing and distance. Continue in this way until you have covered the length of the path.

Plot your results to scale (FIG. 10-6C). You now have a map of straight lines between sighting points. Measure the width of the path at several places. The poles are probably located towards the outsides of bends. Allow for that and mark in the path widths at several points. There may have been parts of the path that were sufficiently straight for sighting, but actually had curves between points. The curves must be put in freehand, but you can complete the map of the path outline with a fair degree of accuracy (FIG. 10-6D).

You can provide a scale to this with a much greater degree of accuracy than with a freehand sketch map. It is a working map, intended to have a greater degree of permanence than a sketch map, so provide it with a north arrow. Draw a border that also encloses a title (FIG. 10-6E).

For the most attractive results, either do all the preliminary setting out lightly so the survey lines can be erased, or trace your first map, omitting the early constructional lines. If others need to consult your map, it is advisable to make prints or photocopies so you do not have to part with your original map.

ROADSIDE SURVEY

A further development of the line survey just described is a survey to produce a map of a road with some of the surrounding features. The road itself can be surveyed with the aid of a compass, in the same way, or by the method described in the next section.

The first task is mapping the road itself. You can measure by pacing, with a tape measure, or a marked rope, but if there are considerable distances to deal with, this could get tedious and may lead to errors. It may be that you have reasonably straight parts for up to 1/2 mile or even more. When you get to that sort of distance you may use a car and note tenths of a mile on the odometer. In any case, measurement of the overall distance by car would provide a check on the intermediate distances, which might include a few errors that build up to a total further out than would be acceptable. You will also have to provide some intermediate sighting positions that may come on a straight part of the road. The effect is to reduce distances between marks.

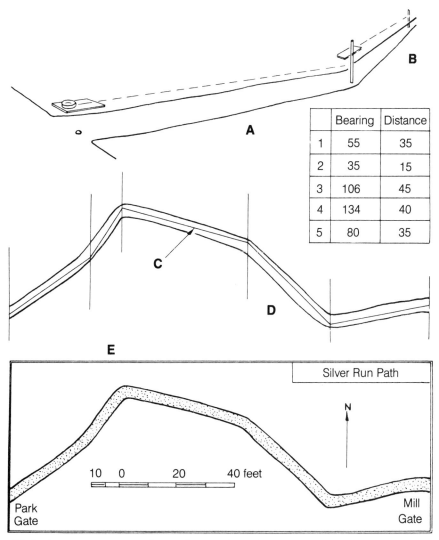

	Bearing	Distance
1	55	35
2	35	15
3	106	45
4	134	40
5	80	35

Fig. 10-6. *A compass survey of a road or trail can be converted to a map.*

A freehand sketch map may serve for preliminary planning. Bends in the road will be places where you change sights along the road. If there are landmarks away from the road, you need sighting positions along the road for them. If there are roadside houses, gates, and other features that you want to put on your map, allow for positioning them. There could be other roads or trails to include. Put all these things on your sketch map and check with this as you progress along the road (FIG. 10-7A). It may be possible to draw the final map as you progress, if you have a piece of paper on a board and use a protractor and rule to transfer every new angle or distance as you obtain them. Alternatively, use a notebook, as previously described, or enter angles and distances on your sketch map. Different colors help to reduce the risk of confusion.

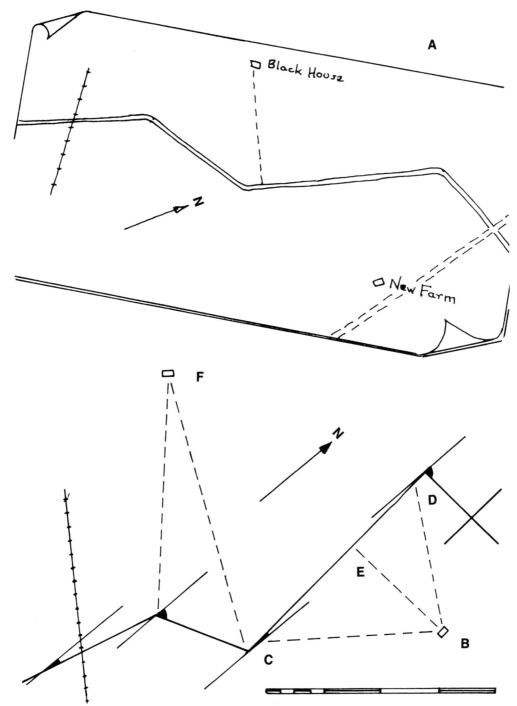

Fig. 10-7. *A sketch map shows what points to sight in a road survey.*

The locations of landmarks away from the road are found by triangulation. As a triangle cannot be distorted, any plotting that involves three angles, or one side of the triangle and two angles, or the lengths of three sides, must be a definite size and shape. In this sort of surveying, we mostly use a measured side of the triangle and the angles at each end of it to project sides to meet at the object being sighted.

As an example, there is a building that we want to put on the map, some distance from the road (FIG. 10-7B). Take a bearing on it, preferably when the angle to the road is about 45° (FIG. 10-7C). Measure a distance along the road until you can sight the building at about 45° the other way in relation to the road (FIG. 10-7D). Plot the sighting places to scale on your map and repeat the sight angles. Your lines give you the scale position of the building. It helps to confirm your result by taking a third bearing, preferably about midway between the other two, so it is about square to the baseline (FIG. 10-7E).

The exact angles are not important, but if you can make the sight lines cross somewhere near square, the crossing is more easily determined than if they cross acutely. Of course, circumstances may decide you have to accept acutely crossing lines. The way the road goes may mean you have to use sights not very different from each other. This could also happen if the building is partly hidden by trees. If sight lines cross acutely, the exact point to draw the building is not so obvious (FIG. 10-7F).

The road probably comes from further back than where you start to map it and goes on further than you want to cover. Determine some marked positions, if possible. Otherwise, establish your own marks, possibly with a pile of stones or a post driven into the verge. If you have to come back for another reading, there will be no doubt where the starting point was.

Start sighting and measuring along the road, in the same way as for the path survey, using an assistant to hold a pole at bends or where you want to take the next bearing (FIG. 10-8A). If you need a point for a landmark bearing along a straight road, it will probably be best to start a new road bearing from there (FIG. 10-8B), even if it is the same angle as the previous one.

Note landmark bearings, and continue along the road. You may have to include some bends before you sight the landmark again, but that does not matter—your sighting each time is related to a north-south line, not to the variations in the road (FIG. 10-8C). Providing you are certain of the locations of the sighting positions, meanderings of the road in between do not matter.

Positions of buildings, gates, signs, or anything else to note alongside the road can be measured and plotted on the map as you progress. If you want to mark the end of a path, track, or other junction with the road, without mapping its course far from the road, you can take a bearing of its angle as it leaves the road. Draw it in for just a short distance (FIG. 10-8D). A railroad crossing is usually easy because it will be straight, or very nearly so. You can take a bearing and draw it on the map (FIG. 10-8E).

If you come to a road crossing, you will have to decide how far you need to map the road in each direction. If it is straight and you can see it going off into the distance, it is simply a case of taking a bearing (FIG. 10-8F). If there are bends in it, and you

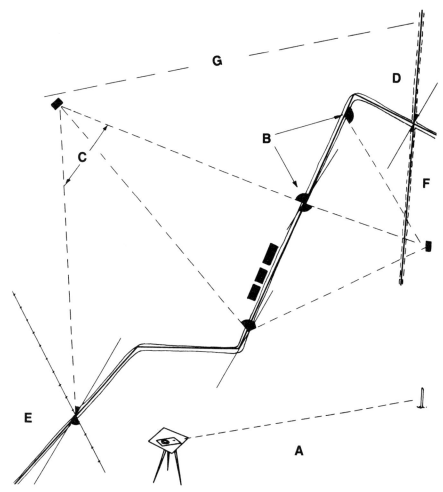

Fig. 10-8. *Bearings from the road, as well as along it, get the positions of all important points that have to be mapped.*

want to map it accurately, you will have to continue taking bearings and measuring in each direction before returning to the principal route.

It may be possible to provide a check from a side road. If you can see a landmark from it, you can take a bearing of it from a known position on the other road. If that does not come close to the first position, you will have to check further (FIG. 10-8G). You may be able to see things on one road from the other. If so, you can take a cross bearing. Any bearing you can take of one thing from another serves to check your previous working and confirm the accuracy of your mapping.

If you make a map with paper on a board as you take sights and measurements, it should be treated as a working copy. A finished map can be made from it, usually by tracing. A border will show the limits of your survey, and you can add the scale and north arrow in the margin.

PLANE TABLE ROAD SURVEY

It is possible to map a road, path, or any series of bearings by direct sighting over the paper that will form the working map. You need a sketch board, or *plane table*, large enough to take the paper that will make the map, and some means of supporting it level for sighting. In its simplest form, you have a piece of plywood nailed to a single post about 4 to 5 feet high (FIG. 10-9A). An assistant holds it upright while you sight. It would be better to have the board on a tripod (FIG. 10-9B). Three legs will stand without wobbling on any surface, and you can work without an assistant.

On this you need an *alidade*. This is a simple sighting aid. One may be bought, but you can make an equally satisfactory one. You need a piece of wood with a straight edge, at least as long as the longest line you will want to draw. The longer the strip is, the more accurate will be your sighting. The simplest sights are two nails driven into the edge and bent upwards (FIG. 10-9C). Rather better are a pair of sights cut from aluminum or tinplate (an old drink can, cut with scissors), bent and nailed on (FIG. 10-9D).

Draw a line across one end of the paper that will serve as the north-south direction of your map. If you know that you will be plotting a general direction that does

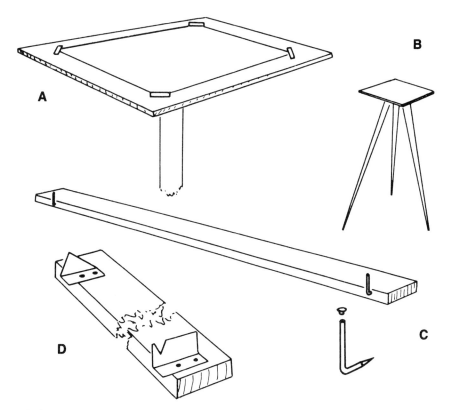

Fig. 10-9. *A plane table is a drawing board (A,B). The alidade to use with it is a straight-edge with sights (C,D).*

not suit having north that way, draw the line as needed. If there is no good reason to do otherwise, having north-south square to the paper is convenient. Attach the paper to the board with adhesive tape or pins.

At the start of your survey, position your board above the starting place and use a compass to set the north-south line true. Mark a starting dot on the paper. Push a pin upright into the dot. Bring the alidade up to the pin so it can pivot against it and sight along it to the post your assistant is holding at the next key position (FIG. 10-10A). When you are satisfied that the bearing is correct, pencil along the alidade from the pin. Measure along the ground and mark the scale distance along the line from the starting dot (FIG. 10-10B).

Move your board to the position you sighted, while your assistant takes his pole to the next position. Set the board so the north-south line agrees with the compass. Put the pin in the new sighting against the pin (FIG. 10-10C). Draw that line and measure along it the second scale distance (FIG. 10-10D). Continue in this way until you have mapped the road as far as you need.

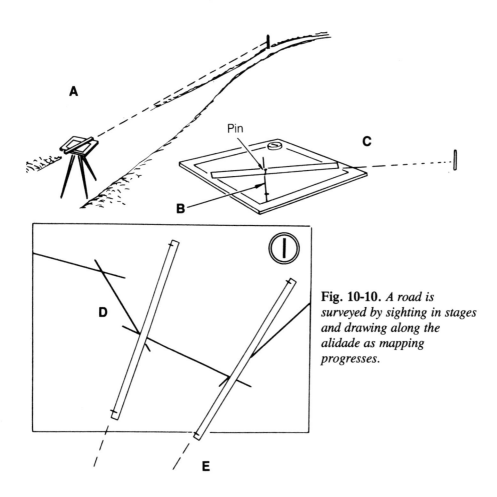

Fig. 10-10. *A road is surveyed by sighting in stages and drawing along the alidade as mapping progresses.*

Similar methods can be used if you want to locate a landmark away from the road. At a suitable point, you sight it with the alidade and draw a line. Later you take another similar sight from another point (FIG. 10-10E) to get the position of the landmark on your map. As with the compass sighting method, a third sighting can be used to confirm the other two.

TRAVERSES

As can be seen, producing a map by sighting with a compass or working on a plane table with an alidade achieves very similar results. In practice, there may be little to choose between the two methods. If you want to make a survey and keep a list of bearings and distances to apply to a map to be made later, a compass survey will be chosen. Using an alidade cuts out the need to read angles and transfer them later with a protractor.

A series of bearings that are linked may be called a *traverse*. The sights along a road or path are a traverse. They could happen in undeveloped country, where you need to map your progress from tree to tree, as you might when working around an unclimbable rock outcrop (FIG. 10-11A). If you do not do this as you go from tree to tree or other landmark, you may be uncertain of your position when you get to the other side of the obstruction (FIG. 10-11B). With clear ground ahead of you, you can set a course for your destination, because you are sure of your departure point. Such a traverse can be drawn on the map you are navigating with, if it is a large enough scale. Otherwise, you may have to make the traverse on a piece of paper, to any suitable scale, then find the bearing and distance of the far end from the start (FIG. 10-11C). Apply that, at the correct scale, to the map you are using as a guide (FIG. 10-11D).

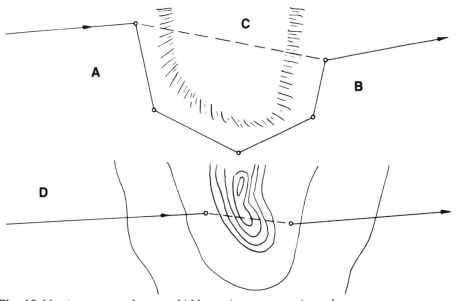

Fig. 10-11. *A route map between hidden points may require a detour survey.*

Sometimes a traverse is needed that brings you back to the starting point. That may be called a *closed traverse*. This could happen if you are laying out the course for a cross country race that will finish where it started. It might happen if you want to map an enclosed space, such as a plantation of trees enclosed by a fence. The fact that the shape you draw on the map should close gives you a check on the accuracy of your surveying. Perfection may be difficult to achieve, but you will have to decide what margin of error the particular project would accept.

You can use similar methods, whether you sight with a compass or an alidade. From the starting position, sight and record the direction of your first mark and measure its distance (FIG. 10-12A). Go to that mark and sight and record from there (FIG. 10-12B). If the fence is straight, the corners are the obvious sighting positions. If there

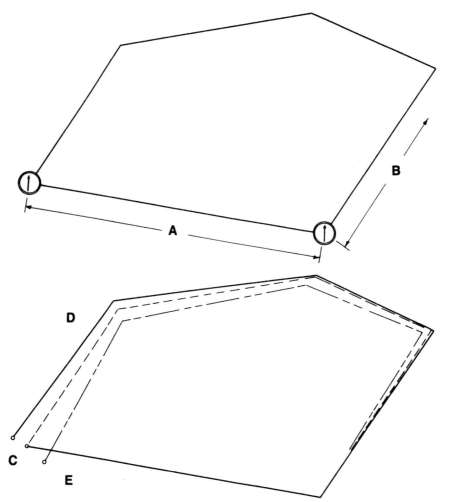

Fig. 10-12. *In a closed transit, survey bearings between points may not be sufficiently accurate to close exactly and have to be adjusted.*

are definite bends in the fence, you may have to use intermediate marks. You may need to put a pole in place temporarily for sighting. However, if you can see past a curve to a corner, a sight on that may be enough and you can estimate the amount of curve when you draw the map.

Work around the shape. It is very unlikely that your final position will fall exactly on your starting position (FIG. 10-12C). Check how far it is out. If it is only a small amount, you will have to alter the map to close it, but do not do that by only moving the last sight line. That would put all the error in that line, bringing it to a very different angle and length from what it was. You have to spread the error, so part of it is taken up in earlier sightings. If there is a gap where the closure should be, with the two positions in line, the fault is probably in the angles, rather than the lengths. Close in each of the earlier angles a little to get the shape right (FIG. 10-12D).

If the final sight line overlaps the first one, you may open each angle slightly (FIG. 10-12E). If the fault appears to be in distances, you can lengthen or shorten each slightly. There will probably have to be a slight modification of lengths and angles.

If the discrepancy at the end is more than you feel is acceptable, you will have to check your surveying again. It would help to go around the route the opposite way. Besides treating this as a new survey, you can compare compass directions, if you were using a compass and not an alidade. The readings should be reciprocals of the first, so each should be 180° more or less than previously. Errors may be more likely in distances, particularly if you are pacing over uneven ground. A reverse survey superimposed on the other survey may disclose one error that is the cause of the trouble.

Making a closed survey is good practice. It could be done on quite a small scale for training young people, where all the points are in view of the start and the instructor can watch for errors as poles or other markers are sighted and measured.

PLANE TABLE AREA SURVEY

Mapmaking depends on starting with a baseline of known length and the means of taking bearings from its ends. In important mapmaking, at national or international level, the methods of measuring and establishing the baseline are extremely advanced, and the degree of precision is such that amateur mapmakers might not comprehend it. Similarly, the instruments used for taking bearings work to such fine limits that they make the instruments we use seem very crude. It is with that sort of equipment that the maps on which we depend are produced.

In the earlier examples, we used a road or path as a sort of baseline from which to take bearings. Making a map of an enclosed area or one with a great many scattered landmarks, but without a road or path, means preparing a baseline from which to work. As an example, suppose there is a field with six sides and two gates that has to be mapped (FIG. 10-13A). The shape is such that the corners and gates can all be seen from near the middle of the field.

The first thing to do is establish a baseline near the center of the field. It does not have to be parallel with a side or in any special position related to north. How long it is depends on circumstances. It would be better not coming too close to any side or cor-

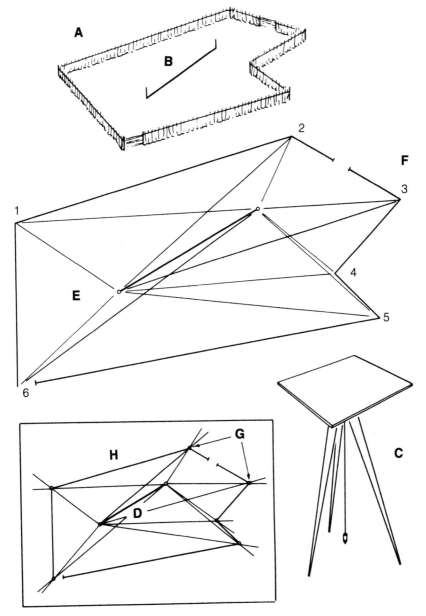

Fig. 10-13. *A plane table survey of a field is made from the ends of a line in the field, with crossing sight lines joined.*

ner, but a long line should produce greater accuracy than a short one, due to the greater spacing between sighting positions. If it is not more than half the distance across the field, that may be about right. If the field is a vast area, you may find something proportionately much less than that easier to lay out and measure. You do not actually have to draw a line in the field—all you need are accurate locations of its ends (FIG. 10-13B).

The final accuracy of the map depends on the accuracy of measuring between the markers at the ends of the line. For some purposes it may be accurate enough to pace the length of the line. For greater accuracy, you may use a pole of known length, turned over along the line, or you may measure with a tape measure. Put a peg in the ground at one end and a vertical pole at the other end. Later you will change them about, but be careful not to lose the marks.

You can make the survey with a plane table and an alidade only. There is no need for a compass in this method. Put your plane table over the peg at one end of the line. It helps to have a weighted line—a *plumb line*—hanging between the tripod legs for accurate centering (FIG. 10-13C). Take your first sight of the pole at the other end of the line and draw a line along the alidade right across the paper. On this line mark the scale length of the baseline (FIG. 10-13D). Put a pin in the end of the line that represents where the table is. Use this as a pivot for the alidade to sight corners, gates, and anything else that should be put on the map. Be careful not to alter the board and make sure you sight everything you want before moving (FIG. 10-13E). The lines you draw are best made longer than they will need to be and you should identify them. It may help to number them in accordance with figures put on a rough sketch map (FIG. 10-13F). Otherwise, you may find yourself using the lines incorrectly later.

Move your table on its tripod to the other end of the line and put the pole where the peg was at the first end. Your first job at the second end is to put the alidade over the baseline drawing of the map and sight back at the pole. Move the table until that line is correctly oriented in relation to the ground. With the accuracy of the baseline established, sight from that end all the positions you sighted before. This will give you a maze of lines, but if you use the numbers to identify them you can mark the crossings you need (FIG. 10-13G).

With all the positions marked, join them to get the outline of the field (FIG. 10-13H). If it is a fairly large field, sightings of smaller sizes, such as the width of a gate, may not be accurate or worthwhile. It is better then to only sight one end of the gate and either go there and measure the width or make an estimate of it.

The project here can be seen to be very similar to the traverse of the fence around a plantation of trees. Because of the trees, it would be impossible to use a central baseline. Traversing would have to be used. In the case of the open field, it would be possible to use either or both methods. If used together, one would make a check on the other. After the area survey with the plane table, one or more sides of the field could be measured and compared with the drawing. Similar bearings could be taken and compared. If a few checks confirm the first method, there may be no need to carry out a full traverse around the field.

COMPASS AREA SURVEY

Bearings taken with a compass, as described for the road survey, could have been used at the ends of the baseline in the field survey. Instead of actually making the map on a board over the two ends of the line, the line could be laid out with the aid of a compass. You know its bearing and can repeat it on the map you make, but which need not be there in the field. Instead, you keep a record of bearings, using the identification numbers on a sketch map, arranged in a separate table for each end of the line.

When you make the map, put north lines through each end of the drawn baseline. Use your protractor to mark the angles of the lines from your table (FIG. 10-14A). As before, do this from both ends of the baseline and identify the correct crossings to link up for the shape of the field (FIG. 10-14B).

That method of surveying is of more use for locating a large number of individual objects in an open area, where there are no roads or enclosing fences. As an example, suppose you want to know the positions of all oak trees scattered over a large area. You need to find somewhere reasonably central where you can see the trees. Ideally, this is higher ground.

At the chosen position, establish your baseline. Mark the ends and measure the length as accurately as possible, as for the previous method. If you have any choice of direction, try to position the ends of the line where you get the best view of the trees, without one hiding another. Take a bearing along the line from one marker to the

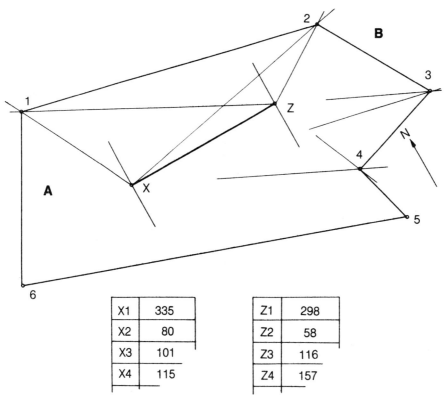

X1	335
X2	80
X3	101
X4	115

Z1	298
Z2	58
Z3	116
Z4	157

Fig. 10-14. *The field could be surveyed using compass bearings from the ends of the lines, listed and joined in the same way as in the alidade survey.*

other. Draw the scale line on the map on this same bearing and put north-south lines through the ends with a protractor. It does not matter what the bearing of the baseline is, or how acutely the north-south lines are to it. Let it come as it will for the best layout of the ground.

Make a rough sketch map as a guide to identifying the trees by letter or number (FIG. 10-15A). Prepare your notebook to list the bearings of the trees, either in a separate table for each end of the baseline, or in a combined list (FIG. 10-15B). Stand over each end of the line in turn and take bearings of all the trees in all directions.

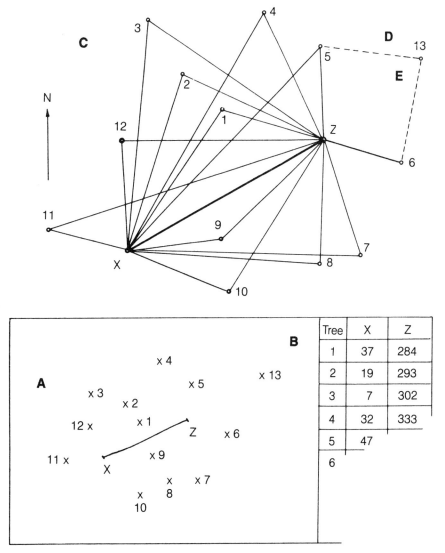

Tree	X	Z
1	37	284
2	19	293
3	7	302
4	32	333
5	47	
6		

Fig. 10-15. *Isolated points, such as trees, can be plotted by sighting from opposite ends of a baseline.*

At the map, repeat these bearings, using the protractor to get scale positions of the trees (FIG. 10-15C). A circle at each place will identify it.

Suppose there is no high ground to sight from, or even if there is, you cannot see all the individual trees from both ends of the baseline. You will have to get all the positions possible with the baseline in the best place. If there are only a few more trees to be positioned, one way is to get bearings of them from trees you have already plotted. Go to a tree and take a bearing of a new tree from it (FIG. 10-15D); then go to another located tree and take a bearing from there. The new tree should be in the position these lines cross on your map (FIG. 10-15E). If you can get a sight from a third tree, it will check both the accuracy of your first plotting and of these latest sights.

If there are many more trees to be located, it may be better to establish a second baseline. If most of the trees can be seen from one end of the original baseline, but not the other, you might take a new line from the first end, at any convenient angle. Measure it accurately to any useful length. It does not matter if it is longer or shorter than the first line. Note its bearing and length; then repeat this to scale on your map (FIG. 10-16A). If the opposite ends of the line are within view of each other, a sight across will provide a check bearing (FIG. 10-16B). If it is possible to measure the distance, that will provide a further check.

Use the new line in the same way as the first to get cross bearings on more trees. That may complete your survey. It may be that the only way to get the bearings of other trees is to use an independent baseline. The problem then is to know the location of the new line in relation to the old on the ground, and to draw it in the correct position on the map.

The first thing to do is to decide where the line must come to get satisfactory views of the remaining trees. This can be anywhere, except you need to be able to see one, or preferably both, ends from the two ends of the original baseline, if that is possible.

Decide where one end is to come and put a pole there. Take bearings of this from both ends of the first baseline and draw these on the map (FIG. 10-16C). You have the spot position. Lay out the line on the ground to the length you want and position another pole. Note the bearing of one pole from the other and repeat that on the map, with the length of the line marked (FIG. 10-16D). If the second pole is within view from the ends of the original baseline, take bearings from them or back to them. Try these on the map. As long as any error is very slight, you have confirmed the location of the second line in relation to the first and can go ahead sighting and plotting the positions of the remaining trees.

In an extensive survey, you may have to repeat similar actions many times. Having plotted all the information you can from one baseline, you establish another and work from that. Remember that any position has to be located by two or more bearings from known locations. This is triangulation, using the fact that a triangle with certain lengths of sides or corner angles can only be one size and shape. If you find you are depending on one bearing or on two bearings to different parts of an object, there is something wrong. Suppose you have bearings to the opposite ends of a short wall (FIG. 10-17A), either by compass or alidade. The direction of the wall could vary and still

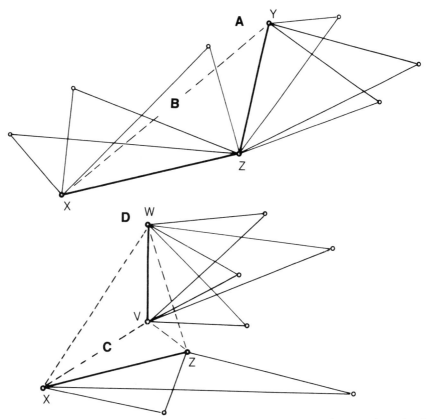

Fig. 10-16. *It may be necessary to use more than one baseline to sight everything that has to be mapped.*

give very close readings (FIG. 10-17B). You need triangulated bearings at both ends of it for accuracy (FIG. 10-17C).

Triangulating can be a building-up process. If you get all you need from one baseline, two objects you sighted can form the ends of another baseline for bearings further away (FIG. 10-17D). Two more might make the baseline in another direction. If it is possible to measure between the objects, that provides confirmation, but you may have to trust the positions found by the original sightings. Extensive surveys of quite large tracts of country are made in this way, but the greater accuracy of instruments makes for less risk of error when triangles build on to other triangles than can be expected when the same processes are done by amateurs with simple equipment.

ELEVATIONS

The methods described for getting horizontal measurements and layouts with reasonable accuracy, using simple and basic equipment, do not have counterparts when elevations have to be measured. There is no simple way of discovering elevations without more advanced instruments.

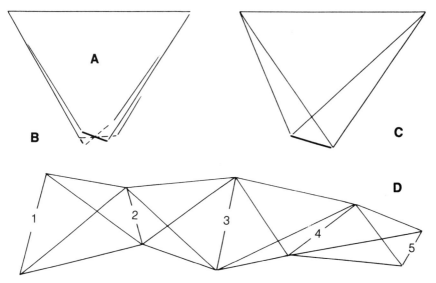

Fig. 10-17. *Sights are arranged to form triangles (A,B,C), and triangles may be built onto triangles in an extended survey (D).*

The basic instrument used is a *clinometer* that looks like a small telescope on a stand. It mounts on a tripod and is used to view a distant pole marked at the same height as the clinometer is above the ground. The clinometer has a leveling device. When you sight through it an object higher or lower than where you are, you can read the percentage of slope. If you know the distance you are viewing, there are tables that will tell you how much higher or lower the distant place is. In this way you can establish heights above or below your starting point. These can be marked as spots on your map. If you get enough of them, they give you elevations that can be joined to provide approximately correct contour lines.

Without a clinometer to allow you to measure elevations, you may have to leave your map without height indications, although if there are great differences in level it would be unsatisfactory to leave the map with no indication of this. You could use hatches around hills. If there is a definite shape to a hill, you might draw contour lines freehand around it to indicate its shape and the relative steepness of different parts. These could be without any attempt to indicate differences in elevation in feet, providing you put a note on the map saying that is the object.

If you have a published map of the area, even if it is to a very different scale and with not much of the information you have put on your map, it may be possible to extract some contour lines from it to put on your map. You might do this freehand through key points, but a more accurate way uses a grid on each map. Suppose you have drawn your map to a scale of 2 inches per mile, but the only other map that covers the area is at a scale of 1/2-inch per mile. It shows roads, but not the features drawn on your map, although there are some contour lines.

Pencil an outline of the area covered by your map on the small-scale map and divide this into a convenient pattern of squares (FIG. 10-18A). Your map scale is four times this size, so divide your map into similar squares in the same relative positions, but four times as large (FIG. 10-18B). Note where contour lines cross the small squares and mark proportionately where they cross the large squares on your map. Join these marks to produce contour lines on the larger scale (FIG. 10-18C).

You might go further and introduce some intermediate contour lines. If you examine the small-scale map, you can see the general pattern of the hill formation and interpret this. Extra lines put midway between the existing contour lines should come quite close to the heights they represent (FIG. 10-18D), although they have only been put there by estimation. At the larger scale they should be of value to users of the map. Include elevation numbers at every line for clarity on a large scale, and note somewhere on the map that the elevations are in feet, meters, or whatever you choose.

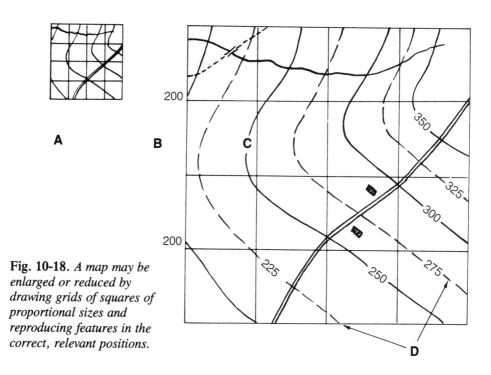

Fig. 10-18. *A map may be enlarged or reduced by drawing grids of squares of proportional sizes and reproducing features in the correct, relevant positions.*

ENLARGED RIVER MAP

Sometimes you need a map of just one feature on a larger scale than the map you have. It could be a map of roads that are to be followed in a bicycle race or time trial. It may be, as in this example, a river which you want to map with information added for canoeists. Maybe it is a special trip you are leading, and you want to give your party an idea of what to expect as they paddle down the river. You may be preparing a more permanent map for the use of canoeists at any time.

Suppose the map on which you have to originate your information shows the river, but does not give any details of it, except two road bridges and contour lines that indicate a moderate fall in river level in the distance between the bridges (FIG. 10-19A). Because you need access for a vehicle, you decide the two road bridges will mark the limits of your enlarged map. With a map measure, or by estimation, you find the distance along the river between the bridges is probably a little over 10 miles.

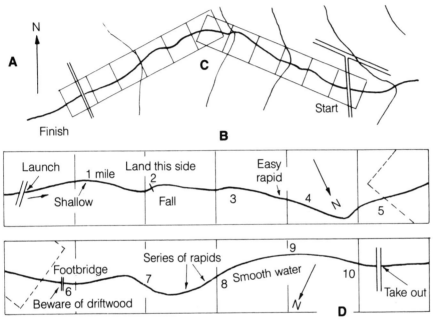

Fig. 10-19. *Strip maps can be enlarged using squares, then arranged in parallel sections.*

You have to decide next how much bigger the new map has to be for you to put on the canoeing information. In this case it could be 2$\frac{1}{2}$ times as big. The proportion could be anything convenient, providing you can draw squares or rectangles over the map and then draw them again to the correct proportion for the enlargement. Usually, a simple proportion and scale will do, but you may want to fit the enlarged map to a particular piece of paper or into the page of a notebook. It does not matter then if the enlarging figure includes an odd fraction, providing you also draw a scale long enough to be useful. If you are using an odd proportion, the map reader will not be able to take measurements with a rule.

You could merely enlarge the whole section of map, as in the previous example, but that would make a rather large sheet, which might not be convenient to handle in a canoe. It might be better to use strips (FIG. 10-19B). In this case two strips will enclose the river, but for a longer river or one with many twists, you may have to use more strips. Draw grids of squares or rectangles on the original map over the part of the river you want. Let them come as they will to enclose the river conveniently and arrange them to overlap slightly (FIG. 10-19C).

Draw two similar grids to the enlarged scale and mark on each where the other overlaps, using dotted lines. It is natural for us to read from left to right, so although the original map has the north direction across the river, we arrange the enlarged grids with the start at the left. They can now be read in sequence from left to right. You will probably want to have them in the same direction as the original map while you transfer the lines representing the river and the bridges. While this way around, mark the north directions (FIG. 10-19D), which are different on the two strips, due to moving them for convenience of layout.

Note where the river crosses the line on the small grid and transfer these points to the large grids. You can join them and get a fair representation of the course of the river. What else goes on may depend on what information you can find and how much you want to tell your readers. You may be able to discover features on the river from shore exploration, but for final details you will have to paddle down the river on a preliminary trip. As a result of either or both explorations, you can add all the notes you think necessary. Put in figures to show miles of progress. Where there are no landmarks it is often difficult to know where you are on a river, but the figures and compass will help.

PROFESSIONAL MAPMAKING

The methods of obtaining information from the land and converting it to a map, as described so far in this chapter, use simple and improvised equipment to produce a reasonable degree of accuracy that may be good enough for many purposes. Professionally produced maps have to be accurate to much finer limits, if they are to satisfy users with a great variety of needs. If the survey is to produce a map that will then be used as a base for making many other maps at different scales, accuracy is of first importance. Any errors will be repeated on the other maps.

The methods of surveying to get the information for these very accurate maps are basically similar to those already described. Very accurate measuring, coupled with triangulation, covers most of the work. Obviously, the measuring instruments for distances and angles are of sophisticated patterns unavailable to the amateur mapmaker.

For a survey of a large expanse of country, there have to be established points at a known distance apart. This distance may be many miles, but the imaginary line between them becomes the base for triangles establishing marking the ends of base lines and with angles measured with instruments capable of giving very fine readings. As can be seen, the techniques are really the same as in earlier examples, although the equipment is more advanced.

That takes care of horizontal surveying, but information is also needed on heights. That is obtained by measuring vertical angles with a theodolite, clinometer, or other instrument from similarly located marked positions—both on the ground and on the map. The elevation of the viewing position has to be obtained with great precision; then other heights recorded are calculated from that.

These actual positions on the ground are marked by metal tablets, called bench marks, or *horizontal* or *vertical control stations*. They are located in higher positions, because a surveyor wants to be able to see as much as possible of the surrounding terrain, as well as one or more similarly marked positions, probably at a considerable distance. The actual tablet is set in concrete or otherwise very permanently secured. It carries a cross in a circle, which is the actual datum from which measurements are taken. The words "U.S. Geological Survey" encircle the tablet and other information about the position is inscribed (FIG. 10-20A), including a warning of the penalty for disturbing the mark!

For anyone using a map, the situation of a bench mark is useful, as finding it gives you a spot check on your position. The locations are shown on Geological Survey Maps. The basic map mark is a triangle with a dot at its center, but other indications show the type of mark (FIG. 10-20B). Marks concerned with elevations only are crosses, with the cross size larger than that used for a spot elevation, which is not a survey mark.

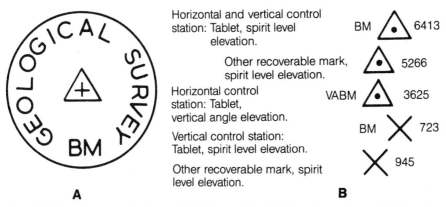

Fig. 10-20. *A survey point is marked with a tablet (A). Locations of spot heights of use to a map reader are marked (B).*

AERIAL PHOTOGRAPHS

Before man was able to fly, all mapmaking had to be done by surveys at ground level, but a map is really a reduced picture of a portion of the surface of the earth as seen from a considerable height. A view from a balloon, airplane, helicopter, or even a satellite, should look like a map. A photograph taken from a sufficient height should not be very different from a drawn map.

The value of aerial photographs was learned during World War I when the science of *photogrammetry*, or the making of maps from aerial photographs was born. As the science has developed, elaborate surveying cameras were created, taking photographs at set angles as well as vertically. With the aid of modern electronics and computers, the information can be brought together to provide mapping information quickly and accurately.

A map based on aerial photography is primarily *planmetric*, meaning it shows features as they are horizontally, but does not show relief in a form that can be measured. Modern methods allow a fairly good idea of relief, but there is still need for accurate surveying at ground level. In addition to its use in originating new maps, an aerial survey can confirm or revise the details on older maps. Such surveys are particularly useful for noting changes in maps. If there has been extensive tree felling or new roads have been made, aerial survey can confirm the alterations noted on a ground survey, or even take its place when details of alterations are needed quickly.

Aerial photography is increasingly used, and many maps have indications in the margin that some parts have been revised by aerial survey. Normally, maps made as the result of aerial survey are completed with the usual symbols, but there are published maps which are formed by the overlapping actual photographs. A map needed urgently for military purposes might be made in this way. With modern methods of photography and printing, the details are clear and the scale quite accurate.

Aerial photographs may be taken so overlapping photographs give a *stereoscopic effect*. With a suitable aid, a picture may be seen to stand out, and a better idea of what is photographed from the air can be obtained. The simplest aid is a stereoscope, consisting of two lenses spaced to suit the eyes and supported on legs, which rest over the photograph.

11

Special Maps

ALL MAPS ARE SPECIAL IN SOME WAY. ROAD MAPS DISCARD SOME information irrelevant to motorists and gives prominence to features that are important to them, or which the compilers of the map want to draw to their attention. Topographic maps of country without roads are obviously of more use to walkers, horse riders, and canoeists, so the information provided is what they may expect to want. Even a general purpose map, which has no particular emphasis, is special in that it is intended to provide a balanced picture of the features of that part of the earth's surface, without emphasizing the needs of any particular users.

Most of the specialized American maps have their origins in the maps of the National Geological Survey or of a state or other more local survey. It is unlikely that the special maps will have started from their own survey, although some of small areas could, particularly if it is a new development with the required details not already available at a sufficiently large scale. Special maps may carry an acknowledgment in the margin to the source of the base map and the date of its survey, which may be important in assessing its accuracy. The new map may show additions and alterations to it at a later date, possibly in the future if it is a project planning map.

A special map may be based on an existing map to the extent of extracting what information is relevant, discarding other details, and drawing in the specialized features for which the map is to be used. Maps to be produced in large numbers may be prepared in that way, with a new independent production, but sometimes a special map is needed as a discussion document or for use for a limited period by a small number of people.

BASE MAPS

There are base maps available of many scales and forms, which are intended to be drawn over. The map is usually drawn in black on white paper, usually with thin lines and no heavy markings so the special features can be drawn in. They will be prominent and not have to compete for attention with details already heavily printed (and possibly not wanted) for the particular use of the new map.

Some of these base maps are very local and may be used in connection with legal documents concerning the transfer of land or the erection of new buildings. The intended changes can be drawn in with a contrasting color, with written annotations. The location is immediately obvious from the already printed details of streets. Such maps may be produced at state, county, municipal, and regional levels. Other maps may have much wider coverage, but they are drawn to provide backgrounds to special features to be added. For instance, there could be a regional map prepared by the Boy Scout Association showing the location of troops, campgrounds, offices, and any other information of use to its members. A trade organization may show the locations of factories and member offices, possibly with symbols indicating their status, number of employees, or anything else appropriate. In both cases, it might be just a one-off map on the wall at the center of administration, with handwritten alterations to keep it up-to-date. Base maps probably have most use in this way, but they could be the first step in a more ambitious project of a separately printed production of large numbers, for general sale or for distribution to members of an organization.

The availability of base maps is not always widely advertised. Such maps are usually cheap, because there is no multicolor printing. They could be of use to individual map enthusiasts, who want to have their own map showing special interests or features discovered while exploring an area. You can draw on bearings of frequently used routes or any other landmark or other feature peculiar to your own needs. You may even name isolated trees or rocks. If an organization regularly uses an area, such maps become something special to members. Base maps can form the background to orienteering maps. Any of the civic authorities concerned with planning at various levels should be able to tell you how to obtain base maps at various scales, if they are available for the area you want.

POLITICAL AND PHYSICAL MAPS

Maps on small scales of large areas cannot show much detail. If there is an attempt to show much, the map becomes confused and difficult to read. Quite often the user does not want to know about everything that has been illustrated, so he gets frustrated. If he wants to know about boundaries of states or countries and the locations of principal cities, contour lines and other indications of physical features would be regarded as irrelevant and a nuisance.

In small-scale maps, it is these divisions that are most often seen. A map is *political* if it shows boundaries, cities, and not much else. Colors are often used, so a selection of a few colors allows adjoining states or countries to have different colors and their outlines become very obvious. In black and white, the borders may be less obvious, but without the confusion of other lines they are still quite clear (FIG. 11-1A).

If the map user is more interested in ranges of mountains, the extents of plains, and other features, and he only wants to find names of important cities and borders as locating guides, the map of the same area becomes very different (FIG. 11-1B). It is called a *physical map*. In atlases, political and physical maps may be printed on opposite pages for easy reference.

A physical map on a small scale can only have contour lines at very wide differences in elevation, but if the spaces between lines are layered with colors, a good picture of the rising and falling of the land over a large area can be seen immediately. If only black and white are used, it is not so easy to see differences, but as lines get closer with steepness, mountains are easily separated from plains.

On a physical map, borders and towns are printed lighter than on a political map. Rivers are more relevant to the physical map, yet only the largest would be on a political map. Roads and railroads may not appear on a very small-scale map, but the more important through routes could be on the political map, yet only on the physical map if they showed the use of passes or some other features connected with physical features.

Globes are obtainable with these differences. Besides the general purpose globes, there are others which give prominence to national boundaries with the use of colors. Other globes are arranged to give prominence to physical features. This also applies to maps of the world. Most are arranged with the use of colors to show national boundaries. Others show physical features, but then only great differences in elevation can be shown. Some of these maps rely on hatching and color shading to indicate mountain ranges, almost pictorially and without very great precision.

AERONAUTICAL CHARTS

With the comparatively fast development of flying has come a need for maps to be used by airplane navigators. These are akin to the charts used for navigation at sea, and it is usual to refer to *aeronautical charts* rather than maps. Early flying altitude was fairly low, and the navigator could refer to things he could see on the ground to get his directions from them. Of course, this is possible with light airplanes, and some navigation is still done by identifying landmarks while flying over them.

The first aeronautical chart was published in the United States in 1927, as a strip covering the air route from Kansas City to Moline, Illinois, but after a few years aeronautical charts became more general. Such charts are basically land maps. Contour lines do not mean much to a flier and hills may be shown shaded, although some spot heights are given. Landing strip and airport details carry information on beacons and lights. Flying by using visual contact is called *contact flying*, and a series of sectional charts covering the whole country by employing this method is available.

As radio navigation aids, air traffic control, plus higher speeds and higher altitudes, and the increasing reliance on instruments developed, there has come a need for charts to provide for these things, with only slight regard for contact flying by those operating suitable airplanes. Special charts are published for *instrument flying*.

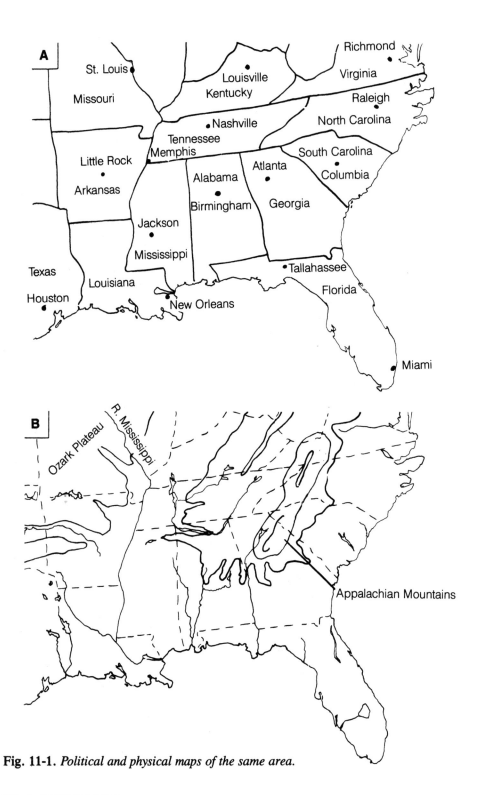

Fig. 11-1. *Political and physical maps of the same area.*

There are radio facility charts, some high-altitude navigation charts with details of instrument procedures, terminal arrivals, and other information important to those handling fast, high-flying airplanes. It is important that only up-to-date information is used, and new charts or revisions are published as frequently as every 56 days.

Even for contact flying there is a need to keep up to date. A motorist who finds a fault in his map may be inconvenienced, but is unlikely to be in danger. A flier using an out-of-date chart could be in serious trouble if facilities he expected were altered or nonexistent. Visual aeronautical charts are not issued quite as frequently as those for instrument navigation, but there is a program of revisions, and a flier of even a small airplane needs to keep his charts up to date.

Ordinary features on the ground, unconnected with flying, do not change much, as can be seen by the very long intervals between revisions and new issues of map sheets. Most features on discarded aeronautical charts are still correct. This means that for the ground-based user of maps for motoring, walking, or exploring, canceled aeronautical charts have value and may be obtained free or very cheaply.

Purple is a color that seems characteristic of aeronautical charts. It is used prominently to border exclusion zones and other limits that have to be drawn to the attention of aerial navigators, who may have to check their positions and progress with only brief reference to their charts.

For flights worldwide, aeronautical charts have much in common with charts used at sea. For long distances, the chart projections have to allow for great circle routes. Navigation may be entirely by instrument with the aid of computers with the course being maintained automatically. The crew spend much of their time as reserves in case of failure of the automatic systems. With radio contact to ground stations, much control can be done elsewhere, but in the ultimate situation, the navigator in the airplane has to understand how to interpret his charts.

RECREATIONAL MAPS

There are a great many national parks, state parks, and other recreational areas, which would not be of much value to visitors if there were no maps to be used with them. Geological survey maps may cover these areas, but there are usually many features of particular interest to visitors that are not shown on them. Fortunately, in all cases where a special map would be of value, there is one. It may only be a rather sketchy pictorial map, without the accuracy of a proper topographical map, but it is intended as a general guide to the majority of visitors, who only want to know the location of view points, marked trails, lakes, and concessions. In that case, the more serious explorer will also want the appropriate large-scale geological survey sheets as well.

The National Parks Service issues visitor leaflets, which consist mainly of a map with additional information. These cover parks, monuments, and historic sites under their control and are available at visitor centers. The map is in a simplified form and its scale varies according to the size of the area it has to cover and the amount of detail that has to be shown. A comparatively small national monument may be shown to a fairly large scale, with 1 mile covering several inches on the map. An extensive park, like Yellowstone, must be at a scale of many miles to 1 inch to get the map on a reasonable size of paper. This affects the amount of detail that can be shown, but there is a uniform pattern used for national park visitor maps.

The standard symbols have been described in chapter 2; they are black and white. There is a general overall green or brown pattern on the map. Green is a characteristic of national park maps, but the shades of color used vary. In the case of a place with little variation in elevation, there may be different shades of green to draw attention to particular areas, with the actual monument or park in a light shade. If there is anything special about the immediately surrounding area, that may be darker. The further area is even darker, but all of the shades allow black print and black or blue lines for streams to be prominent. The roads and trails could be white, if they are not drawn red or black.

If the park is large and contains many hills and valleys, the visitor maps are not given contours, presumably because it is expected that most visitors would not know how to interpret them. Instead, the basic light green has darker green shading added to indicate hills and differences in levels. The shading is arranged as it would be when the sun is low to the west or north of west. This is supplemented by spot heights. Roads and trails on the map of a large park are red. Creeks and streams are blue, but two shades of blue are used if boating is permitted on some water and not others. A dark blue is used where boating is prohibited or restricted, while a light blue shows water where boats can be used.

For anyone with the experience of using geological survey maps, the visitor maps may seem oversimplified, but they contain the information known to be needed by the majority of visitors (FIG. 11-2). If you want to go away from the usual visitor routes within a large park, other maps are advisable. Beside the geological survey map, there may be special maps produced for the area, sometimes with special interests in mind, like natural history or geology. The maps can be purchased at the visitor center. Anyone intending to do more than just visit the standard tourist attractions should spend some time discovering what other maps are available.

A trip with map and compass in a national park would be good practice for anyone new to mapping. With the guidance and backup of park services you always have help and security available.

Much of what has been said about national parks is applicable to state parks, which are usually smaller; moreover, detailed maps may not be available. Sometimes the only map is merely diagrammatic, showing such things as picnic areas and roads. Much depends on the state, as some offer more lavish maps and leaflets than others.

State maps show locations of parks, usually with a marginal list giving details. There are national and regional National Park Service maps showing locations of parks and other properties they control.

FOREST MAPS

The U.S. Department of Agriculture, Forest Service, controls many forests. Many of them allow access to visitors, who need maps of the parts available to them. For their

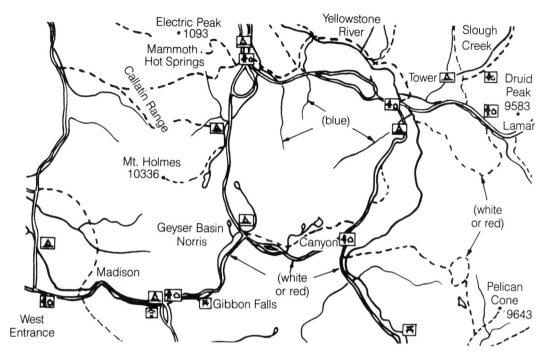

Fig. 11-2. *Part of a National Parks map.*

own use in administration, development, and protection, the Forest Service has a primary base series map of each forest to a scale of 1:24,000. All other maps for the particular forest are derived from this. Some of the maps are for their own work and development use, but others are intended for visitors. Simplest are visitors guides, which are intended to show points of interest, recreational facilities, parking, and other information needed by the visitor not intending to go off marked areas.

Forest visitor maps are available, covering entire forests or other geographical areas at a scale of 1:126,720, which is about 2 miles per inch. Most of the symbols used are the same as on geological survey maps, except that some special markings may be needed for features in particular forests. A comprehensive legend is provided. Color may be used to indicate ownership, where parts of the forest may be privately owned or worked by commercial concerns.

In addition to these maps there are others for wilderness and specially designated areas that come within the national forest boundaries. These are probably of particular value to anyone who wants to go into undeveloped country with map and compass. The forest visitor guides are issued free to the public, but there is a charge for other maps. Forest Service national and regional offices can provide information on the availability and cost of maps covering forests.

A small-scale map of the United States shows the location of areas covered by the Forest Service, with an indication of land besides forest, and the location of national and regional headquarters (FIG. 11-3). This is an example of a map shorn of all but the

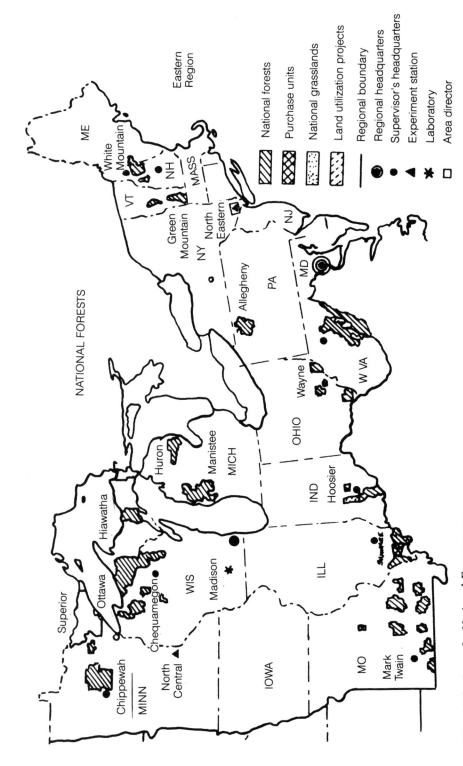

Fig. 11-3. *Part of a National Forests map.*

details needed to provide an index and not intended to take the place of more detailed maps of more local areas.

HISTORIC MAPS

Maps can bring history to life. Anyone studying history soon finds a need to know the locations of places and events. Only a map can give a reliable picture. There are various kinds of historic maps, with some merely picturing places as they were and others relating the older places to modern layouts.

When looking at early maps, or prints of them, notice how early cartographers dealt with the problem of showing features diagrammatically. Some maps are covered with pictorial representations that give general arrangements with little precision. There was also the tendency to go off into fantasy when the mapmakers ran out of facts.

Much early mapmaking of new territory was done by explorers who first had to go there by sea. Many early seafaring navigators had considerable skill in finding their way across oceans, and many of them made a fairly accurate survey of coasts they reached. This information was needed for the safe navigation of their ships and was obviously important to them. When they went inland, their surveying was often not as exact. Maybe they did not have the skills needed for land surveying, or they did not regard inland details as very important, compared with the coast. Because of this, we find many old maps show coastlines not very different from modern maps, but inland, we are uncertain what information to trust.

Other maps of past times are modern products, using current knowledge of mapmaking, but showing details as they may have been during a certain period. Common maps of this type show lands of the Bible, and often bound into Bibles. Our knowledge of those lands about 2000 years ago is fairly extensive. Scholars can identify places, and they can be drawn on a map with a reasonable certainty that they were as shown. Of course, if there are ruins or other remains, location can be positive. Borders between countries may be estimated. In the period being mapped, there were probably no exact borders and certainly no check points as we know them today. Maps can be made to show the land and water concerned with particular events in the Bible stories, such as St. Paul's voyages (FIG. 11-4A). The map may just show details as they were then, or positions of modern places and borders may be superimposed. To avoid confusion, there could be a modern map on the same scale (FIG. 11-4B). A second map on transparent film or tracing paper may be put over the first, for the better relation of new and old places.

The Romans were the great explorers and colonizers of Europe in the centuries before and after the birth of Christ. They built towns and roads where there were none before. Enough evidence of their activities can be found for maps to be made showing fairly accurately the countries in Roman times. Many of their streets and ways have been followed by modern roads; the Roman names are used. This also applies to some modern towns, which owe their foundations to Roman occupation.

As with Biblical maps it is helpful to have a modern map of the area for comparison, preferably to the same scale, especially if you are trying to follow the history of

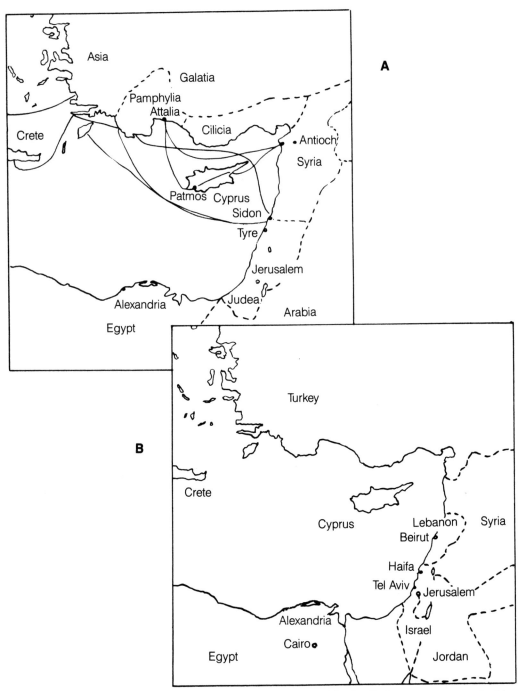

Fig. 11-4. *A map of the Eastern Mediterranean in the days of St. Paul's journeys compared with a modern map.*

your family. There are churches and other buildings that trace their foundations back one thousand years and records going that far back may be found.

In Europe, and particularly Britain, there are visitors maps usually available for many historic sites, very similar to those for national monuments in the U.S., but the period of time portrayed is infinitely greater.

MODERN HISTORIC MAPS

The history enthusiast wants many maps of things as they were, but most map users, with lesser interest in history, are more concerned with relating history to the country as it is. They prefer a map to show them the point on a roadside or elsewhere that something historic happened. They prefer to know, on the land they identify, the situation of a particular happening, rather than study a map of the country as it was when the event took place.

In America, there are maps of the earliest days of settlement, spreading from the east coast to follow the pioneers as they progressed west. At first, our forefathers were more concerned with getting where they were going safely than with accurate surveys, so some early maps are not much more than sketches. As the country became more settled, maps became more accurate. These maps are interesting studies, particularly of areas you know as they now exist.

In areas where major historic events of national significance have not taken place, there may be no maps showing the location of places that figured in the affairs of the area in earlier days. If there is a local history society, they may use a base map and plot on it the situations of places they locate. If there is no society, an interested amateur historian may do this. Local archives may yield information and some local detective work will help to find positions, even if no actual evidence still exists there.

For the affairs of greater importance to the nation, there are maps already published. Where there are national monuments or historic sites, there are National Parks Service maps of the usual type. In places like Gettysburg, where history is the dominant tourist interest, maps and guide books proliferate.

Besides officially published maps, there are others offered commercially and some intended to promote particular interests. Anyone with a more serious interest in maps should usually visit an official information center first. There it should be possible to obtain a map of the area which gives a fair representation of the essential details. The map maintains a certain scale without undue emphasis on features that someone wants to bring to your attention. Having gotten that map, pick up any others that are available, but check their information against your first map. In some places, maps that are primarily advertising may be far from accurate in some details. It is always good policy to check official sources first and work from there.

For wider coverage, such as attempts to follow early trails going west, some modern maps show the locations of historic markers and indicate where modern roads follow the lines of the old trails. If you want more detail, you may have to conduct your own research, both generally and along the way in local archives. There are maps which show the general areas used by particular Indian tribes. Because they were nomadic and rarely built settlements, it is difficult to prepare maps of their very early days in the same way as in Europe where most people settled in their own areas.

There is history everywhere; the land you are standing on has been there for thousands of years. Something must have happened. Anyone carrying out local research needs a base map to mark on if one is available. If not, it is probably better to have a sheet of tracing paper to put over a general map, with some key points marked, so you will put it back in the same place each time. Then you can note your discoveries on the tracing paper and relate them to the map as it is today. You may find it best to have a general map of an area for plotting things away from towns. If you expect to find locations in an urban area, it is better to have a street plan to a larger scale, even if you have to draw it yourself.

When mapping in this way, it is best to keep details in a list away from the map. You might get confused later. It is better to use small circles with numbers in them or near them, with a reference list elsewhere (FIG. 11-5). You may find you want to mark each of a row of past stores and shops close together. With this method there should be enough space for neat marking.

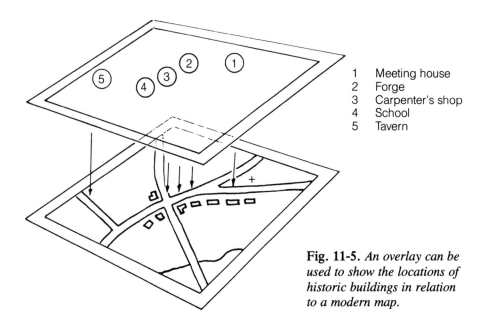

1 Meeting house
2 Forge
3 Carpenter's shop
4 School
5 Tavern

Fig. 11-5. *An overlay can be used to show the locations of historic buildings in relation to a modern map.*

MILITARY MAPS

Of course, a military map has much in common with a map of the same area intended for civilian use. Many of the symbols in general use are the same—roads, railroads, boundaries, and waterways are usually indicated in the same way. Maps normally carry a full legend—there is no assumption that the user has obtained a knowledge of symbols from some other source. Scales show miles, kilometers, and nautical miles—the last because of their use by airplane navigators. (A nautical mile is longer than a statute mile (FIG. 11-6A and appendix B).

An obvious difference, at first glance, is the use of a grid drawn over the map. The grid is not just marked at the borders, so the user needs to put a straight edge across. The squares are there already, and a grid reference is easily obtained (FIG. 11-6B).

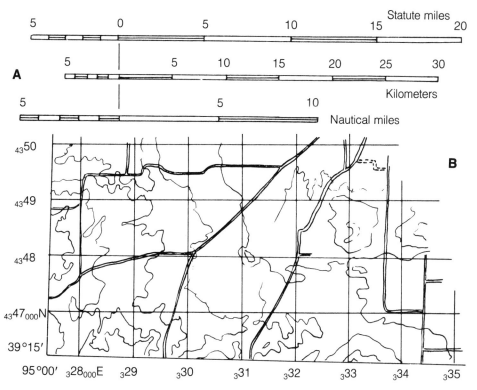

Fig. 11-6. *Comparative scales and numbered grid lines are used on military maps.*

Elevations may be more important to a military user. Contour lines are usually at closer intervals than on many comparable civilian maps. For instance, on a map of 1:250,000 scale (about 6 miles per inch) contour intervals may be at 60 meters for the main contour lines, with supplementary contours 30 meters. Comparable elevation intervals are, in feet, 200 feet and 100 feet for the same in horizontal scale.

The effect of this on the appearance of the map is to give a good picture of the shape of the terrain from the contour lines, where there are great differences in elevation on the area covered by the map. This is further emphasized by the use of tints. There could not be a different tint in every contour gap, but four yellow-brown tints are used to show differences of heights in wide bands of contours, such as 300/1525/

2135/3355 meters or 1000/5000/7000/11000 feet. This has the effect of drawing attention to greater differences in elevation, but contour lines will have to be observed for differences within the bands.

Shading is also applied to steeper slopes to further emphasize them and give the effect produced when the sun is shining low from the west. Where a map is intended for the use of air as well as ground navigators, items of particular interest from the air are shown in purple. These include the various kinds of landing areas, from large air-fields to heliports, with attention drawn to obstructions of various sorts and power lines.

The standard tactical map of the United States Army is at 1:50,000 scale. This can show considerable detail, including individual houses as black dots. Other maps at 1:25,000 (1 centimeter represents 250 meters) and 1:12,500, are used to give a better representation of actual shapes. Roads may be closer to scale widths.

LAND-USE MAPS

Maps are needed to show how the land is used, what crops are grown, what the characteristics of the soil are, where there are minerals, and other information of value to those concerned with the administration of land potential. These may be maps produced locally by developers. They could be wall maps kept up to date by the operators of extensive farmland to show the use being made of certain areas at the time. Details will be altered by hand, as needed.

The maps may cover larger areas, up to maps of the whole country to show the main uses of land in various parts. If the maps deal with minerals, they could range from a map produced by one mining operation to show progress, to countrywide maps showing the whereabouts of known minerals.

Another use of a mineral map comes when a claim is staked and it is necessary to define its legal limits (FIG. 11-7). The map is then more of a plan showing surveyed straight lines of marked length, with their bearings between staked points. Only sufficient natural or other features are given as are necessary to locate the claim. The map is accompanied by notes that may give details of other features, which are omitted in the map or plan if they would confuse survey details.

Soil surveys are scientific documents that give general descriptions of the soil, agricultural and climatic considerations, and background information. They are interpreted for farming and forestry, engineering, and community planning. The reports are accompanied by maps of each area to a large scale on a photomosaic base, showing the parts of the terrain referred to in the survey and soil classifications.

Local maps are best drawn on a suitable base map, if available, or on a tracing paper overlay on a standard map. If colors are used, it is easy to distinguish different crops, pasture, and livestock. A tracing of a part of a large-scale map could be used to draw on a proposed new development, buildings, or a change of use of the land. Prints of the tracing could be colored. This would make a good discussion document between interested parties, even if some users are not accustomed to map reading (FIG. 11-8).

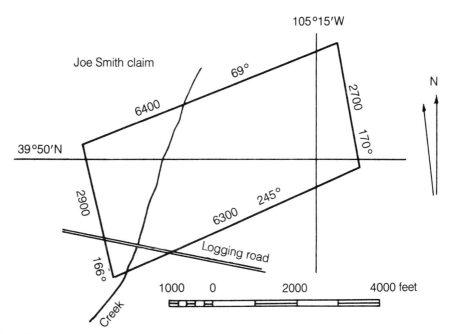

Fig. 11-7. *A map of a mining claim shows the outline and enough other information for locating it.*

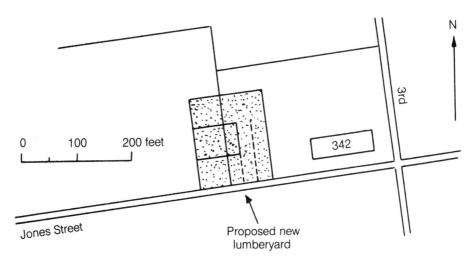

Fig. 11-8. *A simple plan can show intended alterations.*

Anyone with land under cultivation, and who is practicing crop rotation, may make annual maps to show what use is being made of different parts of his land. A small community may be glad of a local map showing the boundaries between land of different owners, with details of what use they make of the land.

At the other extreme, national maps are published to show in a general way what use is being made of the land. Such maps have educational uses in letting the reader see immediately where there are mainly cattle ranges, wheatlands, vineyards, and other less usual crops.

CENSUS MAPS

The distribution of population is important to administrators, those who set up industries, and even to those with only a general touring interest. Areas with a high density of population are mostly industrial, while the thinly populated areas are mostly rural.

Many touring maps give some idea of population by indicating the sizes of towns, either by different symbols or by the sizes of lettering used for names, according to the population bands of the communities (see chapter 2). This is somewhat of a guide, but other population maps give a better guide to the overall distribution of people.

As a result of national censuses, it is possible to extract much information besides just total numbers of people and where they live. One map produced shows the country, or part of it, as if viewed from a satellite at night, with people lit up in white against a dark background. Urbanized areas are then all white, and the extent of the area each covers is given its approximate shape. Outside this, the population density is shown with dots of different size and pattern, ranging down to places in urbanized areas with 25,000 to 50,000 population and dots representing each 500 of the remaining population in rural areas.

The effect is to give an immediate picture of the spread of people by the greater masses of white, indicating big cities, to scattered smaller dots, and even some unmarked places where very few people live.

Other maps produced by the Bureau of Census give the breakdown of such ethnic minorities as Chinese, Japanese, and those of Spanish origin in each county. Other maps show information concerned with housing.

RAISED MAPS

Three-dimensional maps have some uses. If a map can be displayed flat on a table, it may have the surface raised according to the contour lines. It is easy to understand by those with little experience. If it is colored to indicate features of the land it represents, it gives an immediate picture to the viewer, who can go out and see the same thing full size. This sort of map has obvious uses in a visitor center or anywhere that people have to learn about new surroundings, such as a campground or recreation center. It is difficult to construct and may be heavy, but the intended use may justify these disadvantages (FIG. 11-9).

Another use of a raised map is to enable blind persons to learn about a locality. In that case, roads are raised ridges, and other features have their own systems of dots. Names can be provided in Braille. In addition to a general map, there can be a plan to a much larger scale, with raised houses and other features in their actual shapes, plus Braille names and other details.

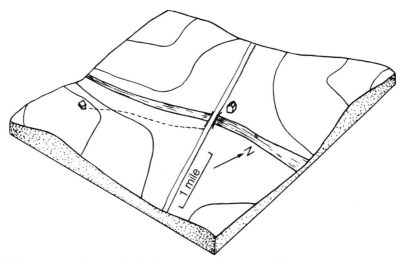

Fig. 11-9. *A map with raised relief gives a good picture of the terrain.*

WORLDWIDE SPECIAL MAPS

The maps described so far have been concerned with our own country or a small group of countries, but we are all part of one world, and there are many things happening in one country that affect others. We cannot isolate ourselves from the rest of the world when we consider such things as climate and communications. With better communications, individual communities, countries and even continents cannot behave as though they need only bother about their own affairs, as seemed possible less than a century ago.

Maps concerned with the whole world can be produced in many ways. The choice of projection depends to a certain extent on what is to be portrayed. If the map is to show such things as agriculture or who lives where, the rectangular Mercator projection, with meridians of longitude all vertical and square to the lines of latitude, probably gives the clearest picture. If the map has to show climatic movements or other movements about the world, the distortion due to that projection may interfere with the accuracy of what is shown. Then it is better to use one of the curved projections, usually one where the outline is elliptical, or a rectangle cut off one. The lines then show longitude curved and converging at the pole.

With the land mass distribution as it is, the most convenient way to present the world map puts Africa near the center, with Europe to the north. This section is square to the viewer. America lies to the west and China and Australia to the east, following the curved contours. In this way, the most distorted parts of the map are in the Pacific Ocean, away from the greater land masses. Similarly, it is usually convenient to cut off the areas north and south of the main land masses and ignore the polar regions. An example shows the main migrations since the seventeenth century (FIG. 11-10).

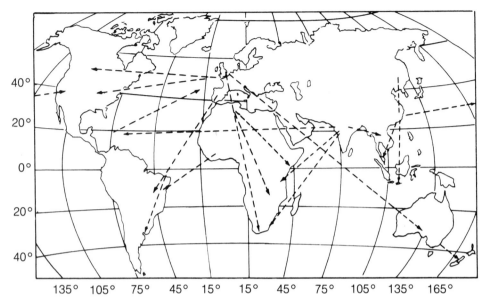

Fig. 11-10. *A map showing migratory routes has north and south cut off, as unnecessary for the subject.*

Another map with this layout may show how wet various places are (FIG. 11-11), either taking the whole year or with a series of maps showing the rainfall each month. For another purpose, it may be necessary to discover differences over a long period. The same sort of plotting can be used to discover how hot, sunny, or cloudy places are, either on average over a year or on a series of monthly maps.

These climatic conditions are comparatively static, but if movements are to be portrayed, such as wind directions, a cutoff map is not so suitable. Some winds come from polar directions, and the winds of the Pacific Ocean are better shown if more of the ocean is on the map. An elliptical outline that embraces all degrees of latitude and longitude is more useful (FIG. 11-12), even if the further limits are not true shapes. Arrows indicating wind directions are unaffected by that.

A projection does not have to be made with Africa at the center. If the map is intended to give more prominence to sea or air routes around the American continent by bringing it to the center, one of the curved methods of projection would not be practical. One way of drawing such a map with a centrally positioned American continent is to use Mercator projection. That may still cut through Russia, China, or Australia, but for purposes of illustration the map could be extended to repeat some features near the side margins (FIG. 11-13). The fact that Australia appears twice should not mislead readers. This arrangement permits some important lines to be drawn in full, instead of inconveniently going off one side to continue at the other.

Not all things are best illustrated by the customary side view of the world. For instance, the supposed movements of mammals in the very distant past may be best shown on a map with the North Pole at the center (FIG. 11-14). As the tracks are

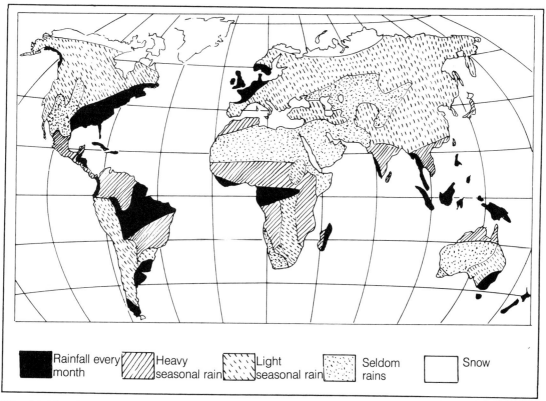

Fig. 11-11. *This map showing rainfall has Africa at the center, and north and south cut off.*

Legend:
- Rainfall every month
- Heavy seasonal rain
- Light seasonal rain
- Seldom rains
- Snow

mostly on the fringes of the polar region, a map in the conventional position would not show them as clearly. A map around the pole gives an increasingly distorted shape to places far from the pole, but for a map to illustrate one particular feature, true shapes are less important providing the places are recognizable or are named.

Birds travel enormous distances, so any map intended to show the routes of bird migration needs to cover most of the world and allow for long distances in many directions. The customary side view would take care of many routes, but a preliminary plot on a globe may show that converting the findings to a flat map is better done with a different view. Much depends on the extent of the survey. It may be better to adopt a circular shape with the North Pole off-center (FIG. 11-15). This allows the greater number of routes over Europe, Africa, and America to be shown. Those that occur around the other side of the pole can also be drawn in full. With this subject there have to be some broken route lines, but the layout keeps the majority of lines whole.

The rectangular arrangement of latitude and longitude lines on the Mercator projection is advantageous when the map is to be used to show time zones in different parts of the world in relation to each other (FIG. 11-16). As time zones are divided along meridians of longitude, the divisions are more clearly shown by having the lines straight.

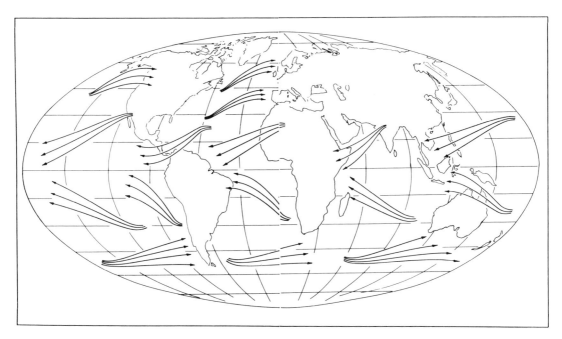

Fig. 11-12. *An elliptical outline allows the whole world to be shown in a map illustrating wind directions.*

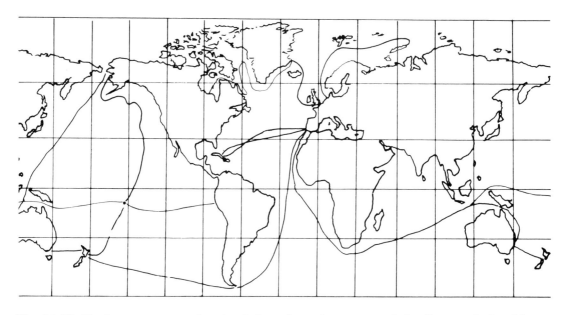

Fig. 11-13. *To show sea routes, America is brought to the center and details towards the sides are repeated to clarify route information there.*

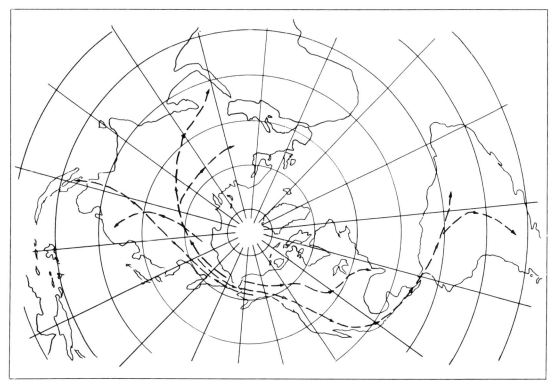

Fig. 11-14. *A map with the North Pole near the center is a better arrangement for showing the movements of mammals.*

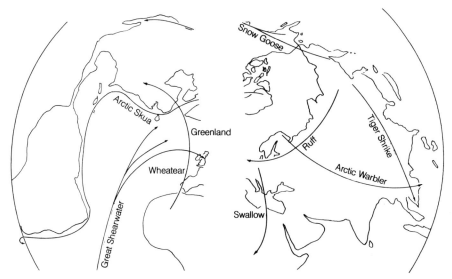

Fig. 11-15. *A map of the north of the world shows the paths of bird migration, but land shapes are distorted the further they are from the pole.*

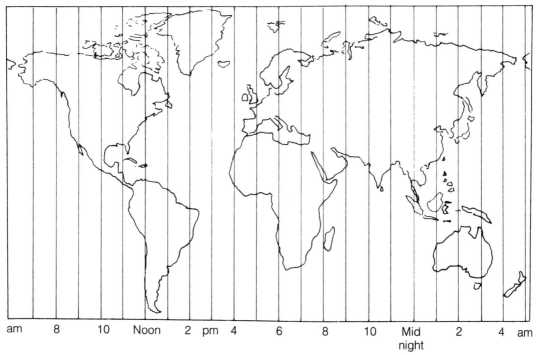

am   8   10   Noon   2 pm 4   6   8   10   Mid   2   4 am
                                                        night

Fig. 11-16. *A Mercator projection map is convenient for marking time zones.*

MAPS IN THE UNIVERSE

For a long time, man has mapped the sky at night, showing the positions of the stars. In many countries, they are related to the North Star, which provides the fixed point about which the other stars appear to rotate. This means that as the earth revolves, the stars other than the North Star seem to move around it, giving different positions in relation to the viewer at different times of the night (FIG. 11-17).

From the earliest times man has given names to various constellations, or formations, of stars. Sometimes it is difficult to see how a particular cluster can be assumed to represent the named thing or person. Astronomers may have separate names for individual stars, but the ordinary viewer tends to use the common, traditional names.

Stars are of varying density, and the relative brightness is usually shown by the size of the drawn star. The tilt of the earth at different seasons causes more stars to appear above the horizon at some times than at others. The planets also move in paths which do not conform to the same pattern of movement as the stars. To complicate things further, there are now some man-made satellites that can be seen.

No one star map is of use at all times. A simple map may show the constellations around the North Star, although the map will have to be turned around to suit various times. This may be all that is needed by anyone wishing to find north by use of the stars. For anyone needing more information, there are *star atlases*, which show the visible star formations at different times and different seasons.

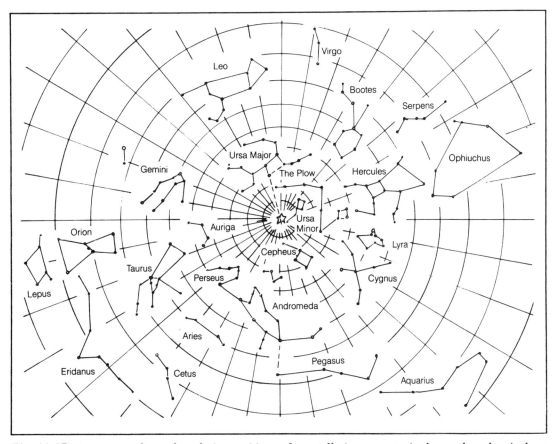

Fig. 11-17. *A star map shows the relative positions of constellations as seen in the northern hemisphere.*

Of course, there are more stars not normally visible to the naked eye. For the user of a telescope, the details are greater, and star mapping becomes possibly more advanced than any land mapping.

Now that man has walked on the moon, maps have been produced as a result of all the findings.

Names are given to features discovered and there are even contour lines. Various orbiters have flown around the moon and taken photographs from different angles. The photographs have been interpreted to allow accurate estimates of the terrain and its heights and hollows.

With satellites going further into the universe, we may expect maps of planets and other heavenly bodies. This is all very far from the man on the ground finding his way with map and compass, but it is another branch of cartography, and we should be aware of it.

12

Nautical Charts and Waterway Maps

A BOATER MUST BE CONSTANTLY CONCERNED WITH WHAT IS BENEATH THE keel. He must know how far it is to the bottom—a sort of elevation in reverse. A marine map may show contours, but these are depths from the surface of the water. A map ashore uses the water level as a datum for measuring heights above it. If the navigator is out of sight of land, his chart may show little except depths. When he comes in sight of land there are a great many aids arranged along most coastlines that he has to be aware of and which should be marked on his chart. He is also concerned with what the land looks like from the sea, so the chart may show hills, prominent buildings, and anything else that he may expect to use in identifying the part of the coast he is approaching.

Even on an inland river or lake, the boater is concerned with the depth of water. If he is using a canoe that only draws a few inches, he can usually see the bottom at the water shoals. Even then he may be glad to know in advance that one side of the river is shallower than the other, or that there is a sandbank very near the surface in the middle of the river. Anyone sailing needs a keel to prevent leeway. A very small sailing craft may need 30 inches of water in which to float, so a small-boat sailor needs to know about shallows and shores that shelve gradually. Larger craft may draw perhaps 20 feet, and they have to be navigated very carefully in shallow water, where a dredged channel may not be very wide. Besides the contours and spot figures showing depths, a coastal or river chart will show where there are buoys and other marks as guides to keeping a deep-draft vessel on course.

Navigating by checking the depth of water is a practice that goes back into early history. In the Bible, in the Acts of the Apostles, chapter 27 and verses 27 to 30, we read of St. Paul's shipwreck on Malta. The sailors sounded and found 20 fathoms; then they sounded again and found 15 fathoms. They realized they were moving into shallow water, and then they lowered four anchors to prevent the ship drifting ashore, possibly onto rocks. That chapter is worth reading for the seamanship involved.

Those Biblical sailors measured depth by lowering a weighted marked line and noting the mark nearest to the surface when the weight touched bottom. A fathom was the spread of a man's arms, now standardized as 6 feet.

Today there are electronic devices that give instant readings of depth under the keel, but sounding with a weighted line is still used with some small craft in coastal waters. A *sounding lead* (FIG. 12-1) is a long heavy lead block attached to an ample length of line, which is marked at intervals to show depth. Differences in the type of bottom are shown on the chart. A hollow in the bottom of a lead may be filled with tallow to bring up a sample of the bottom for identification.

There was a traditional way of calling the depths, so they could be understood even in the noise of wind and waves. The best-known call to Americans must be "by the mark twain," meaning two fathoms. Mark Twain became the pen name of the famous Mississippi author, Samuel L. Clemens.

The oceans are international waters and there has been a move towards metrication that has been more rapid in other countries than in the United States. Consequently, most ocean charts have depths in meters, not fathoms. Our own coastal charts

Fig. 12-1. *A sounding lead, used on the end of a line for checking the depth of water.*

are moving the same way. Depths will be prominently marked in the margin of a chart, so always check that before using a new chart. A large-scale chart may have depths in feet or meters. An ocean chart may have depths in fathoms or meters. An inland chart may be in feet.

Charts are produced like maps, with a wide border that carries a considerable amount of information, but there may not be a detailed legend on every chart. It is assumed that the user is familiar with the standard symbols. Latitude and longitude are more important to anyone afloat than to a person ashore, so divisions are given in more detail around the margin. At least one complete compass rose is printed on the chart, instead of the simple arrows on most shore maps. You'll learn why later. Charts are printed on fairly strong water-resistant paper. Creases would be a nuisance, so most charts are supplied and stored rolled. Very large charts may be folded across once.

In general, there are two broad divisions of charts. The deep-sea charts are intended for professional navigators. There are others more suitable for amateur sailors. They have more color and special symbols to make chart reading simpler, particularly where inset plans of harbors help the user in popular small-craft sailing areas.

Of course, it is important that a chart is up to date. Hazards and navigational aids change. Charts are supplied through agents who correct any charts they sell, up to the time the customer takes them away. After that, they offer a correction service, or the owner can obtain the notices of corrections and make the changes himself. Anyone doing more than just boating around a limited local area should make sure he has charts that are fully corrected.

PUBLICATIONS

The National Ocean Survey is responsible for the production of nautical charts, as well as aeronautical charts and publications related to both of them. Charts are produced at many scales. Sailing charts with scales smaller than 1:60,000 are used for planning and navigation in open waters. General charts are from 1:150,000 to 1:60,000 scale and are intended for offshore navigation using visual and radar navigation aids as landmarks. Coastal charts are from 1:50,000 to 1:150,000, and these are the most widely used charts, intended for navigation near the shore, in inlets and bays, and some inland waters. Harbor charts are to scales larger than 1:50,000 and give greater detail of smaller areas, such as anchorages and lesser waterways.

Small-craft charts are to scales between 1:10,000 and 1:80,000, and they show information needed by users of small craft, with tides and currents, as well as marinas, shelter, and anchorages. Where the other charts are presented mostly in sheets, these may be bound for convenience in handling in the restricted space on small boats.

There are books known as *pilots* that cover particular areas as supplements to the charts. They give detailed navigational information that could not be conveniently put on a chart. Anyone navigating on tidal waters needs *tide tables*, which give the forecast times of high and low water at many places. Another publication gives the movements of tidal streams at various states of the tide. If there is much rise and fall of the tide in a particular area, this information is important because the depths shown on the chart are to a mean water level, as indicated in the chart margin. There are places that dry out as islands at low water, yet at high water there is a good depth of water over them.

Some charts are published commercially, often accompanying guide book information. Some of these publications are primarily advertising, although often very comprehensive. It is best to treat them as planning guides, but refer to official charts for actual navigation.

The United States Coast Guard publishes several navigational aids. One of them is a *lights list* that gives details of all navigational lights in a particular area.

For many lakes and rivers, The Corps of Engineers of the United States Army issues navigational information on the waters they control. Charts of the Great Lakes are government publications.

"Notices to Mariners," is a weekly publication giving corrections to charts and relevant publications produced by all official agencies.

CHART SYMBOLS

The number of symbols used on charts is far greater than that used for maps of land areas. In a book on general mapping, it is impossible to show more than a few samples. Complete lists are available from the publishers of charts. Symbols are not normally shown as a legend on a chart because there are too many.

Depths are shown by contour lines where that is possible, especially near coasts. The depth each line represents is inserted as a figure in the line—at every line, not only some of them, as on a land map (FIG. 12-2A). Other depths are shown by isolated figures (FIG. 12-2B). Away from the fairly even shoaling towards the coast, the bottom does not usually follow a sufficiently even pattern for lines to be shown. Remember that depths could be in feet, fathoms, or meters and this will be stated somewhere on the chart. The actual depth at a particular time will have to be found by making a conversion from a tide table.

Anyone navigating at sea will need to know how to recognize dry land features as he approaches them. In most places, his most useful guides are man-made lights, lighthouses, daymarks, and similar fixed things on which he can take bearings, or there may be floating buoys, which carry lights.

Lights can be recognized because most of them do not show a steady beam, but may flash or otherwise break the sequence of dark and light in a timed pattern. Details are given alongside the symbol on the chart, as well as in a lights list. The symbol used is a dot for the actual position and a *flare sign* like an exclamation pointing at it (FIG. 12-2C).

At the entrance to a harbor or the approach to a channel, a light may be arranged to show different colors at different angles of view. If you can see a white light you know you are on the correct course, but if you see red you are heading for danger and must change course until you see white. Other lights are obscured in some directions. Light lists show the angle of view, if that is not indicated on the chart.

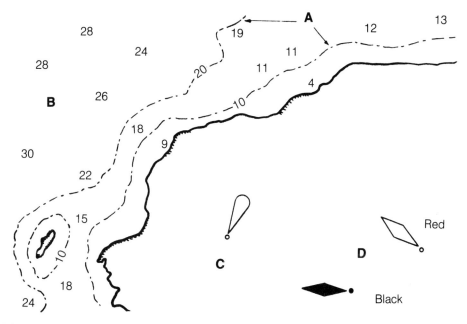

Fig. 12-2. *Spot depths are marked on a chart. Attention is drawn to the buoy and other positions with symbols.*

The flare is shown in a magenta color. Floating light aids to navigation are within magenta discs, but some old charts are not marked in this way.

Buoys may be individually placed to mark an obstruction or the edge of a shallow area. They may be used at the sides of a dredged channel to indicate the bounds within which deep-draft vessels should keep. Most buoys are marked with a dot that indicates its position and a diamond shape pointing at it (FIG. 12-2D). If the buoy is black, the symbol is solid black. If it is red, the black outline of the diamond is filled with magenta. For other colors, the diamond is open and a letter indicating the color is inside it or alongside it.

There may be *top marks* on buoys, and their special shapes are all indicated on the chart. Most navigational buoys carry lights, and these are arranged to a timed light-and-dark sequence different from all others in the vicinity, so they can be identified. A buoy may carry a bell or a fog signal. This is shown in words on the chart. Buoys usually carry a large number for identification, and this is shown at the symbol on the chart.

Safe courses near the shore may be ensured by using *ranges*. Marks are provided that have to be kept *in transit* (in line). For suitable positions ashore, there may be a high lighted mark some way inland and a lower one near the water. A navigator holding these in line knows he is keeping his vessel in the correct channel. There might be a similar arrangement with buoys to be kept in line, if shore marks cannot be used. Directions may be to keep other features lined-up, such as a tall chimney behind a distinctive house.

BEARINGS

As with finding your way ashore, you must relate bearings as viewed on the actual terrain with compass directions on the map or chart. It is not usually feasible to set a chart with a compass in the same way as a map is set ashore. Instead, you have to read a bearing directly and transfer it to the chart, possibly inside a cabin, where you cannot see anything outside. You may have to do it the other way around, by getting a bearing from the map and converting it to the way the boat is headed, or the direction in which you expect to see a landmark.

Most craft are navigated with a compass mounted rigidly in the boat, so its lubber line is in line with the direction the boat is heading. The helmsman, who is usually directly behind it, keeps the boat on course by adjusting his steering to the oscillating compass card so that the desired heading stays opposite the lubber line. In most craft, that compass stays there and is not used for taking bearings. Its location does not usually permit easy sighting across. In a few small craft, it is possible to put a sighting arrangement like an alidade across the steering compass and make sights over it, but that is unusual.

It is more usual to have a separate handheld bearing compass. It can be any type, but quick and accurate readings are important. The boat may be moving through the water and probably rolling, so it is not a stable platform for working, like taking a similar sight ashore. The most convenient bearing compass allows you to sight through a prism and immediately read the bearing there from a liquid-damped card (FIGS. 3-5 and 6).

On the modern chart, there is at least one fairly large compass rose, marked in degrees. The outer circle of markings is in degrees (marked every 2 degrees), with 0 at true north. Another inner circle is oriented on magnetic north (FIG. 12-3). The date of the drawing is indicated together with the annual changes. For utmost precision, the changes in magnetic north direction must be allowed for, but for short coastal trips they may be ignored, as errors in keeping the boat on course will be greater than any change in magnetic north. Visual sighting will allow corrections when you get within reach of your destination.

INSTRUMENTS

There are several ways of transferring a bearing to or from a compass rose on the chart. One way is to use a drawing triangle sliding on a straight edge, or another triangle, arranged so one of its edges can be slid from the nearest rose to the point where the bearing is needed (FIG. 12-4A). There are long rules mounted on rollers that can be moved across the chart to transfer bearing lines in a similar way.

Several devices for obtaining bearings on charts are based on protractors, where the arm or outer part can be moved around the calibrated disc. Charts have many meridians marked and a convenient one can be used to position the protractor so the other part can be moved through the position sighted and the angle read. That is based on true north and may have to be converted to magnetic, which is what the bearing compass will register.

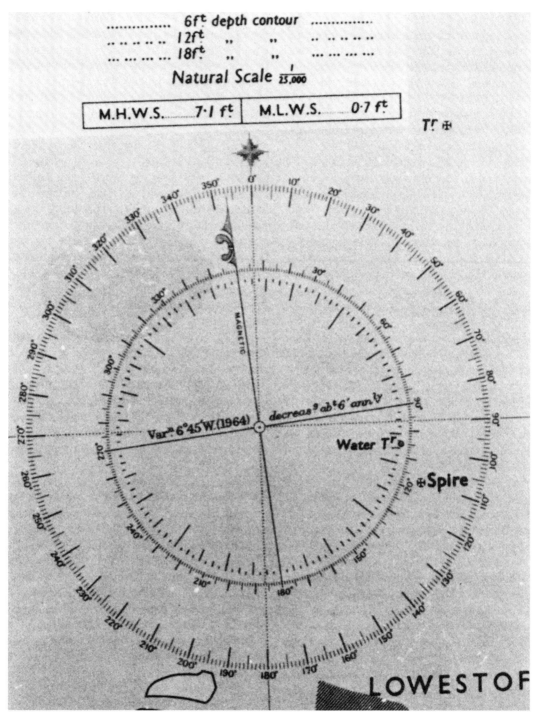

.... 6ft depth contour ....
... . 12ft „ „ .. ..
... ... 18ft „ „ ... ...

Natural Scale $\frac{1}{15,000}$

| M.H.W.S. | 7·1 ft | M.L.W.S. | 0·7 ft |

Tr ✠

Varⁿ 6°45'W (1964) decreas⁹ abᵗ 6' ann'ly

MAGNETIC

Water Trᵉ

✠ Spire

LOWESTOF

Fig. 12-3. *The standard compass rose on a nautical chart, used for obtaining bearings by means of parallel rules.*

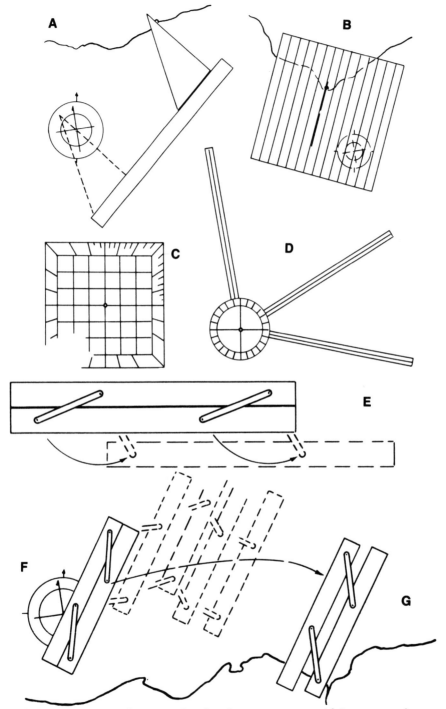

Fig. 12-4. *Bearings on a chart are related to the compass rose with instruments in several ways.*

One simple aid is a large piece of transparent plastic marked with a large number of parallel lines. Its value is only apparent when it is big enough to cover both the position being plotted on the chart and a compass rose (FIG. 12-4B). If one line on the plastic sheet is put through the bearing on the compass rose, another line should be close enough to the plotted line position for it to be checked.

Some other aids have the effect of bringing a compass rose to the plotting position. One is a large square protractor, with degrees around its edge and a grid of squares over its main area (FIG. 12-4C). If it is large enough to cover the sighted object on the map and the expected position of the boat, it can be located by a meridian to set it correctly, using a grid line on it as a guide. The underside is matted and can take a pencil line, which may be erased later.

A device that works in a very similar way is a *station pointer*, which has a central protractor to place in position and three arms which can be set to bearings (FIG. 12-4D). The applications of both devices is described later (FIG. 12-8).

Parallel rules are the traditional chart instrument for transferring bearings on a chart (FIG. 12-5). Two similar rules are joined with arms, and they have knobs for gripping. Lengths may be upwards of 9 inches, but 18 inches is a useful length. It is possible to "walk" the rules across the chart for any distance, without losing the angle. Practice is needed, but one rule is held firmly while the other is lifted very

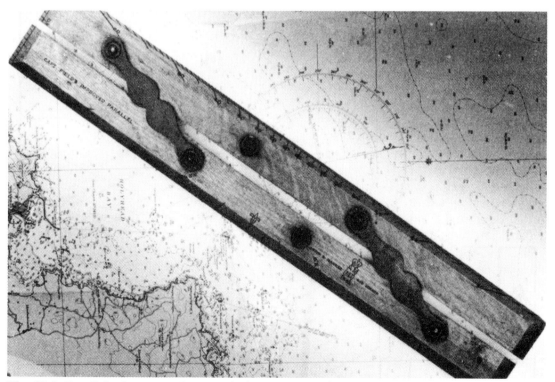

Fig. 12-5. *Parallel rules are used to transfer bearings on a chart.*

slightly, and swung away from the first (FIG. 12-4E). That position is held firm while the other is swung up to it, and so on until one of the straight edges comes where you want it.

Suppose you stand on deck and sight a lighthouse, which you can identify with your bearing compass. The reading is 245°. On the chart, you find the lighthouse symbol. Take a compass rose fairly close and put one edge of the parallel rules through that bearing (FIG. 12-4F). Walk the rules across the chart to get one edge through the symbol and draw a line (FIG. 12-4G). You have transferred the bearing sighted to the chart; your boat is somewhere on that line.

Much coastal navigation or pilotage applies the technique you have just used. You have to do this efficiently and quickly, because the boat is moving through the water. In even a low-powered boat, you will have moved some way from where you took the sight if you spend a long time transferring the fix to the chart.

Soft pencils are important navigation instruments. Do not use hard pencil or ball point pens on a chart. Have a good eraser available. You may need to alter a line, and you will want to clear the chart of lines when you have completed your voyage. Lines which will not erase or the grooves caused by hard pencils may cause errors in later use of the chart.

A chart is provided with a scale, in a similar way to shore maps, but distances are in nautical miles or meters. (A few charts of inland waters may be in statute miles.) Measuring on the chart is best done with *dividers*. Traditional dividers are fairly large and have friction joints, with most of the construction in bronze or other saltwater-resistant metal, and only the points are steel. Modern dividers would be better in stainless steel. Simple school twin-point compasses or dividers could be used, but the friction joint should be smooth to allow both easy adjustment and the ability to stay firm when set. Spring-bow dividers can be used because they lock at any setting, but many of them do not have much movement.

Most charts are arranged on Mercator projection, in which scale distances get greater towards the poles. The difference is slight on local charts, but on a chart of a large area, the scale is made accordingly and drawn up the side margin. Distances should be read from it at a point opposite the area concerned.

If a distance is within the capacity of movement of the dividers and less than the chart scale, one setting is all that is needed (FIG. 12-6A). If the distance is greater, the dividers are set to a convenient distance and stepped along a line (FIG. 12-6B). Any difference to make up the distance is checked at the end. If the dividers are swung in arcs on opposite sides of the line (FIG. 12-6C), you can move them along alternate ways between finger and thumb of one hand.

POSITION FINDING

The simplest position finding method uses two known recognized objects, which may be marked points ashore or buoys afloat. Buoys are less reliable because, although they are tethered to the bottom, they move a little with the tide. Take bearings of both objects at one time, so there is no appreciable interval between sighting them. Then use the parallel rules, or other device, to draw a line through the symbols on the map.

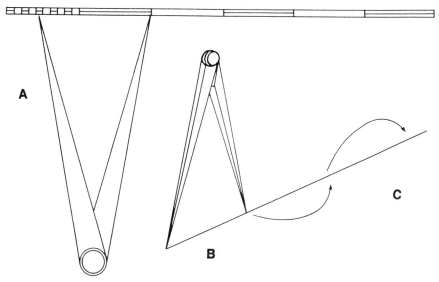

Fig. 12-6. *Dividers are used for stepping off and comparing distances.*

Assuming perfection, you are exactly at the point where the lines cross (FIG. 12-7A), or were at the time of the sighting.

There are too many factors militating against perfection, so you have to assume you are in the vicinity of where the lines cross, but may be away from it by an amount you estimate for errors. It is better to get sights of three objects and draw three lines (FIG. 12-7B). Almost certainly the lines will not meet at a point. If it is only a small triangle where they cross, you can assume you are near the center, but if the triangle is large, it will be better to start again with three new sights that may show one or more of the first sights are slightly out. If you have tried to plot your position because of a nearby danger, it is wiser to assume you are at the part of the "cocked hat" triangle nearest to danger.

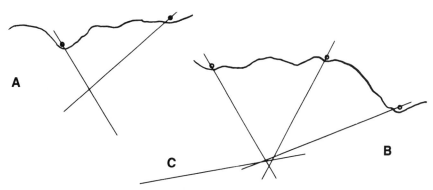

Fig. 12-7. *Two bearings (A) are better with a third (B) to confirm a fix; then a course can be set from that point (C).*

Ideally, two sights will come at about 90° to each other and three sights at about 60° to each other. It is very unlikely that you will find such angles, but these figures show you ideals to aim at, particularly if you have a choice of landmarks. If viewing angles are acute, it is difficult to ascertain exactly where two lines cross; on a small scale, two thick lines from a blunt pencil could give you an error of several miles.

When you have a fix in relation to the shore or buoys, check your position as you progress by dead reckoning. You know the course the helmsman is steering and either know from instruments or by estimation what the speed is, so you can plot the direction and progress from the known point, so long as that course is maintained (FIG. 12-7C). This assumes your movement is unaffected by tide. Correction for tide is dealt with later.

It is always better to plot your position from sights than to rely on dead reckoning, so bearings of located objects should be taken whenever an opportunity occurs. Besides being good practice, a coastwise navigator should try to know as exactly as possible where he is at all times. Fog or mist is not then such a hazard, if you can set a course, knowing with reasonable accuracy the position from which you are starting.

The method of getting a fix by reading bearings from a compass rose, either with parallel rules, a roller rule, or a lined plastic sheet can be modified if you have a large square protractor or a station pointer. These devices are particularly useful where the physical size of the part of the chart that concerns you is not large and where you are in a small craft with inadequate facilities for spreading the chart flat and working out bearings in comfort.

Suppose you take bearings of two objects ashore. If you have a large square protractor, you can pencil the bearings on the matte underside and move the protractor so the grid lines are north and south according to a meridian, and the pencil lines project through the symbols of the sighted objects (FIG. 12-8A). Sighted magnetic bearings will have had to be corrected to true. Your position on the chart is where the center of the protractor comes. A small hole there allows you to pencil through. Better still, work with three bearings, if there are suitable features to be sighted. Maneuver the protractor to get them on the pencil lines when the protractor is square to north-south lines. This will give your position on the chart, with a degree of accuracy dependent on your reading of the bearing compass. As with the drawn sights that produce a small triangle instead of an exact cross, you may have to accept an average position if you cannot match all three sight lines.

With the station pointer you can get a greater coverage of the paper the chart is printed on, so it may be better suited to longer sight lines. With the three bearings, set the moving arms to the readings around the protractor. Put the instrument over the chart and move it about until the lines on the arms are through the marked features sighted when the protractor has its north-south line the same way as a meridian drawn on the chart (FIG. 12-8B). When you have done this, the center of the protractor is your position; mark through to the chart in the same way as with the square protractor.

Instead of just taking bearings of two or three individual landmarks, it is helpful to look for possible transits to use instead of one individual mark. The advantage of a transit is that it establishes a definite line for you to follow. Other bearings sighted then

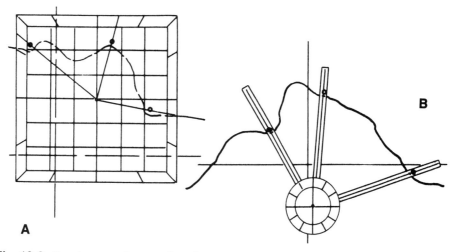

Fig. 12-8. *Bearings can be transferred to a chart with a protractor or a station pointer.*

show where you are on that line, reducing the risk of error to a position on a definite line instead of a triangle, where you have to estimate the actual position.

This could happen as you approach a harbor, where leading marks are set up for you to keep in transit as you enter. A sight of another object will tell you how far you are from the harbor, but you may be able to use other features when you are off a stretch of more open coastline. The chart may show you a radio mast some way back from the coast and a house much nearer. If you wait until these two are in transit and at the same time take a bearing of something else, you can plot an accurate position (FIG. 12-9A). A third sighting at the same time will confirm it.

RUNNING FIX

In many situations, there are not many landmarks to use as you travel off a coastline. If there is only one mark you can identify ahead, there is a simple geometric method of finding your position with sights of it, depending on how accurately you can settle on your course direction and distance traveled. Take a sight of the mark and note the time. Note the angle between the line of sight and the course the boat is taking (FIG. 12-9B). Continue on course until you can take another sight that shows double the angle of the first one (FIG. 12-9C), and note the time again. The distance you are from the mark is the same as the distance you traveled since the first sighting. From the speed of the boat and the time between sightings you can work out the distance (FIG. 12-9D). Of course, it is the distance travelled over the bottom that counts. Distance through the water will not be the same if there is much tidal or wind effect, and you may have to estimate how much these factors might alter the result. However, doubling the angle on the bow is a useful method as a rough guide when you cannot find marks to give a more precise position. If you can arrange the first sight at 45° to the course, the other sight at 90° will be directly abeam and easily observed.

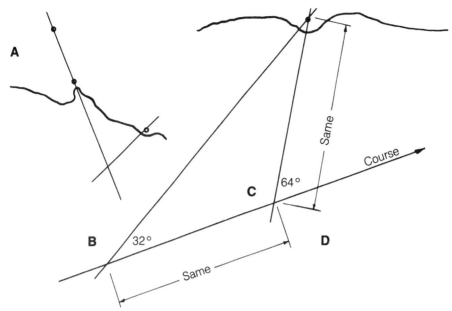

Fig. 12-9. *A transit sight gives an accurate position line. Doubling the angle on the bow is a way of obtaining a position from one landmark (B,C,D).*

That method is a form of *running fix*. In another form, when there is only one mark on which you can get a reliable sight, take a bearing and check the time. Draw the line on the chart with a note of the time (FIG. 12-10A). You need a point on this line as a start for working, so estimate where you are on the line, either from observation or from previous calculations and dead reckoning. Draw a course line through the point (FIG. 12-10B). Later, take another bearing of the mark, preferably when the difference between the two sightings is near 90° (FIG. 12-10C). From the time of this sighting and that of the other, calculate how far you have traveled and mark the distance on the course line (FIG. 12-10D). Draw a line parallel to the first sight through this mark, so it crosses the second sight line. That crossing is your position (FIG. 12-10E). Remember, your course line is based on an estimate and could be some way from your true course. This final transferred position is more accurate, and you could move to a new parallel course line to run through it, if your boat is to continue on the same course bearing.

SEXTANT ANGLES

When any vessel is navigated offshore, its latitude is found by observation of the sun and stars, using an instrument called a *sextant*, which is a device for measuring angles very accurately. Celestial navigation is outside the scope of this book, but if there is a sextant on board it can be used for measuring horizontal angles, instead of using a compass for bearings. There are certain limitations due to the instrument. Differences between bearing lines are best if kept greater than 30°, and three sights are necessary.

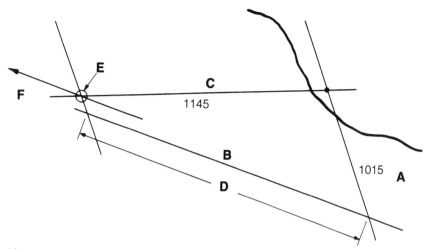

Fig. 12-10. *A running fix allows a position to be obtained from a single mark.*

In sighting, two objects have to be superimposed on each other in their mirror reflections. That becomes difficult if their heights are very different.

The results you get are the angles of two sights each side of a central one. A square protractor or a station pointer would be convenient for plotting. In this case, there is no reference to north-south lines. The 0° of the protractor goes through the central mark, and the instrument is moved to get the other bearings correct and to locate the sighting position at its center (FIG. 12-11A).

A simpler way, but similar in principle, uses a *pelorus*, which is an arrangement of sights over a protractor base (FIG. 12-11B). Turn it so the 0° direction is sighted at the middle mark; then take and read sights each side of it of the other marks. Note the angles and transfer them to the chart, in the same way as using sextant angles.

With a sextant and suitable tables it is possible to find the distance from objects of known height. Charts show how high the lens of a lighthouse is above sea level, and there may be heights given of other man-made or natural objects. If such an object is within view, take its bearing and draw a line to match on your chart. Use the sextant to measure the angle between an observation of the top of the object and sea level (FIG. 12-11C). From the height and the angle you can read the distance away from the table. Measuring this to scale along the line on the chart gives you your position. Large craft have radar, which can be used to measure the distance, and it is possible to use a rangefinder. Either device, used with the compass bearing, will give you a fix.

ELECTRONIC AIDS

Much modern navigation at sea is done with the help of radio. Direction finding of special radio transmitters is used instead of visual observation of marks with a compass, but the principle is the same. It is also possible to read the range from a station, so plotting from one station will give a fix.

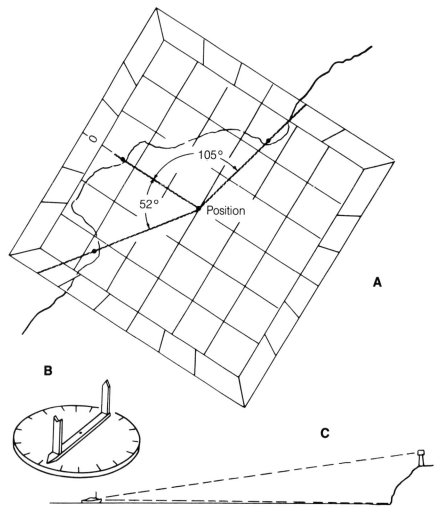

Fig. 12-11. *A large protractor allows a position to be plotted from bearings each side of a central one (A). These sights could be with a pelorus (B). A sextant allows a distance off to be converted from a height angle (C).*

Radio beacons transmit signals that are easily identifiable and serve in the same way as lighthouses for visual navigation. Some operate from lighthouses.

Direction finders are radio sets with vertical or other directional aerials or antennas, which can be turned while the operator listens with headphones. The direction finder is turned and the signal strength noted between zero and maximum. The bearing is read when the signal is brought down to zero, with progressive moments each side of it by reduced amounts.

DRIFT

The methods of navigation described so far assume that the boat is moving in still water, with no air movement. Unfortunately, both wind and water movement will affect the progress of a boat, so the actual passage over the bottom or between two shore points may be very different from what it seems to be on the surface.

If the wind is directly ahead or astern of a boat, it should not have much effect on the direction of the boat's progress, although it may slow or speed it. If the wind comes anywhere from the side, it will cause *leeway*. Persistent wind over the surface of the water may also cause the water to drift, but that is difficult to measure and is more a feature of open ocean than of waters closer inshore.

A sailing craft has a deep keel to resist leeway, but when it is sailing with the wind abeam, it will be blown sideways to a limited extent, besides being driven forward by the wind. This also applies to a motor cruiser, particularly if it has a high superstructure. Relatively, leeway is greater and of more importance in the navigation of slow craft than of fast ones. With a high-speed planing boat, leeway might often be ignored. Most displacement craft, such as sailing yachts and fishing craft, often do no better than 5 knots (nautical miles per hour); therefore, leeway may alter courses considerably. The error after a few hours would be serious if ignored.

As a hull passes through the water, it leaves a wake. If the helmsman holds his course and notes the bearing of his compass, you can stand facing over the stem and sight with a bearing compass on the furthest part of the wake, to take its bearing. If you compare a reciprocal reading of this with the actual heading of the ship you can find what the angle is between the wake and the course being steered (FIG. 12-12A). From this, you can see that although the ship is being steered in a particular direction, its actual track is to one side of it (FIG. 12-12B).

If the course is altered so the wind comes at a different angle, or the wind itself shifts or changes in strength, the effect will differ. Therefore, any observation of leeway cannot be regarded as precise or effective for very long. If you are in any craft that is known to make considerable leeway, you must take this factor into account.

Fig. 12-12. *The wake may indicate a course different from the boat's heading.*

TIDAL CORRECTIONS

Tides are affected by the moon. Not only does the water level rise and fall, but it moves horizontally, sometimes at quite high speeds. In most places, the times of high water are slightly more than 12 hours apart, with low water just after midway between. Tide tables tell you the forecast tide times. A tidal atlas shows you the relative direction and speed of the water at various states of the tide. If you are navigating in tidal waters, this information has to be taken into account when you lay off a course on the chart. You may know what the direct course is between your point of departure and your destination, but the actual course steered may have to be very different. It will not be the same at different times, if there is more than minimal tidal effect in the area.

If you are crossing the tidal stream at about low water, and the trip is expected to take about 12 hours, you may head for your destination and get there, but instead of travelling in a straight line, you will go sideways for about 6 hours and be swept back for another 6 hours. The greatest effect comes about halfway between high and low water (FIG. 12-13A).

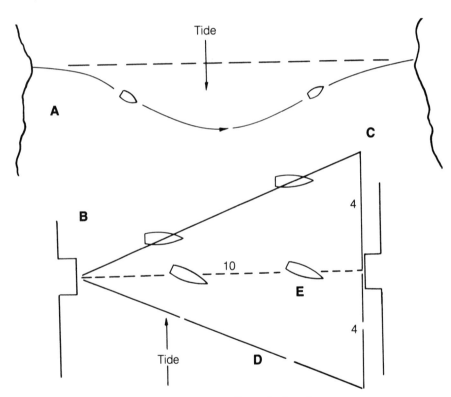

Fig. 12-13. *A tidal stream across a course affects the boat's passage.*

If you are travelling with or against the tide, water movement will not affect direction, but it will affect speed or the distance covered in a given time. Along an average coast, the tide may make 3 knots, but if it is compressed between headlands it could reach 6 knots. If your boat is low-powered, you might not be able to make progress against it. By using the tide, you might travel about 30 miles with little use of power or even with little wind in your sails. If you tried to go the other way, you might be lucky to manage 10 miles in the same time. It is always advisable to wait and use a favorable tide.

Problems come when your course is across a tidal stream. The *course made good* will be different from the way the boat is heading.

In a simple example, suppose you are doing a ferrying trip across a stretch of water 10 miles wide, and your boat will do 5 knots. You expect the trip to take 2 hours (FIG. 12-13B). From the tide tables you see that the tide is about half-ebb, when the tidal stream will be averaging about 2 knots across your course.

If you head straight across, by the time your 5-knot boat has done 10 miles, the tide will have moved you sideways 4 miles, which is quite a long way from your destination (FIG. 12-13C). To allow for that, you must set a course by that same amount towards the tide and hold that course by compass (FIG. 12-13D). Although your boat will be forging ahead through the water, the water is moving sideways over the bottom, so you are moving crabwise across the channel in relation to the bottom (FIG. 12-13E).

In fact, the movement of water also affects its friction against the bottom. Because of this, close to shore it does not move as fast as it does where it is deeper near the middle of the channel. Neither does it keep up a steady speed for long. You cannot take all these variables into account when laying a course, but when you are in the boat, practice will show you how to vary the course you steer to take advantage of probable variations in water movement. If there is a beam wind, you may also have to allow a few degrees for leeway, increasing the angle if wind and tide are together—or decreasing if the wind is against the tide.

With the different water speeds at different states of the tide, allowance for tides becomes complicated for a voyage of many hours. If possible, divide the cruise into stages, each of a few hours. If you are to be within sight of land, you can get your position at intervals by observing marks. Allowance for tides can then be corrected, and you start again with fresh calculations from a new departure point.

Suppose you estimate that a crossing from one harbor to a buoy off another, about 20 miles away, will take about 4 hours under sail. The wind is on the beam, so you do not expect to have to tack (FIG. 12-14A). From the tide tables and the tidal stream atlas, you see that the flow is diagonally across your course at about 1 knot for the first hour, increasing to $1^1/_2$ knots during the next hour, holding that for another hour, and dropping to 1 knot for a fourth hour. This is obviously enough to affect your crossing.

At any point on the chart, draw a line in the same compass direction as your course. From the point representing the start, draw another line in the direction of the tidal flow (FIG. 12-14B). Decide on a scale—it could be 5 miles per inch, but anything will do. From the tidal speeds you can see that in the 4 hours you estimate for a crossing, the water will have moved 5 miles. Mark the 1 inch to represent this on the tidal line (FIG. 12-14C). Set your dividers to 20 miles (4 inches) and mark from the end of the tide line to a point on the course line (FIG. 12-14D). Draw a line to join these points; that is the course to steer. Get its bearing from the compass rose (FIG. 12-14E). If you keep the boat headed on that bearing you will closely follow the intended course, but your bow will be turned slightly towards the tide.

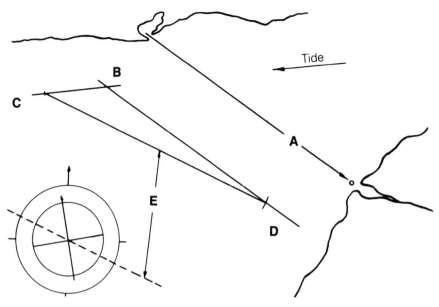

Fig. 12-14. *A tidal diagram shows the course to take for the necessary correction.*

INLAND WATERS

Where inland waters are extensive, such as in the Great Lakes, charts and maps are very similar to those used around the coast. Navigation is also very similar, particularly on lakes large enough to take shipping of considerable size, and where it is possible to be out of sight of the shore. Some symbols differ from those used on coastal charts, and there are specialized publications concerned with navigation, with which a boater should be familiar. For these waters, it is necessary to equip and deal with navigational problems as seriously as when going to sea, except that there are no tides to contend with.

There are a great many other waters open to navigation. Charts are available for many lakes, some officially issued and others commercially published. What buoys there are and other marks to aid navigation may not conform to standards elsewhere, so the local chart and its legend should be consulted. Where the lakes are artificially dammed, they probably form part of a longer waterway, with locks for passing dams. In that case, the U.S. Army Corps of Engineers, or other authority, will provide river and lake navigation charts. A special route, which is affected by tides, but has much of the character of an inland waterway is the Intracoastal Waterway.

River navigation charts tend to be to a fairly large scale, and made as a book, with a spiral metal binding to allow opening to bring the chart in use flat on top. An example is the Ohio River Navigation Charts, issued as book by the United States Army Corps of Engineers and which has the charts on stiff paper, with each page about 8 inches by 14 inches, carrying a section of the river to a scale of 1 inch to 2,000 feet.

Charts are accompanied by a legend and explanatory notes. Symbols are particular to the river system and not the same as on nautical charts. The water is colored blue, with a black edge showing the normal level limits. Within the blue, another line backed with black dots shows where there is less than a 9-foot depth (FIG. 12-15A). Buoys are used to mark the navigable channel. A small circle marks the actual position, but a diamond shape draws attention to it, with black for *can* (black) and red for *nun* (red) buoys (FIG. 12-15B). If the buoy is lighted, there is a large red circle, with black at the center of it, if it is a can buoy (FIG. 12-15C).

A light on the bank is also shown as a red circle with a black center. A daymark is a red triangle, but only marked that way if it is not accompanied by a light (FIG. 12-15D). Letters indicate the shape of the daymark. There is a code that shows the characteristics of each light. For instance, "Gp. Fl. W, 5 sec., 2 flashes," means it is a group flashing white light, showing 2 flashes each of 5 seconds. Some lights may be fixed or arranged to flash at different rates, so they cannot be confused with other lights in the vicinity. Colors may be white or red on the left descending bank, white or green on the right descending bank. Gauges showing water level may be in the vicinity of a lock, and the arrival points for locking are indicated (FIG. 12-15E). Other symbols are self-explanatory (FIG. 12-15F).

A prominent broken red line shows the channel line for large craft, and an arrow indicates the direction of water flow. Mile posts are shown. Lights and daymarks are

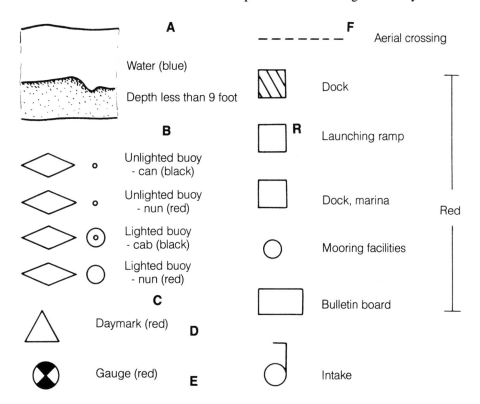

Fig. 12-15. *Inland waterways maps and charts have their own symbols.*

positioned where they can provide guidance to the main channel. They come towards the outsides of bends where they can be seen from the approaching straighter parts (FIG. 12-16A). These, and the buoys, indicate the channel line, which is important to deep-draft vessels.

Each section of map carries a north arrow and scale. As the sections are arranged so the river is across a page, their relevant compass directions vary as the river twists, so north on adjoining sheets may not be the same. Each section overlap is marked on the next by a match line across the river (FIG. 12-16B). Only enough shore details are given to indicate bridges and main urban areas, with tributaries and riverside docks. For further information on the surrounding country, the user needs a general map. Names of docks, bridges, and other marked places are listed and keyed to the map symbols with letters and numbers.

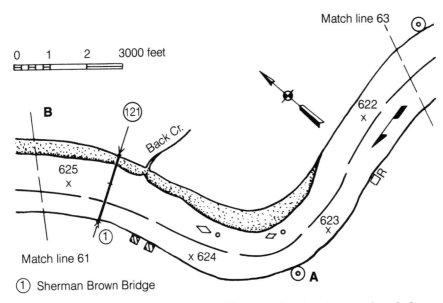

Fig. 12-16. *A section of the map of a navigable river, showing the use of symbols.*

Bridges are pictured on the backs of charts, with dimensions and clearances. Similar information is provided on aerial power crossings. All of this is important to operators of large craft, but the details provide recognition for those with smaller boats.

Maps of the majority of rivers are prepared in similar ways. They provide very full navigational information, but the user should have topographic or other maps if he is to get the most out of his exploration of a river and its valley.

In some cases, as when a lake or a river forms an extensive recreational area, a chart is produced with the main channel and its markers shown by the usual symbols. The rest of the lake and some of the surrounding land is given color and more detail, with underwater contours drawn and shaded. Access points and other information needed by recreational boaters are shown, as they can use parts of the water away from the main navigational channel. In that case, the chart shows all that may be needed by anyone approaching from the shore as well as by water, although the shore information does not go far back from the water.

Navigation on inland waterways is mostly an extension of map and compass work described throughout this book. There is much more to the use of nautical charts for navigation and pilotage around and away from coasts. Anyone interested in deep-sea navigation should add to the information in this chapter by reading specialized books.

13

Care of Maps and Compasses

MAPS ARE VALUABLE. IF YOU ARE IN NEED OF A MAP AND IT IS NOT THERE to be used, you cannot put a value on it in dollars. Besides that consideration, you may have marked a map to suit your needs, so a replacement would not be the same. You want to preserve your original map as long as possible. Map care requires common sense.

This care also applies to compasses and other navigational equipment. Fortunately, most of these things are fairly tough, but damage or loss could be serious. In the field, they should be protected from damage, yet be easily available for use. In storage, they should be kept carefully—steel and brass will corrode in a damp atmosphere. Many plastics get brittle if they become extremely cold.

MAP FOLDING

Some maps are supplied folded, but many topographic maps are supplied flat or rolled. They are unsuitable for field use in that form, except for plotting your own survey for a special purpose, or for another use when the map could be temporarily mounted on a sheet of plywood. An unfolded map is the choice if you want to mount it on a wall for reference. In some cases you can specify if you want the map folded or flat, but many maps can only be obtained unfolded. They are mailed in a roll.

Do not rush into folding a rolled map. Many nautical charts are only supplied unfolded. It has probably been rolled for some time and become set in the curve. It will help to roll it the other way until it stays reasonably flat when you release it. Consider what size you want the folded map to be. If you have a map case, it must obviously fold to a size that will fit into it. If you do not have a map case and intend using the map uncovered, the size should be convenient to handle. Not covering the map will soon cause it to become creased and curled at the corners. Folds will wear and surfaces will deteriorate. It is better to give the map a plastic cover, which may be one of the transparent folders intended for filing papers. The folded map size should be less than 8 inches by 10 inches.

If the map is small enough, it may come down to a suitable size folded in four (FIG. 13-1A). Then, you can consult any of the four quarters easily, without having to open the map fully; two are already outside, and you can put the other two outside by reversing a fold.

When you have settled on the fold positions, it helps to rub them down hard, so there are very positive creases that the map will automatically resume when you want to reduce its size. Much depends on the paper. You may get a hard enough fold with finger pressure, but the quality of paper used for most maps needs more pressure. Use a piece of wood (FIG. 13-1B), the handle of a knife, or anything firm, but preferably not metal, which could leave a dirty deposit on the paper. Whatever you use should have rounded edges.

Many maps are too big to come down to an acceptable size by folding in four. If you further fold on four, you get extra thicknesses at the folds, which do not lay flat very well. You will have to fully open the map and reverse some folds if you want to use any of the inner surfaces.

Concertina folding can bring a large map down to a reasonable size so any part can be examined without the need to fully open the map. It also avoids thick multiple folds that get unwieldly. Plan ahead so you do not put folds where they are not needed. Pencil marks on the borders are advisable.

Fold the map across its center (FIG. 13-1C) with the printing outside, and rub the fold down hard. Fold each end alternate ways into an even number of panels, depending on the final width you want (FIG. 13-1D). Rub down the double thicknesses, so when you push the parts together you get a tight close pad. This gives you a tall folded map. For convenience in stowing, fold it in half again (FIG. 13-1E), but this time do not rub down the folds. If you fold into six panels across, you can now open the map half-height and zig-zag it open to any panel, viewing whichever side you need, without at any time having to handle a package too big to control in a wind or protect from rain (FIG. 13-2).

That map may be kept in a plastic cover or a map case when not being consulted. It can be turned so the panel you need is visible through a transparent cover. Alternatively, you might give the map its own protective card cover. Cut a piece of card large enough to extend over the folded map about 1/4 inch all around and give it two flaps to glue to the map (FIG. 13-1F). Glue these to the back of the map edge, so the cover extends and there is enough slack on the fold to close over the map without creasing it. This is best done with the map and cover fully closed. Put the whole thing under pressure to harden the folds and compress the map as much as possible. A title and any other details you wish to add on the cover completes the transformation to a good

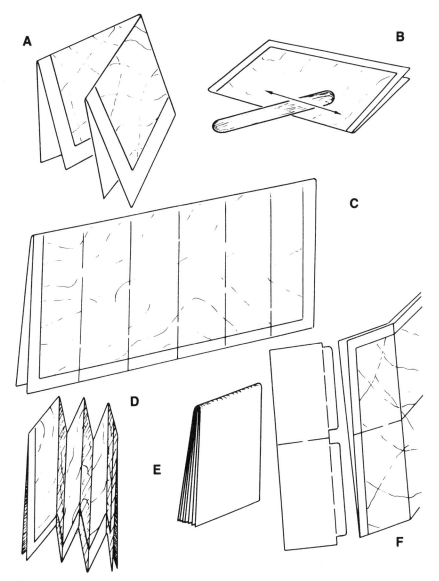

Fig. 13-1. *A map may be folded into four or zig-zagged into more parts.*

working map from one that was only suitable for display or surveying. The inside of the cover will take notes, or you could glue a note pad on it.

In some other methods of folding, there have to be cuts along some fold lines. The advantage of this is that some parts can be folded back to show another surface, without moving other parts. The disadvantage is the weakening of the map. The paper may tear at the cut unless the map is backed with another piece of paper. This may be done in military mapping, where convenience is more important than the long life of the map, but it is inadvisable for general map use.

Fig. 13-2. *If a map is folded in half and then in a zig-zag manner the other way, any part can be brought to view without opening the whole map.*

Maps that are cut into segments of the size that would be obtained by folding to a convenient size are obtainable. The segments are glued to a fabric backing, with slight gaps so the fabric will fold without creasing the paper of the map. This allows the vital surfaces of the map to remain flat. The gaps result in slight breaks in continuity of features that cross folds, so distances that run across cannot be scaled, and there may be difficulty in identifying some things that come just over cuts. Advantages tend to be outweighed by disadvantages, so this arrangement is rarely seen. Of course, one major disadvantage is the cost of production.

Folding a map so its printed surface is inward may provide protection to the important part, but the sheet has to be opened fully for the map to be read. That may not matter if the sheet is small, but would be a nuisance with the majority of maps. Also, it is the more usual practice to fold with the working surface outwards.

MAP CASES

When a map is out of use, it may be given sufficient protection to put it in a pocket of a coat or pack, but corners will curl and surfaces may crease and become marked. With the amount of plastic film and sheet that is used for wrapping almost everything today, it is better to salvage some and wrap the map in plastic before putting it away. Even better is a stiffer plastic envelope or folder, probably originally intended for filing office papers. If this is clear plastic, you can examine the map through it.

If you want to mark your map, it helps if you provide a stiff backing. A floppy piece of paper in your hand will not encourage the accurate marking of courses. If you want to draw a straight line, the surface must be held flat. If the map is without a card cover, a piece of stiff card in the envelope with the map will serve as a simple drawing board. It could be double size and folded, then you can open it and it will be stiff enough if you hold it so lines are drawn across the direction of the fold.

Map cases may be bought. They vary in complexity. The simplest type has a stiff back and a transparent plastic front, with a flap to close over the map. There is a cord to go around your neck. A typical size is about 10 inches square (FIG. 13-3). If obtainable, the size should be related to the folded size of your map. Then, it is possible to secure the map inside so it does not slide, and you can mark on the transparent cover instead of on the map. If the map can move, your marks would go out of register. A wax pencil will mark on the plastic surface, but you have to be careful not to rub marks off before you have finished using them. Soft pencil marks on the actual map are less liable to inadvertent removal.

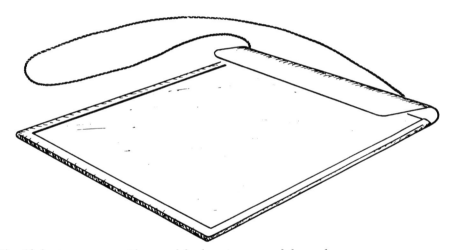

Fig. 13-3. *A map case with a cord for hanging around the neck.*

That type of case may be made entirely of plastic and is fairly light. For harder use, it is better to have a canvas cover. The military pattern is one version that has a protective flap over the transparent front, with divisions inside for carrying pencils, scales, and other instruments (FIG. 13-4).

There is a stiff backing and the case on its strap around your neck can be lifted horizontally and used like a drawing board in front of you, with what you need ready at hand. If you are surveying the mapped land to lay out a competition course or to record some new features, this is a convenient way to carry map and instruments. If you are only carrying a map for occasional reference in navigation, the simpler case, or none at all, may serve.

Maps in book form are convenient if you are travelling long distances. One of the

Fig. 13-4. *This canvas map case has the map under a plastic sheet, and there are compartments for instruments in the cover.*

many road atlases may serve you better than individual maps for motoring. One problem is balancing the ease of reading large pages against the convenience of carrying and stowing a book with smaller pages. Large pages certainly make for simpler and quicker reading with greater accuracy, but can you stow something, probably 11 inches by 16 inches? A map half the size, or less, will be easier to put on a shelf or in a glove compartment, but it may be more difficult to read and you may have to run over several pages, with a greater risk of error.

Decide for yourself, but if there is a choice between limp and hard covers, it will probably be worth the extra cost to have hard covers for the greater protection of the maps. Note how often the atlas is revised. Roads and other features change. Maybe a limp cover will stand up to use long enough, if you ought to buy a new edition in a year or so. You might get two different editions in soft covers for the cost of one in hard cover.

PRESERVING MAPS

Nearly all maps are printed on paper. Some are on plastic or plasticized paper. Cheaper maps, particularly state and similar maps, are on paper that has little resistance to dampness or misuse. Better maps are on stronger paper, with some resistance to dampness. Nautical charts have even greater resistance to dampness.

If a map has to be used for exact measurements, it is important that the paper cannot expand and contract, or at least be only restricted to the absolute minimum. That is one reason why better maps are damp-resistant. Untreated paper can vary in size considerably between its very dry state and when it has absorbed moisture from the atmosphere on a humid day. This could be as much as a $1/4$ inch in 30 inches. When that is related to a small scale, the difference is more than enough to matter.

If a cheap, untreated paper map becomes damp, there is not much you can do to return it to its original state. Mop off actual water. Do not try to dry it rapidly, as that will almost certainly cause it to wrinkle. If possible, put it flat between pieces of blotting paper and leave it to dry at normal temperatures. When it is dry you can fold it along the original creases and press it under a weight or in a vise. It may be better to replace it.

If the map is on water-resistant paper it is unlikely to be permanently damaged, if you can remove surplus moisture fairly quickly. Avoid excessive heat and leave the damp map to dry naturally. Much depends on the paper and printing, but you may be able to use a moderately warmed domestic iron over a piece of cloth to draw the final dampness out of the map. Water can also be drawn out of paper by wiping with a cloth soaked in alcohol, but that might affect the printing ink. It could be used on the plain back of a wet map.

A map used in all conditions may get sand and grit within the folds. Quite a small amount of grit can damage the surface of the map to a surprising degree if it is left to move about within the folded paper, so shake out a map if you suspect sand or other grit has gotten inside. When you get home, wipe the surface with a slightly damp cloth before finally folding the map for storage.

When a map is out of use, store it in the same way as you would a book. Standing on edge between books will keep folds tight and prevent corners from curling. If you have penciled on any map, use an eraser before putting the map away. If you get into the field later and find old pencil marks you do not want still there, you will probably not make as good a job of clearing them.

CARE OF INSTRUMENTS

Fortunately, compasses need little maintenance. The way a compass is made should allow it to be turned in any direction without the needle coming off its pivot. If the compass is liquid-damped, the chamber should be absolutely full of liquid. Sometimes an air bubble develops. Providing it is small, it will not affect the performance of the compass, although you may regard the sight of the bubble moving about as disquieting. Air in the compass does not affect the way the needle points. Excessive air would reduce the damping effect and its swirling would further affect this, so the needle may gyrate more before settling on north. There is no easy way of removing the air and topping up the liquid. The liquid used is not the same in all compasses. Usually it contains alcohol. (The compasses on ocean-going sailing ships were topped up with gin.) Compass makers have their own choice of liquid, and it would be advisable to return a compass to the makers for topping up. At extremely low temperatures, a vacuum bubble may form, but that will clear itself as the temperature rises.

A bearing compass, or a large one of traditional construction, has many parts of brass, with some surfaces painted and others left bright. The bright parts were probably lacquered during manufacture, but lacquer will chip off if knocked. If a bare part has been left for some time it will usually have corroded to a green color. If only part of the lacquer has come off, you can rub the exposed part with fine abrasive (a domestic cleaning powder will do); then repolish it with any liquid metal polish. A suitable touch-up lacquer is clear nail polish, if you do not have a proper metal lacquer. If you need to repolish and relacquer an entire surface, it may be possible to chip off old lacquer with a knife, but you can soften and remove it with alcohol or nail polish remover.

Many compasses are made of plastic, which does not have a very good resistance to abrasion. It may not matter if an opaque part of a case gets scratched, but if a transparent part becomes dulled due to abrasion or something sharp digging into it, visibility through it is impaired. It is possible to bring the surface to a clear state again, but that is done by wearing the surface away slightly. If it is a lens, that would affect its performance. On a flat clear piece of plastic, the very slight distortion of the view through may not matter. This could apply to the base of a Silva compass or to the plastic covering disc over the needle.

If there is only a slight dulling of the plastic due to general abrasion in use, without contact with anything that severely roughened it, you can use any metal polish intended for silver. Rub it on with one cloth and polish it off with another clean one. If the abrasion is more than this will remove, use a polish intended for brass and get the surface as bright as you can. Make sure all traces of the brass polish are removed; then polish again with silver polish.

If there is a scratch that goes very deep, it may be unwise to try to remove it completely because you will have to rub down the surface around it and thin the plastic. That would cause a distorted view and might weaken the material if not much thickness will be left. If the scratch is slight, you can treat it in the same way as a general abrasion, with brass and silver polishes. If necessary, start with another abrasive. Pumice powder on a damp cloth will work quicker than brass polish. When that, or domestic scouring powder, has got down to the depth of the scratch, clean it off and follow with the two grades of metal polish. There are some special polishes produced for plastics, which could be used instead of the suggested metal polishes.

When a compass is out of use, it is best stored the right way up and away from iron and steel, although most compasses seem to survive unharmed however they are kept.

Scales and protractors need no special treatment; just keep them clean and avoid misusing them. Do not be tempted to use a scale as a guide for a knife when cutting cardboard. You want these instruments to be as clear as possible, sometimes in conditions far from ideal, so wipe them clean. Use a mild detergent if necessary. If the graduations become indistinct, you can revive them by wiping over with a cloth soaked in black ink or paint. Follow this immediately with a clean cloth, preferably wrapped around something flat, so it cleans the surface without going into the graduation impressions.

A mechanical pencil may be better than a woodcased one, but carry a small piece of sandpaper for rubbing a fine point on it. This can get very messy and mark other things. It helps to have a piece folded along its center, with the abrasive surface inside. Alternatively, glue a strip of sandpaper to a thin strip of wood and make a sheath for it to slip into—folded cardboard held with adhesive tape will do. If you prefer a wood-cased pencil, make sure you always have a knife for sharpening.

Dividers and drawing compasses need stiff joints. Usually, the friction joint has a screw adjustment. If not, there may be a rivet through it that will have to be hammered tightly. Adjust the joints so they move smoothly throughout their range and stay put wherever you leave them. Dividers that cannot be relied on are a nuisance.

Divider points must finish level and be sharp. You cannot get an exact reading if a point is blunt and rounded, and for measuring short distances uneven projection will make setting difficult. Needle points may be replaceable in some dividers, but these and fixed points can be sharpened on a whetstone (FIG. 13-5). Hold the divider leg diagonal to the stone and rotate it as you rub it along. If you have dividers with solid legs that come together with triangular points, your final sharpening may be with the legs closed and rolled as they rub along the stone.

Fig. 13-5. *Divider points should be kept sharp by rubbing them on a whetstone.*

Having sharpened the points, protect them, so they do not get damaged and cannot cause damage. Pushing them into a cork is a simple treatment (FIG. 13-6). Little pieces of plastic or rubber tubing pushed over the points can be used—insulation pulled off electric wiring will do. If the dividers push into a pocket in a map case, that may be sufficient protection.

Oil and grease are substances you do not want to bring into contact with maps, but if you have any steel instruments that need protection, you can rub them with wax or a

Fig. 13-6. *Divider points may be protected by pushing into a cork.*

piece of candle, which will not be so messy. For steel in storage, place silica gel crystals or treated paper nearby to absorb any moisture from the air. Most modern steel instruments are stainless, so they should not give any trouble. Some stainless steel is also nonmagnetic, so anything made from it should not affect a compass.

More advanced instruments, such as theodolites and sextants, come with their own lined boxes and obviously should be kept in them. They are precise measuring instruments, which are comparatively delicate, and their accuracy must be preserved by careful storage.

Other instruments, such as parallel rules, station pointers, and homemade equipment like the plane table do not need much maintenance other than obvious care in storage. You cannot throw things aside until you need them and expect them to be ready for use.

Appendix A
Map Suppliers

The following list of suppliers of maps, atlases, and related publications is given as a guide to availability. In some cases, the address is of an agent, and not the publisher, who may not supply directly.

The list does not include state publishers and agencies, but a comprehensive list of *State Mapping Information Sources* is available from the National Cartographic Information Center.

United States Department of the Interior
Geological Survey
National Mapping Program
Reston, VA 22092
   Topographic and many other maps.

Send orders to:
United States Geological Survey
1200 South Eads Street
Arlington, VA 22209

United States Geological Survey
Branch of Distribution
Box 25286, Federal Center
Denver, CO 80225

National Cartographic Information Center
United States Department of the Interior
Geological Survey
507 National Center
Reston, VA 22092

Information on sources of all kinds of maps. List of state mapping information sources.

Superintendent of Documents
United States Government Printing Office
North Capitol and H Streets, NW
Washington, DC 20402

Census, Civil War, treasure, Indian reservations, national park system, transportation, weather maps, and some mapping books.

United States National Ocean Survey
Distribution Division (C-44)
Riverdale, MD 20840

Aeronautical charts, nautical charts, world maps.

Defense Mapping Agency Topographic Center
Attn: Code 55500
Washington, DC 20315

Arctic and Antarctic, foreign waters, time zones, and world maps.

United States Forest Service
Information Office, Room 3238
Post Office Box 2417
Washington, DC 20013

National forest regions.

United States Soil Conservation Service
Information Division
Post Office Box 2890
Washington, DC 20013

Soil survey maps.

United States National Parks Service
Office of Public Enquiries, Room 1013
Washington, DC 20240

National parks.

United States Army AG Publications Center
2800 Eastern Boulevard
Baltimore, MD 21220

Army mapping manuals.

Rand McNally & Company
Post Office Box 7600
Chicago, IL 60680
   Road maps.

United States Army Engineer District
Corps of Engineers, Nashville
Post Office Box 1070
Nashville, TN 37202
   Cumberland River.

United States Army Engineer District
Corps of Engineers, Chicago
219 South Dearborn Street
Chicago, IL 60604
   Illinois Waterway to Lake Michigan, Mississippi River (Upper).

United States Army Engineer District
Corps of Engineers, Vicksburg
Post Office Box 60
Vicksburg, MS 39180
   Mississippi River (Lower).

United States Army Engineer District
Corps of Engineers, Omaha
6014 U.S. Post Office and
Courthouse Building
Omaha, NE 68102
   Missouri River.

United States Army Engineer District
Corps of Engineers, Louisville
Post Office Box 59
Louisville, KY 40201
   Ohio River.

Tennessee Valley Authority
Mapping Services Branch
Ill Haney Building
Chattanooga, TN 37401
   Tennessee River.

Ordnance Survey
Romsey Road, Maybush
Southampton, S09 4DH
England
   English topographic and many other maps.

Appendix B
Units of Measure

1 statute mile = 1760 yards = 5280 feet
1 nautical mile = 2026.8 yards = 6080 feet
1 fathom = 6 feet
Knots are nautical miles per hour
(quote speed as X knots, not X knots per hour)

Metric Measures of Length

10 millimeters (mm) = 1 centimeter (cm)
10 centimeters (cm) = 1 decimeter (dm)
10 decimeters (dm) = 1 meter (m)
100 centimeters (dm) = 1 meter (m)
1000 meters (m) = 1 kilometer (km)
(decimeters are rarely used)
(metric abbreviations are written without a period)

Approximate Conversions

1 millimeter = 0.039 inch
1 centimeter = 0.394 inch
1 meter = 39.37 inch
1 meter = 3.28 feet

1 kilometer = 0.62 mile (5/8 mile)
8 kilometers = 5 miles
1 inch = 25.4 millimeters
1 inch = 2.54 centimeters
1 foot = 304.8 millimeters
1 foot = 0.305 meter
1 yard = 0.914 meter
1 mile = 1.609 kilometers
5 miles = 8 kilometers
(Metric fractions are always decimal; for instance, 0.75 not 3/4)

Equivalent Units of Angular Measure

A circle = 360 degrees = 6400 mils = 400 grads
1 degree = 1/360 circle = about 17.8 mils = about 1.1 grad
1 mil = 1/6400 circle = 0.5625 degree = 0.0625 grad
1 grad = 1/400 circle = 16 mils = 0.9 degree or 54 minutes

Glossary

aerial mosaic—Pattern of overlapping photographs taken from the air.

aerial survey—Survey made by aircraft and based on photographs.

aeronautical chart—Map intended for use in navigation of aircraft.

aiming off—Plotting a course to one side of the final destination to make use of a feature that will lead in to it, in case of error.

alidade—Sighting device used in surveying, consisting of sights arranged over a straight edge.

altimeter—Instrument for measuring elevations or altitudes.

Antarctic Circle—Line of latitude 66¹/₂° south of the equator.

Arctic Circle—Line of latitude 66¹/₂° north of the equator.

atlas—Book of maps.

attack point—Identifiable position from which approach to destination can be made.

azimuth— Bearing direction, normally in degrees.

back azimuth—Directly opposite to the azimuth direction. A reciprocal bearing.

base map—An outline map on which other maps can be based.

bathymetry—Science of measuring water depths to produce chart of the bottom.

bearing—The direction of one point from another as determined with a compass.

bearing compass—A compass with sights so the compass bearing can be read at the same time as the object is sighted.

bench mark—A relatively permanent mark used in surveying and mapmaking.

bezel—The rim of a watch or compass.

binnacle—The stand for the compass used for steering a ship, usually containing gimbals to keep the compass level.

boundary—Limit or dividing line shown on a map, but which may not be marked on the ground.

boundary survey—Survey to establish the position of a boundary line on the ground.

boxing the compass—Reciting the traditional points of a compass, clockwise around the card.

cadastral survey—Survey of boundaries in relation to a register of land quantities, ownership or value. Property survey.

card—The calibrated disc of a compass, particularly the type that revolves with the needle.

cardinal points—N, S, E, and W on the compass.

carrying contours—Contour lines that run together at a cliff or vertical face.

cartography—Science and art of making maps.

catching feature—Easily identified feature that is an indication that the intended destination has been missed.

celestial navigation—Finding the way by using stars and sun, particularly in ocean crossings.

chain—Unit of length equal to 66 feet.

chart—Map intended for navigation at sea or in the air.

clinometer—An instrument for measuring the percentage of slope, used to determine relative heights when used with a suitable table.

closed traverse—Traverse that comes back to the starting point.

cocked hat—The triangle of crossed bearing lines that may occur when plotting three bearings that do not coincide.

compass—Instrument with a needle that points north.

compass card—The calibrated disc of a compass, particularly the type that revolves with the needle.

compass rose—Drawn compass circle marked in degrees, particularly on a chart.

conic projection—Map made from the development of a cone that touches a globe.

contact flying—Flying within sight of landmarks on the ground.

contour—A line on a map passing through places of the same elevation.

contour interval—Difference in elevation between two contour lines.

contouring—Passing along a route at a constant elevation.

control—A point that must be visited in orienteering.

control card—Card carried in orienteering that must be marked at each control.

control station—Point on the ground, with a known position, used as a base for surveying.

conventional sign—Symbol on map.

coordinates—Identifying lines on a map, such as latitude and longitude.

datum—Reference point. Plural: data.

dead reckoning—Computing progress from distance, time and direction only.

declination—The angular distance of a celestial body, used in celestial navigation. The angular difference between true and magnetic north at a particular point.

deliberate offset—Intentionally set course to one side of destination.

deviation—Compass error on a particular heading.

dividers—Twin-pointed adjustable instrument used for comparing map distances with the scale.

Douglas protractor—Large square protractor with a grid, used for position finding on a chart.

drift—Tendency to move sideways, due to water or wind at sea.

echo sounder—Electronic device for measuring depths from a boat.

ecliptic—Apparent path of the sun around the earth.

elevation—Vertical distance of a point above a datum, usually at sea level on a map.

errors of parallax—Errors due to not looking directly over two lines that should coincide.

estuary—A river mouth into which sea water can flow.

fathom—Length of 6 feet.

feature separation—The preparation of separate drawings during the preparation of a map.

field—The area in which action takes place.

field sketching—Making a map or sketch in the field.

fix—To obtain a position on a map or chart as a result of taking bearings.

flood plain—Land adjoining a stream or river that may be flooded when there is excessive water coming down.

form line—Lines added between contour lines to help give an idea of the form of the land, but not at surveyed heights.

gazetteer—List or index of places on a map, usually with references.

geological map—Shows the composition and structure of geological features.

getting a fix—Taking sights to plot a position.

gimbals—Pivoted rings used to support a compass so it remains level when a vessel pitches and rolls.

graphic scale—The scale printed in the margin of a map.

grid—System of crossing lines, used for reference.

grid reference—Numbered location obtained from the margin numbering of grid lines across a map.

handrail—Orienteering route guide.

hatchure, hatching—Lines drawn as shading to indicate slopes.

hemisphere—Half the globe, usually divided at the equator.

high water—The highest level reached by a tide.

hydrographic survey—Survey of a water area.

hypsometric map—Map showing relief by any means.

index contour—The drawn contour line with an elevation figure shown on it.

intermediate contour—Contour line added between the regular contours.

International Date Line—The meridian of longitude 180° from the meridian of Greenwich.

I.O.F.—International Orienteering Federation.

isogonic line—Line joining points on the surface of the earth, which have the same magnetic declinations.

knot—Nautical mile per hour.

landmark—Man-made or natural feature that can be used to determine a location in surveying or navigation.

large-scale map—Map on a large enough scale to show considerable detail.

latitude—Angular distance of a point north or south of the equator.

layer tinting—Coloring a map between contour lines to emphasize differences in elevation.

lead line—Weighted line used for sounding the depth of water.

leeway—Moving sideways through the water.

leg—The distance or route from one point to another.

legend—An explanatory list of symbols used on a map.

line feature—Any feature that extends across a map.

line survey—Survey based on a line of known position and length.

liquid-damped compass—Compass in which the needle moves in a liquid that reduces its tendency to oscillate.

lodestone—Ore containing iron and having magnetic properties.

longitude—Angular distance of a point east or west of Greenwich.

low water—The lowest level reached by a tide.

lubber line—A mark on a compass bowl, particularly on a ship steering compass, indicating the heading, against which a reading can be taken.

magnetic azimuth—The direction towards the magnetic pole.

magnetic lines—Lines on an orienteering map pointing to magnetic north.

magnetic north—The pole to which a compass points.

map measure—An instrument for measuring distances on a map, usually by rolling along the route.

map memory—The skill of remembering map detail, particularly valuable in orienteering.

map projection—Method of using lines on a map to represent a corresponding system of imaginary lines on the surface of the earth.

master map—In orienteering, the map from which competitors extract information.

mean high water—Tidal datum based on average high water levels.

Mercator's projection—Method of projecting a map so latitude and longitude lines are square to each other.

meridian—Great circle on the surface of the earth passing through the poles, so all points on it have the same longitude.

monument (surveying)—Permanent structure, making the position of a survey point.

mosaics—Assembly or aerial photographs.

nautical mile—1 minute of latitude (6080 feet).

navigable waters—Waters suitable for navigation by craft of moderate size, usually for commercial purposes.

neatline—Border between the map and its margin.

needle compass—Compass in which the calibrated disc is in the bottom, or calibrations are on the rim and the needle alone is pivoted.

offset course—Course to one side of the eventual destination.

Ordnance Survey—The British governmental publisher of maps.

orientation (orient)—Establish a correct relation of map, compass, and the part of the earth's surface concerned.

orienteering—Sport combining map, compass and cross-country running.

orienting a map—Setting a map the same way as the land it represents.

orthophotomaps—Maps made of color-enhanced photographic images.

overedge—A part of the map taken over the neatline.

overprint—Extra information printed over an existing map.

panoramic sketch—Sketch made in the field to show an area pictorially.

parallel of latitude—Line parallel to the equator through all points having the same latitude.

parallel rules—Linked rules used to transfer bearings between the compass rose on a chart and the points concerned.

pelorus—Sighting instrument for getting relative bearings.

photogrammetry—The obtaining of reliable measurements from photographs.

photomosaic—Map formed with a pattern of aerial photographs.

physical map—Map featuring elevations and natural features.

pilotage—Navigation at sea within visual or radio contact of the shore.

plain—Any area which is comparatively level.

plan—A very large-scale map of a small area.

plane table—Supported drawing board, used with a pelorus or compass for making a survey.

planimetric map—Map showing only horizontal features with no relief indications.

plat—Scale diagram showing information concerning the boundaries and subdivisions of a tract of land.

plot—To mark on the map the results of bearings and sights.

plumb line—Weighted cord, used to get an instrument over a spot.

point feature—In orienteering, a single recognizable feature.

political map—Map showing borders, towns, roads, and usually without contours and other physical features.

premarked map—In orienteering, a prepared map showing controls.

prime meridian—Longitude 0° at the meridian of Greenwich, England.

protractor—Instrument used for measuring degrees.

quadrangle—Four-sided area bounded by meridians of longitude and parallels of latitude.

quadrangle map—Geological Survey map based on a quadrangle and described in minutes or degrees.

quadrantal points—NE, SE, SW, NW, on a compass.

radio direction finder—Radio set used for finding the direction of the transmitting station.

reciprocal bearing—Direction opposite to a bearing: 180° more or less.

relief—Heights and hollows of land or the sea bottom.

relief shading—Emphasizing relief by adding shadow effects.

representative fraction—The scale of a map expressed as a fraction relating distance on the map with distance on the ground.

road map—Any map primarily concerned with roads and towns, particularly intended for motorists.

roamer—Device for measuring intermediate distances in a grid system.

runability—In orienteering, method of showing ease of passage on parts of a map.

running fix—Method of getting a fix from a single shore object, on a course passing it at sea.

scale—Relation between a distance on a map and the distance it represents on the surface of the earth.

scale rule—A rule marked to suit the scale of a map.

sea level—Height of the sea, which varies with tides.

section—Unit of subdivision of a township. Cut through contour lines showing rise and fall vertically.

segmented map—Map cut into sections and glued to a fabric backing.

setting a map—Arranging a map in the same direction as the part of the surface of the earth it represents.

sextant—Instrument for measuring angles, particularly of celestial bodies when navigating a ship.

sighting compass—A bearing compass, where the bearing can be read at the same time as the sight was taken.

sketch map—Freehand map, drawn as a rough guide or as a preliminary to a survey.

small-scale map—Map of a large area at a scale that does not permit much detail.

sounding—Finding the depth of water at a particular point. Soundings are underwater contours of spot depths.

spot elevation—Point on a map where a specific height is noted.

station pointer—Instrument based on a protractor, having three arms that can be set when plotting a position from landmarks on a chart.

steering mark—Point ahead and on course, which can serve as a guide to direction.

supplementary contour—Contour drawn between two normal contour lines to provide additional information on elevations.

survey—Obtaining information that will be used in making a map.

symbols—Conventional signs used to indicate features on the surface of the earth.

template or templet—Alternative name for a roamer.

terrain—Tract of land.

theodolite—Surveying instrument for measuring angles.

tide—Periodic movement of the water at sea, involving horizontal movement as well as a rise and fall.

topographic map—Map presenting the vertical as well as the horizontal positions of the features shown.

town plan—Large-scale map showing streets and other details in a town.

transit—Getting two landmarks in line to establish a position line. A special type of theodolite.

traverse—Surveying by taking bearings and distances between a series of points.

triangulation—Surveying by taking bearings and distances in the form of triangles.

trig point—A bench mark: abbreviation of trigonometrical point.

Tropic of Cancer—Parallel of latitude $23^1/2°$N.

Tropic of Capricorn—Parallel of latitude $23^1/2°$S.

universal Mercator grid—Worldwide system of grid references.

variation—Angular difference between true and magnetic north.

vertical datum—Base from which vertical control stations are measured.

world geographic reference system—Worldwide position reference system, primarily used on aeronautical charts.

Index

leads, wilderness travel, 129
legends, maps, 4, 8, 104-108
light lists, nautical maps, 220
line surveys, mapmaking, 169-170
local noon, 37
longitude, 3, 71-75
    degrees, minutes, seconds, 72
lubber lines, compasses, 33

M

Magnetic North, 36
map-memory orienteering events, 161
mapmaking, 163-191
    aerial photographs, photogrammetry,
        190-191
    alidade, 174
    area surveys, compass use, 181-185
    area surveys, plane tables, 179-181
    bench marks, 190
    compass use, 181-185
    control stations, horizontal and vertical,
        189-190
    detailed sketch maps, 165-167
    elevations, 185-187
    estimation aids, 167-169
    line surveys, 169-170
    plane tables, 174-177, 179-181
    professional mapmaking techniques,
        189-190
    river maps, enlarged, 187-189
    roadside surveys, 170-174
    roadside surveys, plane tables, 174-177
    sketching basic maps, 163-165
    traverses, 177-179
    U.S. Geological Survey markers, 190
maps (see also mapmaking), 193-215
    aeronautical charts, 195, 197
    atlases, 5
    azimuth, 47
    base maps, 194
    boundary lines, 14-16
    cases for maps, 244-246
    census maps, 208
    charts, 2, 83
    color use, 9
    conic projection, 80
    contour lines, 4-5, 53-67
    declination, 36
    distortion of landmasses, 213
    elevation, 4
    folding procedures, 241-244
    Forest Service maps, 16-18, 198-201
    globes, 2
    grids, 75-78

    height indicators, 53-67
    historic maps, 201-204
    land-use maps, 206-208
    latitude and longitude, 3
    legends, 4, 8
    measuring distance on maps, 24-28
    Mercator projection, 80, 214
    metric system measurements, 19-21
    migratory routes of birds, 210
    military maps, 204-206
    nautical (see nautical maps)
    orienteering events, 150
    pelorus to find direction, 49-51
    physical, 1, 194-196
    plans, 2
    political, 1, 194-196
    preservation of maps, 246-247
    prevailing winds, 212
    projections, 2-3, 78-82
    proportions and scale, 21-22
    protractors to find direction, 44-48
    rainfall distribution, 211
    raised relief, 208-209
    recreational maps, 197-198
    relief maps, 4, 208-209
    road maps, 6, 9-11, 97-120
    scale, 1, 3-6, 17, 19, 23-24, 73
    sea-routes, 212
    setting or orienting a map (see setting a
        map)
    star maps, 214-215
    statute miles vs. nautical miles, 24
    structures shown on maps, 14
    suppliers/sources, 251-253
    surveying and map-making, 5
    symbols, 4, 7-17, 151-152
    time zones, 214
    topographic survey maps, 6
    town plans, 6, 118-120
    Universal Mercator Grid (UTM), 76
    uses of maps, 1-2
    water shown on maps, 11-13
    worldwide maps, special maps, 209-214
measurements
    measuring distance on maps, 24-28
    metric system, 19-21
    statute vs. nautical miles, 24
    units of measurement, 255
Mercator projections, 80, 214
metric system measurements, 19-21
migratory route maps, 210
mileage charts, road maps, 106-107
military maps, 204-206
milligrads, compasses, 33
minutes, latitude and longitude, 72

N

national park maps (*see* Forest Service maps)
nature signs to find direction, 40-41
nautical maps, 11-13, 60-61
  bearings, 222
  cans and nuns (buoys), 237
  contour lines, 60-61, 64
  depth charting, sounding leads, 218
  depth curves, 64
  direction finders, electronic, 232
  dividers, 226
  drift or leeway, 233
  electronic navigation aids, 231-232
  flare signs, 220
  in transit, 221
  inland waterways, 236-239
  instruments needed, 222-226
  lights, light lists, 220
  National Ocean Survey publications, 219-220
  navigation techniques, 217-218
  parallel rules, 225
  pelorus use, 231
  pilot books, 219
  position finding, 226-229
  ranges, 221
  river maps, mapmaking, 187-189
  running fix, 229-230
  sea-route maps, 212
  sextant angles, 230-231
  sounding leads, 218
  station pointers, 225
  symbols, 220-221, 237
  tidal corrections, 233-236
  tide tables, 219
  top marks on buoys, 221
nautical miles, 24
night orienteering, 161
noon, local noon, 37
North pole, true vs. magnetic North, 36
nuns, nautical maps buoys, 237

O

offset courses, wilderness travel, 129
orienteering, 147-161
  catching features, 158
  compasses, 149-150
  compasses, Silva protractor-type, 147
  contouring, 158
  control points, 158
  distance measurements, 154-155
  equipment needed, 148-149
  International Orienteering Federation (IOF), 148
  lay-out of course, 155-156
  map memory events, 161
  maps needed, 150
  night orienteering, 161
  relay events, 160
  scale, 150-151
  score events, 160-161
  setting a map, 151-154
  slow runs, 158
  symbols on maps used, 151-152
  typical orienteering event, sequence of event, 156-161

P

parallax errors, compasses, 150
parallel rules, nautical maps, 225
park maps (*see* Forest Service maps)
pelorus, 49-51, 231
photogrammetry and mapmaking, 190-191
physical maps, 1, 194-196
pilot books, nautical maps, 219
plane tables
  area surveys, 179-181
  roadside surveying, 174-177
planmetric mapmaking, aerial photography, 190-191
plans, 2
plotting positions, 94-96, 226-229
political maps, 1, 194-196
position finding, 87-89, 94-96, 226-229
preservation of maps, 246-247
prevailing winds maps, 212
profiles, 64-65, 66-67
projections, 2-3, 78-82
  conic projection, 80
  Mercator protection, 80, 214
  time zones, 214
proportion and scale, maps, 21-22
protractors, 44-48, 248-249

R

rainfall distribution maps, 211
raised relief maps, 208-209
ranges, nautical maps, 221
recreational maps, 197-198
relay orienteering events, 160
relief maps, 4, 67, 208-209
river maps, mapmaking, 187-189
road maps, 6, 9-11, 97-120
  city and town plans, 6, 118-120
  elevation, 100-101
  international roads, 101-103
  legends, 104-108
  location and position finding, 116-118

Other Bestsellers of Related Interest

THE LOG OF CHRISTOPHER COLUMBUS
—translated by Robert H. Fuson
"I decided to write down everything that I might see and experience on this voyage, from day-to-day, and very carefully . . . " So begins the most influential journal in nautical history. Robert H. Fuson, an eminent Columbus scholar, has painstakingly assembled the patchwork of notes and theories surrounding this historic voyage, resulting in an exciting tribute and moving story of this courageous accomplishment. Complete with handsome maps, photographs, woodcuts, and pen-and-ink illustrations. 272 pages, 15 illustrations. Book No. 60660, $14.95 paperback, $29.95 hardcover.

BLIGH: A True Account of Mutiny On Board His Majesty's Ship *Bounty*—Sam McKinney
In this special Bicentennial Anniversary Edition commemorating the actual event, gifted storyteller Sam McKinney takes you aboard the *Bounty* to experience one of history's most extraordinary tales. Described and illustrated in authentic detail are the mutiny, Bligh's incredible 3,600-mile open boat voyage, the fate of the mutineers, and the British Navy's relentless pursuit to bring them to justice. 244 pages, 45 illustrations. Book No. 60132, $22.95 hardcover only.

Goin' Fishin': The Story of the Deep Sea Fishermen of New England—Wesley George Pierce
Captain Pierce's vivid recollections of the daily life of New England's salt-water fisherman have been rare and sought-after volumes since first published in 1934. This fascimile edition, featuring Pierce's elegant drawings, takes you back to the days of chebacco boats, heeltappers, racing fishermen, and high-line mackerel killers. 336 pages, 70 illustrations. Book No. 60217, $17.95 hardcover only.

GOOD FRIDAY—Robert Lawrence Holt
". . . excitement in the flying scenes and in the fight for power among the Saudi royalty . . . the author does know [his] flying!" —The *New York Times Book Review*
In this gripping novel, award-winning author Holt takes the evening news one step further. Combining both fact and conjecture he sets up a believable confrontation between the Soviet Union and the free world over the richest oil-producing nation, Saudi Arabia. You'll find this exciting, realistic work of fiction almost impossible to put down. 224 pages. Book No. 22399, $14.95 hardcover only.

SWEETWATER GUNSLINGER 201
—Lt. Commander William H. LaBarge, U.S. Navy, and Robert Lawrence Holt
Set aboard the U.S. Carrier *Kitty Hawk* during the Iranian crisis of 1980, this fast-paced novel details the lives, loves, dangers, trials, tribulations, and escapades of a group of Tail Hookers (Navy carrier pilots). As much fact as fiction, it's a story that is both powerful and sensitive . . . by authors who do a masterful job of bringing the reader aboard a modern aircraft carrier and into the cockpit of an F-14! 192 pages. Book No. 28515, $14.95 hardcover only.

Prices Subject to Change Without Notice.

Look for These and Other TAB Books at Your Local Bookstore

To Order Call Toll Free 1-800-822-8158
(in PA, AK, and Canada call 717-794-2191)

or write to TAB Books, Blue Ridge Summit, PA 17294-0840.

Title	Product No.	Quantity	Price

☐ Check or money order made payable to TAB Books

Charge my ☐ VISA ☐ MasterCard ☐ American Express

Acct. No. _____ Exp. _____

Signature: _____

Name: _____

Address: _____

City: _____

State: _____ Zip: _____

Subtotal $ _____

Postage and Handling
($3.00 in U.S., $5.00 outside U.S.) $ _____

Add applicable state and local
sales tax $ _____

TOTAL $ _____

TAB Books catalog free with purchase; otherwise send $1.00 in check or money order and receive $1.00 credit on your next purchase.

Orders outside U.S. must pay with international money order in U.S. dollars.

TAB Guarantee: If for any reason you are not satisfied with the book(s) you order, simply return it (them) within 15 days and receive a full refund.   **BC**